Praise for *The Intuitive Advisor*

"**The Intuitive Advisor** is a new kind of healing tool that provides a different perspective on challenging health issues. In her signature no-nonsense, humorous style, Dr. Mona Lisa guides the reader through a process of understanding his or her illness on an energetic level and then offers practical strategies to address each health problem. If you're tired of tolerating pain and stress, you'll want to use this book to learn a whole new way of welcoming health into your life."

— **Cheryl Richardson,** the author of *The Art of Extreme Self-Care*: *Transform Your Life One Month at a Time*

"**The Intuitive Advisor** is a magnificent, wise, bracing, and extremely helpful book. It puts anyone with goodwill in touch in the most sparkling way with their own powers of intuition. It is written with directness, hilarity, and savvy; and will have you sometimes laughing out loud and sometimes gasping for breath. I loved this book and recommend it heartily."

— **Andrew Harvey,** the author of *The Hope: A Guide to Sacred Activism*

"Dr. Mona Lisa Schulz is a rare genius. With stunning clarity and insight, she shows how health issues are guides to emotional healing. Brilliant, funny, and completely down to earth, she provides a chakra- based map of the human energy system with the power to evoke your best self and bring your body back to balance. This book is a must-read for every human being."

— **Joan Borysenko, Ph.D.,** the author of *It's Not the End of the World*: *Developing Resilience in Times of Change*

"Dr. Mona Lisa normalizes, simplifies, and helps you implement tools that can transform your body while entertaining the reader (helping the brain make all those good neurotransmitters) while doing it. She also makes the best cookie batter on the planet. From teenagers to those of us who remember when pong was the only video game on the market, Dr. Mona Lisa has a voice to reach everyone (and every cell!)"

— **Laura Day,** intuitive business consultant ~~and~~ ~~best sellin~~g author

"Dr. Mona Lisa Schulz is an a. [...] iant scientist who delivers lifesaving wisdom [...] re. You'll be so entertained you may be amu [...] t you to use your own intuition to solve [...] *Intuitive Advisor* is the most important and [...] ook on health and intuition ever."

— **Barbara Carrellas,** the author of *Urban Tantra*: *Sacred Sex for the Twenty-First Century*

Also by Mona Lisa Schulz, M.D., Ph.D.

Books
Awakening Intuition
The New Feminine Brain

Audio/Video Programs
Igniting Intuition, with Christiane Northrup, M.D.*
Intuitive Listening, with Christiane Northrup, M.D.*

Online On-Demand Download
Where Medical Intuition Meets Mysticism, with Caroline Myss*

Miscellaneous
*Mind/Body Makeover Oracle Cards**

●–●–●

the intuitive ADVISOR

A Psychic Doctor
Teaches You How to Solve
Your Most Pressing Health Problems

Mona Lisa Schulz, M.D., Ph.D.

HAY HOUSE, INC.
Carlsbad, California • New York City
London • Sydney • Johannesburg
Vancouver • Hong Kong • New Delhi

Published and distributed in the United States by: Hay House, Inc.: www.hayhouse.com • *Published and distributed in Australia by:* Hay House Australia Pty. Ltd.: www.hayhouse.com.au • *Published and distributed in the United Kingdom by:* Hay House UK, Ltd.: www.hayhouse.co.uk • *Published and distributed in the Republic of South Africa by:* Hay House SA (Pty), Ltd.: www.hayhouse.co.za • *Distributed in Canada by:* Raincoast: www.raincoast.com • *Published in India by:* Hay House Publishers India: www.hayhouse.co.in

Editorial supervision: Jill Kramer • *Project editor:* Alex Freemon
Design: Amy Rose Grigoriou • *Interior illustrations:* Colleen Daley

Library of Congress Cataloging-in-Publication Data

Schulz, Mona Lisa.
   The intuitive advisor : a psychic doctor teaches you how to solve your most pressing health problems / Mona Lisa Schulz. -- 1st ed.
      p. cm.
   ISBN 978-1-4019-2393-8 (hardcover : alk. paper) 1. Intuition. 2. Healing. 3. Mind and body therapies. 4. Chakras. 5. Self-care, Health. I. Title.
   RZ999.S3675 2009
   615.5--dc22
                              2008047706

Tradepaper ISBN: 978-1-4019-1907-8
Hardcover ISBN: 978-1-4019-2393-8

13 12 11 10   6 5 4 3
1st edition, May 2009
3rd edition, May 2010

Printed in the United States of America

In my Portuguese background, we have *madrinhas*—godmothers who we always turn to in times of joy and pain. Caroline Myss and Lisa Gorman truly fit the *madrinhas* bill. They love and hug when appropriate. They scream, yell, and threaten when critical. They tell me to save my money when I'm going nuts with my credit cards. They tell me when I'm driving my car "too damn fast." They tell me when I'm not eating enough good food or when I'm eating too much sugar.

Madrinhas are always great cooks—Caroline with her brussels sprouts, carrots, and chicken; and Lisa with her banana–chocolate chip bread and rugelach.

Both Caroline and Lisa could be counted on to be brutally honest when it came to giving me feedback about the first drafts of this book. ("This intro is @#%$#, ML." "I hate this. I don't understand this. What are you trying to say?") Both Lisa and Caroline can make me weep like a baby or laugh like a hyena, all within five seconds.

Not only would this book not have been written without either of these great *madrinhas,* but I probably wouldn't be alive without them, either. Caroline sat down and helped me distill my voice from that of a stiff academic to the one in this book. Most people know her as a brilliant writer and medical intuitive but are not aware of her capacity to be a brilliant book editor. Caroline also gives me "the look" whenever I'm doing things that wreck my health. Lisa has been a singular force to be reckoned with in my personal, private, and health life. The loving support, the long car drives, the deli food . . . I just don't know what I would do without her.

Both *madrinhas,* Lisa Gorman and Caroline Myss, my closest advisors, it is to you with great love and devotion that I dedicate this book.

•–•–•–•–•

Contents

Foreword

We are all born with intuitive abilities. That we may not all be attuned to our inner voice is another matter, but we are all born with an intuitive survival instinct that activates, for example, our fight-or-flight mechanism and our gut response when we meet someone new, telling us whether we trust this new person or not. This survival sense is also attuned to our health. Through ways both awesome and at times annoying, we're alerted that we should be exercising more or watching what we eat more carefully. So attuned is this inner voice that it will reach us through dreams, if necessary, conveying messages that we're heading into serious health problems unless we change what we're doing or get a medical checkup. We don't really need the help of outsiders for as much information as we think, if we would only just pay more attention to our survival intuition. Indeed, our survival intuition is the inner physician that nature herself has provided each of us.

In *The Intuitive Advisor,* Mona Lisa Schulz has expanded the voice of our inner physician, scripting a guidebook complete with a basic template of the chakra system that outlines the relationships between these seven centers of power and their related stress disorders. Your intuition is enhanced most by bringing into your conscious mind the knowledge that is inherent to its own system, and this profile of the chakra system is precisely the type of data that you need to educate your own intuition. In learning this system, you provide your intuitive abilities with a vocabulary and an inner reference library that validates your gut responses.

Most often we dismiss intuitive hits because they're rapid, fleeting bits of energetic data that are difficult to anchor in physical proof. Or we dismiss intuitive hits because we don't like the information we're receiving. This is frequently the case with matters of health, as I've personally experienced many times as a teacher in this field.

Medical-intuitive readings are by far the most challenging type of intuitive readings to master, certainly because you're dealing with matters of health, but also because the field of health is inclusive of so many factors. It is extremely complex, covering the realm of emotions, mental dynamics, psychic factors, sexuality, and physical disease. There is nothing simple about a medical-intuitive reading.

Yet your intuitive system is attuned to every fiber of your psychic field, to every memory, to every fear, to every hope, to every cell in your body. And, amazingly enough, you actually know this. How much you really *want* to know about yourself is much more of a challenge than having the ability to tap into this information. I already know that every person is born wired to tap into it.

Amazingly, as the years have gone by in my own work, I find that I look for different things in people. I used to focus more on issues related to illness, and now I'm drawn more to study other things—for example, why we're so attached to our patterns of suffering. Suffering is a central theme in our culture, and among the many reasons why people remain in suffering consciousness is that we cannot bring ourselves to respond to our intuitive guidance. Acts of self-betrayal, without a doubt, are the cause of more self-inflicted pain than can be measured. And the irony is that we consider ourselves an intuitive society now, yet listening and responding to that intuitive voice remains the most frightening act for most individuals.

I see this book as yet another milestone toward helping people get over the hurdle of a profound discomfort with their own intuitive voice. Toward that end alone, Mona Lisa has made a most necessary contribution to the field of healing. But in addition, she has written this richly inspiring and informative book on how to become attuned to your own health system with humor, insight, and solid information—the type that can actually make a difference in your life. The stories she shares of her many client readings are not only entertaining, but they each have a jewel of genuine wisdom. And beyond that, it's worth appreciating how much each person was helped within the course of one reading, using the level of information that Mona Lisa is now sharing in this book.

As a medical intuitive, I've worked with the chakra system for 25 years with my colleague, C. Norman Shealy, M.D., Ph.D. The combination of physical anatomy with energy anatomy positioned matters of health in a completely new light. To be able to discuss how and why a patient is losing power because of a fear pattern, spiritual crisis, or trauma that continues to live on in the psyche, and thus the cell tissue, has redefined our approach to healing itself. We have an entirely new and far more complete understanding of who we are and how we function because we know about the human energy system and its relationship to our physical anatomy.

In truth, you cannot afford *not* to know your energy anatomy, your chakra system. You cannot afford *not* to read this book. Mona Lisa has written what I consider to be an essential work on the human energy system that is more than a textbook, because it's aimed at educating you, the reader, while simultaneously attuning you even more to your survival intuition. As someone who watched her write this book with passion, fury, panic, and devotion, I can say without a doubt that her heart and soul are woven into every page, as is her uncompromising genius. She is a magnificent medical intuitive, scientist, and physician; but more than that, she is my dear friend.

I'm not unbiased when it comes to Mona Lisa's word, obviously, but I'm tough when it comes to my standards as a teacher, writer, and medical intuitive. I deeply believe that this book will help you awaken your inner abilities and perhaps even help you avoid serious illness. And given that, I believe this book is needed now more than even Mona Lisa realizes.

— **Caroline Myss**

PART I

Working with Medical Intuition

Note to the Reader

The information in this book is not meant to be a substitute for medical care. If you have a medical or emotional problem, see your physician or other licensed practitioner in your area. Medical intuition does not diagnose illness, nor does it prescribe specific medical treatment. You should make medical decisions only in a trusting relationship with your doctor.

Human vulnerability to disease cannot be reduced to a single physical or emotional cause. Numerous genetic, nutritional, environmental, emotional, and other unknown factors contribute to the development of illness and disease. There are limitations to any scientific inquiry. Patients should work with their health-care practitioners to examine for themselves which problems, relationships, habits, and situations in their lives contribute to disease and which medical, herbal, and nutritional solutions are available to create health.

The client studies and medical-intuitive readings presented in this book are composites of several similar cases. None represents a single identifiable individual. Sexes of partners and children have been switched frequently; and occupations, names, and locations have been changed. Any similarity to any real person's name or identity is coincidental.

●–●–●–●–●

Introduction

How I Got into This Intuition Business Anyway

Ever since I can remember, my mind has wandered into the private lives of other people. You can call it being inquisitive or caring, but this characteristic led me into my profession as an intuitive advisor as well as a physician and scientist.

I've been in the intuition business since the second grade. In fact, being a quasi–yenta/busybody was responsible for my getting a failing conduct grade on my report card that year, with the added comment: "Finishes work quickly, but seems overly concerned with solving the problems of everyone else in the room." Thus began my career.

People's lives, their problems, and the solutions to those problems have always popped into my head in one form or another. When I first learned how to write, I'd pen pages about a specific person's life, as well as about his or her trials and tribulations. My parents would ask me who these people were and how I knew them. I would answer that I'd never met the people I was writing about, but I just seemed to know everything about their lives.

When my sister didn't know the answers to her math homework, the numbers would pop into my head and then out of my mouth just as quickly. Such behavior didn't win me friends, but instead caused concerned stares. It also resulted in a psychological evaluation at the age of five—this was in the '60s, I might add, at a time when no children really got psychological evaluations unless they were schizophrenic, psychotic, or "mentally retarded," as they used to say. Apparently, my brain fit into none of those categories, and I was dismissed with a diagnosis of being only very bright and creative.

Figuring that a more traditional source of information scared people less, I decided by the age of seven to focus on being a physician and scientist so that others wouldn't be afraid of me anymore. I chose those professions so that people could come to me with their health problems and I could tell them how to get better. Oh, so naïve!

So during the next several decades, I more or less avoided intuition altogether, trying to get perfect grades so I could become a perfect doctor. I actually overshot it a little by becoming *two* doctors instead of one—an M.D. *and* a Ph.D. Nothing succeeds like excess! I figured that if I learned all the facts, I could solve all the problems.

As an encyclopedia wannabe, I entered my first year of medical school with a head full of facts and the pockets of my new white coat equally filled with little medical reference books. I was totally overwhelmed. When a stressed-out medical resident barked out an order for me to go down to the emergency room and pick up a 46-year-old female patient, I froze. The facts and intelligence weren't enough. Desperate for survival in a circumstance where I felt I was intellectually way over my head, I returned to my intuitive roots—quite unintentionally. I simply saw an image pop into my head: in my mind's eye, I saw this 5'4", moderately obese middle-aged woman in these lime-green stretch pants screaming, "Doctor, doctor, it's my gallbladder! Do something!" as she clutched the upper right part of her abdomen.

So in the elevator on the way down to the emergency room, I distracted myself from my nervousness and impatience by looking up gallbladder disorders in my little reference book. By the time I arrived in the ER, I had a clipboard crib sheet outlining how I'd work up a patient with gallbladder disease.

I found Betty, my first patient, waiting for me: this middle-aged, moderately obese woman wearing lime-green stretch pants was lying on a gurney and screaming, "It's my gallbladder! Do something, doctor!" I thought, *Wow!* I'd gotten an intuitive head start on Betty, and as a result, I was able to work up my patient in record time and get out of the hospital three hours faster than the other medical students.

As time went on, I was also able to "see" specific emotional situations in my patients' lives that aggravated their health. For example, when a patient named Nora was admitted to the hospital after precipitously going into kidney failure, I got a strong intuitive hit that her kidneys weren't her only problem—she had a seriously broken heart as well. In fact, Nora soon told me that her husband had recently left her for a woman 15 years younger.

I wasn't sure exactly how I knew these things, but I did. And so I began to regard medical intuition not just as a trick to help me imagine my patients' problems before I met them so I could get them out of the hospital faster, but rather as a system inherent in all patients' bodies that let them know when something in their personal lives was spiraling out of control.

Other than that, I wanted nothing to do with medical intuition. Remember, my intuitive abilities had landed me, at the age of five, in a psychologist's office. Even though that was decades earlier, I didn't want to repeat the experience during my medical training. Essentially not much had changed in people's minds about intuition since then. Left-brain intellect was worshipped at the altar, but right-brain intuition was still suspect. Intuition was considered unprofessional, fringy, paranormal, or just plain nuts—and I certainly didn't need anyone questioning my sanity.

A few people were actually intrigued. When ob-gyn Christiane Northrup found out that there was this medical student (me) who was also a medical intuitive and had survived the training, she agreed to let me work with her. I began to follow her in her clinic. After testing my intuitive accuracy on a series of 19 women (17 of whom I read accurately), she started to send people to me for medical-intuitive readings. And after that, I began to live truly in both worlds. By day, I was a physician and a scientist, running in and out of the hospital and scientific laboratory; and by night, I worked as a medical-intuitive advisor—both roles that I continue to balance to this day, more than two decades later.

Intuitive Advisor Principles

In order to maintain these two careers and keep both my integrity and my sanity intact, I developed a series of principles along the way that I have come to live by. I call them my *Intuitive Advisor Principles,* and Intuitive Advisor Principle #1 is, as the poet Robert Frost once said: *Good fences make good neighbors.* This has to do with legally setting up boundaries between my two careers. (All the people who have medical-intuitive readings with me sign consent forms ahead of time acknowledging that they understand that a medical-intuitive reading is not a physician/patient relationship and that I will not give them medical diagnoses, prescribe treatment, or do psychotherapy. I don't want people coming to me for treatment when they should be going to their own physicians.)

As my intuitive capacity to see, hear, and sense people's physical and emotional lives continued to develop over the next two decades, it often did so in fits and starts—two steps forward and then sometimes one step back. For example, when I did a reading on Katherine, 38, the only intuitive image I got was a piece of Swiss cheese stretched across her chest. I later learned that she had metastatic breast cancer. This intuitive reading was visually accurate, but how helpful could it actually be to the client? It was, as they say, all sizzle and no steak. It was flash . . . and flash is trash.

This led to Intuitive Advisor Principle #2: *An intuitive advisor should help the client connect the dots between mind and body.* By that, I mean that just intuiting the client's physical ailments isn't enough. My goal became to educate clients about the connection between the physical symptoms in their bodies and their emotional issues.

Readings that emphasize the phenomenon of intuition instead of helping clients understand their bodies' intuitive guidance systems run the risk of putting the intuitive in the middle of a circus act— a dog and pony show. I've demonstrated medical intuition twice, in fact, on international TV. The first time was on *The Oprah Winfrey Show* in 1991, and the other was on a Discovery Channel program called *One Step Beyond* in 2004. In both situations, the client and I were each on camera in totally separate locations. Knowing only the person's name and age, I was asked to accurately describe both the client's emotional pattern and physical health problems, specifically pinpointing each person's illness. After nailing both readings, I promised myself I'd never again have to prove on TV that I could accurately read someone intuitively. After all, there is always going to be someone who doesn't believe in intuition, no matter how much you turn yourself into a psychic pretzel to try to prove it.

Even so, the physician and scientist in me wanted to know if scientific studies supported the idea that certain emotional patterns are associated with specific health problems. So in the midst of helping Chris Northrup research her first book, *Women's Bodies, Women's Wisdom,* I went to Harvard's Countway Library of Medicine and looked up every single organ in the human body and identified what psychological factors were associated with the diseases of that body part. In the back of my silver Honda Civic hatchback with the front bumper falling off, I filled milk crate after milk crate with research files. You name the organ or the disorder, I had a file researching its psychological influences catalogued in the back of my car. Over the next few years, I scoured the scientific literature demonstrating the connection between emotional patterns and physical illness, the same patterns that I was seeing in my medical-intuitive readings.

Around that time, Chris introduced me to Caroline Myss, a medical intuitive who had worked with her on hundreds of her patients. Caroline brought a theology background to her medical-intuitive readings, and she talked about spirituality and an energy anatomy. You might think that this would be far less threatening for me. But the first time I was supposed to meet Caroline, I was so terrified by the stories I'd heard about her that I hid behind a ficus tree in a conference hall. I wanted to watch her interact with other people before I decided if it was safe to come out from behind the foliage.

I eventually got the guts to meet her, and she became a great mentor to me. For about a year and a half, I talked to her once a week on the phone, going over my readings for that week and learning how I'd blown certain details.

For example, when I did a reading on Donna, 36, I saw that she was involved with some man who had a balancing act going on with relationships. It was as if he were juggling two bowling pins over his head, but he was dropping one all the time. I assumed he was the source of her health problems. When I looked intuitively at her body, I saw that her eyes, head, ears, neck, thyroid, heart, breasts, and lungs weren't the issue. But when I got to her abdomen, it felt like a bloated water balloon. So when I asked Donna if she was in a bad relationship, she said, "Yes. Actually, I'm involved with this married man who keeps blowing me off." And then when I asked if she had a weight problem, she said no, although she mentioned that she was being treated for an eating disorder.

Later, when I spoke with Caroline, I asked her to take an intuitive look at Donna.

"Hmm . . . she's anorexic," Caroline said.

"How can you say that?" I responded. "When I look at her abdomen intuitively, it appears so bloated."

"Mona Lisa, you're looking at her body through *her* mind's eye," Caroline explained. "You're seeing how she distorts her body image."

This experience led me to Intuitive Advisor Principle #3: *An intuitive advisor learns to see intuitively through the perspective of another person—through the client's eyes, not through the advisor's eyes.* It's never enough to just intuitively describe a situation and explain it to someone. To have the experience be truly meaningful, creating an "Aha! moment," it's always important to step inside someone and see the world through that person's eyes and from his or her point of view.

I called Donna back after my discussion with Caroline, and I started to ask her about her distorted body image. That's when, of course, she began to talk to me about how she would always look in the mirror and think that she looked fat. *Bingo.*

Because Caroline already had more than a decade of medical-intuitive experience under her belt, she knew all the pitfalls and mistakes, which led me to my next two Intuitive Advisor Principles—#4: *Practice makes perfect;* and #5: *Follow the leader.* In case after case, Caroline gave me great advice, explaining the energy anatomy underlying the medical intuition of each of my readings. She also helped me not get discouraged when I couldn't see specific details as precisely as I wanted to.

"You just need to practice," Caroline would assure me, adding that I shouldn't be hard on myself because I was still a "baby" intuitive (a phrase I truly hated, I might add). She told me that I would be fine after a few thousand readings. *Gee, thanks!* I thought.

Now I, too, teach medical intuition. And when my students explain that they hope to develop a virtuoso level of intuitive ability in a weekend workshop, I tell them to forget it. It's not possible. The idea that anyone can instantly become an expert intuitive is a myth. Look at it this way: Intuition is a practiced skill, like singing, that is a normal by-product of a functioning brain and body. All of us, if we open our mouths, can instantly sing. And if we're motivated to spend hours practicing with an instructor, we could develop adequate vocal technique. However, some people's brains and bodies just aren't conducive to becoming top-level singers. The most successful opera stars, for example, are usually heavy and known for being emotionally temperamental. It just seems to go with the territory. Similarly, medical intuitives tend to have an emotional tone and physical temperament that's specifically adapted to being intuitive, which leads me right into Intuitive Advisor Principle #6: *Mind your mood, and watch your health.*

I've found that people who work in the field of intuition, myself included, are some of the moodiest, most anxious, irritable, high-strung, blunt, and passionate individuals I have ever met. I've been told, for example, that I would never win any awards in diplomacy. And how I feel about something is never a mystery, despite the fact that the real Mona Lisa smile was quite mysteriously deadpan.

Many of the great saints who were medically intuitive (St. Catherine of Genoa, St. Teresa of Ávila, St. Catherine de' Ricci, and St. Thérèse of Lisieux among them) were notorious for not being what you would call ordinary housewives. They were often eccentric, temperamental, anxious, and very direct and cutting when they delivered their prophetic or intuitive information.

As is the case with many people who work as intuitive advisors, their health was also poor. For starters, they all had epilepsy. Other examples of the types of very hard-to-treat, reactive, complex health problems that medical-intuitive advisors often seem to have include anxiety, migraine headaches, weight and thyroid issues, and immune-system disorders.

My own numerous health problems have been bizarre and quite dramatic, starting with a 120-degree double curve in my spine at the age of 12 that required fusion and a nearly yearlong stay in the hospital. Later, I had to have my spine re-broken and re-fused from my neck to my tailbone with ten rods and several four-inch nails. I've also had epilepsy, narcolepsy (once I actually fell asleep while jogging and got run over by a truck), bilateral invasive breast cancer that required a double mastectomy with reconstruction, Graves' disease, and most recently, asthma (although the jury is still out on that one).

When I had to go into the hospital in Boston for breast-cancer surgery, I tried to poke fun at my ridiculous medical history as I handed the surgeon my list of health problems. "None of these illnesses are real," I joked. "I have Munchausen syndrome [a psychiatric disorder where the patient fakes one or more illnesses to get attention]. It's all a cry for help!"

Suffice it to say that whenever I'm told about other medical intuitives, the first thing I ask is not how intuitive they are, but what they're like: moody, anxious, irritable, cranky, or easy to get into an argument with? What's their health like? How many surgeries have they had? How many times have they almost died? Have they ever nearly bled to death? Do they have migraine headaches, epilepsy, autoimmune disorders, or thyroid problems?

If the answer is yes to many of these questions, I just know these individuals are the real thing. All the shamans and native healers of the indigenous tribes, as well as the intuitive healers who came later in history, had a lot of health problems because the tendency to be intuitively porous also makes a person emotionally and physically reactive. So those who work as medical intuitives have to pay special attention to their emotional and physical health, which tends to go down the tubes at times.

Nonetheless, my knowledge and experience as a medical intuitive has become refined and has evolved over the past 20 years. The more readings I do, the more I realize this vital truth: no matter how much knowledge I have and no matter how good an intuitive I am, I still have to have contact with some higher power in order to help people.

It is with that mind-set that I lay down the last principle, Intuitive Advisor Principle #7: *Consider the source.* Intuition is from God or from some other higher power that you recognize. It's a way of getting information that's related to love and empathy. By keeping the source of intuition in perspective, you learn not to manipulate; alter; make politically correct; or color with your own personal opinions, ideas, or agenda what you see. Intuition isn't what we think in our brains. It's a message from a higher source that pops into our heads and into our hearts about someone we care about.

There you have them, my seven Intuitive Advisor Principles. Now let me take you inside the experience of what it's like for me to do a medical-intuitive reading—starting from the first moment someone calls.

An Insider's View of a Medical-Intuitive Reading

Let's say that Edward, 28, schedules a reading. After he signs and faxes back his consent form, he calls me on the phone. Knowing only his name and age, I start to look intuitively into his emotional life for a problem that could trigger a health crisis. I might say to him, "I see you at a workplace, surrounded by people—your gang. This doesn't seem to be a problem." Then I look around to see a relationship. I ask the question in my head: *Whom is he going out with? Is he living with someone?* Then I'll start to see pictures. The more I come across, the more problems there are in that area.

I start to describe what I see. "I see a woman, always on the phone, always calling, calling, calling," I might say. I'd probably get a bit derailed in my reading because of this woman and her phone calls, because that is very likely a significantly aggravating feature in Edward's health. The woman seems moody and irritable, and she wants an awful lot of contact. In fact, she's probably escalated the amount of time she needs with Edward as their relationship has progressed. This woman makes me nervous.

Then I say to my client, "I see this situation aggravating you *and* your health. Although all illness is in part due to the environment, genetics, or injury, every instance of it also has an emotional, behavioral, and intuitive component. I see you becoming increasingly concerned about a relationship with a woman who calls you a lot. I hope you have an unlimited phone plan, Edward!"

He laughs nervously and says, "That's my new girlfriend."

Now I turn my attention intuitively to Edward's physical body. If you were sitting opposite me while I was doing this reading, you'd see me look up to the right, as if there were a holographic image of the client's body hanging there from the ceiling. Then, mechanically, I describe what I see clairvoyantly, hear clairaudiently, or feel clairsentiently from head to toe. I'd say something like, "I look at your head, your eyes . . . I see problems with attention and distractibility. I look at your ears, neck, thyroid, throat . . . they're not the issue. I listen to your heart . . ." And if Edward were to have an irregular heartbeat or some other cardiac problem, you'd hear me talk about it.

I'd continue down to Edward's left lung, right lung, esophagus, stomach, liver, gallbladder, colon, and rectal area. Then I might say to him, "I see problems with redness along the lining of your esophagus and stomach. I can't figure out if this is due to excess acid or excess bacteria, but it gives you a burning feeling and makes you nauseated. I look at your prostate, kidneys, and bladder; and again, this isn't the issue. I look at the joints in your hands, wrists, elbows, shoulders, hips, knees, and ankles. I see something different about your right knee and your right shoulder. I can't figure out if this is due to an old injury or something else." Finally, I'd see that Edward struggles with melancholy and sadness, but he won't admit this to other people because he wants to look cool. And then I might see him having problems with falling asleep and staying asleep.

Then I would ask, "Can you please tell me your health concerns?"

Let's say that Edward tells me he has the beginning of a gastric ulcer, which of course is the redness I see in his esophagus and stomach. He might also mention having some trouble with nausea and vomiting, but before I went over his digestive issues, I'd return to some of the other things I picked up on during his reading—the problems with attention, focus, and distractibility. Edward might tell me at this point that he was diagnosed at age five with ADHD and that he has taken Ritalin ever since to help him pay attention and stay on task.

How about the issue I saw in his right knee and right shoulder? Did he have an accident? Edward might laugh and say that actually, it's his left knee, left arm, and left shoulder—he broke them in an automobile accident in high school. It's not unusual for me to get the side wrong. I don't know why this is, but it happens.

Edward might tell me next that he had his appendix taken out when he was seven, but I didn't see this. When I do a reading, I'm more likely to describe what's going wrong in someone's health that threatens his or her survival right now. The more major the concern, the easier it is for me to pick up intuitively. I'm not very good at all at picking up what I call "ticks and fleas"—the smaller, more annoying, day-to-day aggravations that we all experience, such as bunions, age spots, or eye floaters.

For the rest of the reading, I'd explain the connection between Edward's gut intuition—which is what his ulcer really is—and the annoying phone calls from his girlfriend (who, frighteningly enough, Edward is considering becoming engaged to).

● ● ●

Some readings are incredibly rewarding. For example, when I did one for a woman named Francine, I saw a hormonally sensitive lumpiness in her left breast, which occurred within a year of a failed marriage. When I mentioned this, Francine told me that she'd noticed this lump and was nervous about it, too. She'd already gone to her doctor, but once he'd seen the mammogram results, he told her that he wanted to watch the lump over time.

After the reading, Francine went back to her doctor and insisted that he do a needle biopsy. When he did, it came back positive for invasive breast cancer. What I love about readings like Francine's is seeing medical intuition confirm what a client already intuitively knows in his or her heart of hearts but hasn't yet trusted him- or herself enough to act upon.

Then there are the readings that don't go as well. I call that "bagging a reading." If what I read intuitively about a client's emotional life and physical body doesn't make sense to the person—doesn't match his or her experience—I end the reading and return the fee in full. In fact, at the beginning of every reading, I say that there are some people I simply can't read. It's no one's fault when that happens, but if it does, I just end the reading and return the money.

The first reason this sometimes occurs is human error. I am, after all, a human being, not an MRI machine. There are two other reasons why I occasionally can't read people—either the information is not what the client wants to hear or I'm not relating it in a way that's *safe* for him or her to hear. Whatever the reason, I have failed, and these readings are never fun. Ever the perfectionist, I always try to figure out what went wrong.

Some readings are doomed before they even start. This happens when I get the sense that the clients want me to relay only what they want to hear. These people either aren't interested in hearing anything difficult or painful or don't want to be encouraged to engage in a variety of more strenuous approaches to helping themselves, such as changing their diets or starting to exercise. I call these "blow-job readings" because all that these people are calling for is to feel good. They want me to reassure them that everything will be all right. These clients aren't interested in any intuitive advice on how their health problems may be indicating that certain areas in their lives need to change.

I don't do blow-job readings, because they don't follow my principles as an intuitive advisor. And even if I did do them, these clients would just keep calling back day after day for more reassurance. What these people really need is to investigate faith and spirituality, and medical intuition is not a substitute for that.

Finally, there are the readings where the clients have been dragged into them kicking and screaming. These folks would never have signed up for a reading on their own—instead, they were coerced into it by a well-meaning loved one.

Gary, 68, is a perfect example. The first thing that came to me in this reading was that this man didn't want a reading at all. He didn't even believe in intuition. The only reason he called was because his wife nagged and nagged and nagged him until he scheduled one just to shut her up. In cases like Gary's, I always say, "You don't really want a reading, do you? You're only doing this because your wife told you to do it. Isn't that right?"

Invariably, these clients will laugh and admit, "You're right. My wife told me to call."

"No one should have to do anything that he or she doesn't want to do," I tell these clients. "I'm refunding your money in full." This usually leaves them stunned.

●–●–●

This, in a nutshell, is how I got into the intuitive business. Maybe after reading my story, you can see yourself using intuition to advise yourself about your life, trials, and problems and others about theirs. But one of the reasons I wrote this book is to let you know that you don't have to be a medical-intuitive advisor to be intuitive.

I've come to recognize three basic truths that I want to share with you here: (1) everybody's body is intuitive, (2) medical intuition is a natural form of body intelligence that lets us know when something in our lives is out of balance, and (3) learning how to apply a series of seven intuitive rules will help you guide your life toward lasting health.

So at this point, you're probably sitting there with this book in your hands, thinking, *Well, what now? How am I going to use these pages to become more intuitive? How am I going to use intuition to gain physical and emotional health?*

Here's what you do. The first part of *The Intuitive Advisor* shows you how medical intuition works, starting with an overview in Chapter One of what I call the Seven Rules for Intuitive Health. Each rule governs a different specific area called a *chakra* or *energy center* in the human body and involves the delicate balance between issues in daily life that you (and everyone) find challenging—your needs versus your family's, going for the money versus going for the love, staying in the relationship versus maintaining your sanity. You'll learn how following these seven intuitive rules helps you create balanced health in these seven energy centers, where emotional, physical, and intuitive wellness are all interconnected.

Then in the second chapter you'll learn about a technique that I call the *mind-body makeover,* which will help you use the intuition you receive from your seven energy centers or chakras and transform it into grounded, actionable steps to create lasting health in your mind and body.

As you proceed to the second part of this book, you'll get the opportunity to take a closer look at your health in each of your seven chakras, with a chapter devoted to each one. You'll learn the physical and emotional health challenges associated with the corresponding area of the body, but you'll also see the four personality extremes that tend to predispose us to having medical problems in that chakra. I'll also suggest a mind-body makeover specifically tailored to each personality type that is designed to improve the health of that area of the body.

There are a variety of ways you could approach this part of the book. First, if you want intuitive guidance on a health issue you're having right now, you could skip ahead to the chapter that discusses it. For example, if you have problems with your lungs, you might want to start with the chapter on the fourth chakra to try to figure out which of the four emotional styles you tend to identify with. We all have a little bit of each of the extreme personality styles within us, but one usually predominates. Following the steps of the mind-body makeover for that type will help you "triage" your current medical crisis or concern.

Second, if you want to get along with the other people in your life—including your mother, father, mate, kids, boss, co-workers, friends, and so on—you could read, chapter by chapter, the descriptions of all the personality extremes and the mind-body makeover suggestions given for each one. Because everyone has seven chakras of their own, as well as a unique blend of personality styles and health concerns, reading about all the different styles will give you a better grasp of how to navigate and interact with the people in your life in an understanding, loving, and healthy way. In addition, learning about each of these personality styles will make you better able to continually decipher the messages from your own inner intuitive advisor, and that puts you in a better position to live your own life and help the people around you live theirs.

•—•—•—•—•

Chapter One
The Seven Rules for Intuitive Health

M any people have had the sense that their health is affected by their emotions. You've probably heard friends or relatives say, "You're going to give your father a heart attack if you keep going on the way you do," or "I could just feel it in my bones that something had happened to you," or even "That job has given me an ulcer." It may sound like an exaggeration, but the truth is that they're onto something. Science shows us that there *is* a connection between emotions and illness—whether it's high blood pressure, depression, or immune-system problems.

Back when the practice of medical intuition began, the original medical intuitives noted that physical health problems corresponded to specific emotional issues, which followed a map called the *seven chakras* or the *seven energy centers*. They found that a specific anatomical area of the body, called a *chakra,* corresponded to a particular energetic and emotional issue in a person's life. When the client had an emotional problem that needed attention, an organ in that chakra territory would begin to signal disease and stress.

As I wrote in the Introduction, when I started my medical-intuitive career, I flew roughly by the seat of my pants. I merely told clients what emotional patterns and physical symptoms I saw in their bodies, leaving any further analysis for their own reading and meditation. Late in the '80s, around the time that Caroline Myss became my mentor, she was working on *Anatomy of the Spirit,* a book that would eventually be the first of her five *New York Times* bestsellers. In that work, she calls our seven chakras or energy centers "our spiritual anatomy" or "the biology of our biography." She writes that these seven basic energy centers are associated with the specific territory of one's health.

Initially, as a Ph.D. candidate in neuroanatomy, I resisted the idea of both chakras and energy centers. Being knee-deep in academia, I had no interest in either spiritual or energy anatomy because neither was a department in the medical school. But as I discovered while filling all those milk crates in my car with studies I dug up in medical journal after medical journal, there is indeed a scientific basis behind the ancient chakra system. And there's also an emotional basis behind illness that corresponds to these chakras. Lo and behold, as I wrote in 1998 in my first book, *Awakening Intuition,* I found that all the health problems tended to cluster in seven basic centers—emotional patterns that parallel Caroline Myss's spiritual or energy anatomy (see Figure 1 on next page).

I spent the next two decades teaching people how to intuitively read their bodies, listening to how their physical symptoms were letting them know that a specific emotional issue in their lives was out of balance. By and large, people did very well. But over time, many hit the wall with their progress, unable to make those changes in their emotional patterns that could help them heal their illnesses.

The First Chakra/Energy Center

People with first-chakra concerns, for example, typically have health issues in the area of their bones, joints, and immune systems. These individuals soon learn that their bodies' symptoms tend to act up when a problem occurs in their families or somewhere else in their lives. If they don't feel safe or secure, the physical problems in the regions of their first chakras simply get worse. Eventually, those with chronic first-chakra health issues—such as fibromyalgia, osteoarthritis, rheumatoid arthritis, and chronic fatigue, among others—tend toward one of two extremes, two polar opposites of behavior.

First-Chakra Pattern I: Norma Ann

The one extreme includes people who feel safe and secure only if they can be very keyed in to their own individual needs. They tend to avoid the public, other people, and even their own families. Handling politics of groups becomes overwhelming for these folks.

I learned a lot about healing first-chakra issues when I did a reading for a woman named Norma Ann. This 61-year-old woman was a

CHAKRA/ENERGY CENTER CHART:
CONNECTING THE HEALTH PROBLEM WITH THE EMOTIONAL SITUATION

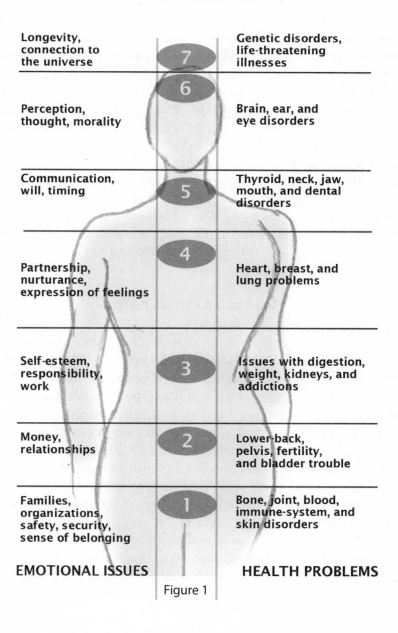

EMOTIONAL ISSUES		HEALTH PROBLEMS
Longevity, connection to the universe	7	Genetic disorders, life-threatening illnesses
	6	
Perception, thought, morality		Brain, ear, and eye disorders
Communication, will, timing	5	Thyroid, neck, jaw, mouth, and dental disorders
	4	
Partnership, nurturance, expression of feelings		Heart, breast, and lung problems
Self-esteem, responsibility, work	3	Issues with digestion, weight, kidneys, and addictions
Money, relationships	2	Lower-back, pelvis, fertility, and bladder trouble
Families, organizations, safety, security, sense of belonging	1	Bone, joint, blood, immune-system, and skin disorders

Figure 1

19

very intuitively and emotionally porous person who was "the sensitive one in the family." In fact, her family always told her that she was *overly* sensitive. Norma Ann was very poor at tolerating environments with a lot of chaos and interpersonal drama.

After a childhood of first-chakra immune and autoimmune problems, such as eczema and chronic colds and flus, Norma Ann went from job to job, having trouble figuring out a way to fit into the group politics in the workplace. Eventually, not only did her childhood first-chakra eczema issues reemerge in adulthood, but she also eventually developed allergies to a variety of office products, including copier ink, perfumes, oils, and rug glue. Eventually, the only way that Norma Ann could feel safe and secure was to live completely alone in a special dwelling in Santa Fe, New Mexico.

Although Norma Ann knew that her first-chakra intuition was telling her through her immune system that she didn't feel safe and secure in group politics, she didn't have any way of handling her health problem other than leaving groups completely. But that wasn't really working either, because she wasn't living a full life.

First-Chakra Pattern II: Otto

The other extreme of people with first-chakra issues includes the folks who only feel safe and secure ensconced in a family, surrounded by constant support—the opposite of those like Norma Ann. These people find that their health is best when they're immersed in families or other organizations. They are masters of blending and belonging, while being alone makes them feel very insecure and unstable.

A perfect example of this was Otto, a 24-year-old party guy and man-about-town who was always on the go. Everyone in New York City's Greenwich Village knew him. Whether it was at afternoon tea, a movie opening, a dance club, or the new "in" restaurant, Otto could be seen schmoozing. In the midst of the crowd, being the life of the party, Otto was in his element, and he shone.

But once the party was over and he went home alone, my client was a mess. Without being constantly surrounded by loving support and the contact of friends, family, and colleagues, Otto's first chakra—his mood and immune system—would sink into the pits. And when that happened, his human papillomavirus (HPV) and herpes ran rampant. Otto could only feel safe in the world if he was plugged into a group, so much so that he lost his capacity to have any confidence in his own personal identity. His only ability to be an individual in the world was when he was surrounded by others.

• • •

If you, like Norma Ann or Otto, tend toward either extreme—you need to be isolated or need to be surrounded by lots of other people—you'll tend to have chronic first-chakra ailments such as joint pain, colds, flus, or other immune-system problems.

The Second Chakra/Energy Center

What about people with second-chakra challenges—those with lower-back, hip, pelvic, uterine, ovarian, fibroid, prostate, and fertility concerns? These folks soon learn that their health issues work as part of their intuitive guidance systems, letting them know when they're having difficulties with finances, money, their marriages, or some other relationships. Eventually, these people tend toward two polar opposites as well.

Second-Chakra Pattern I: Presley

On the one extreme are those who are very good at relationships, whom I call the "nest featherers." These people tend to be very confused about, and avoid the world of, competitive finance.

Doing a reading on Presley, 38, really drove the nest-featherer syndrome home for me. Presley, who had a 12-year-old daughter and a 14-year-old son, had just found out that her husband of 16 years had been leading a double life. He'd been living with another woman in a different state, having an affair that spanned a decade. Presley had put everything, including her heart and her soul, into her marriage and her family. She was devastated.

After a lot of prodding on my part, she admitted that she'd turned a blind eye to her suspicions that her husband had been cheating for years. Presley told me that she ignored her intuition because she was 100 percent financially dependent on her husband and had zero job skills. Despite the fact that Presley had contracted herpes three years before and had had a recent scare with cervical cancer (both second-chakra issues), she was trying to convince her husband to give marital therapy a try, even though he had admitted that their marriage was completely dead.

Presley's capacity to build relationships was fabulous, but she had absolutely no idea how to build a solid base of financial support. Her inability to balance these two second-chakra skills (relationships and money) was putting her health—and her life—at risk.

Second-Chakra Pattern II: Leanne

The other extreme in people who have chronic second-chakra issues includes the Donald Trump (or "Donna" Trump) look-alikes. These born entrepreneurs are always comfortable wheeling and deal-ing, but they tend to have quite the challenge when it comes to hav-ing enduring and stable relationships.

A good example of this came from Leanne, 34, who called me for a reading when her lower back started acting up. Upon first glance, I wondered why this very successful CEO of a Fortune 500 company would have any second-chakra back problems—particularly because she'd just gotten a raise, and her marriage seemed healthy.

When I looked deeper, however, I saw that Leanne's husband had never had a job in the entire time they were married. And although it was certainly convenient that he was a stay-at-home dad for their year-old daughter and four-year-old son, Leanne felt an undercurrent of resentment and discontent in their relationship. As her husband started to get bored, gain weight, and spend more and more money, my client began to carry the financial stress of this situation in her lower back. Leanne was having trouble managing both a stable rela-tionship with her husband and stable finances.

If you're toward one end of the spectrum, like Presley (all love but with money problems), or more at the other end, like Leanne (a financial wizard with relationship failures), you'll tend to have continual, unrelenting problems in the second chakra, with either lower-back, pelvis, or reproductive sex-organ problems.

The Third Chakra/Energy Center

Now let's take a look at people with third-chakra issues—digestive disorders, weight, kidney, or addiction concerns. These individuals soon learn that when their symptoms worsen, their intuitive guidance systems are alerting them that something needs to change in the areas of responsibility, work, and self-esteem. And again, after a while, people with chronic health problems in the third chakra tend to have two opposite personas.

Third-Chakra Pattern I: Suzanne

The first persona includes people who have what I call the "hyperactive responsibility gland." These individuals are forever compelled to take on financial, physical, and other types of obligations for everyone around them, but they tend to neglect doing things for themselves or things that make them feel good about themselves.

For example, Suzanne, 32, was the family angel. If you needed someone to babysit for an evening, you could ask her. If you needed someone to bake a dozen cupcakes for a school party, Suzanne was your woman. If you were upset and needed someone to talk to, Suzanne was always there for you—but who was there for *her?*

When I did Suzanne's reading and tried to suggest a mind-body makeover schedule of healing activities, her calendar was already booked months ahead of time. Exercise every afternoon at 4? "I can't," she told me. "I'm a meals-on-wheels volunteer, and that's when I make my deliveries." How about exercising 30 minutes in the morning? "Oh, I can't. I have to drive my kids to school," she said.

Whenever I pressed her on one of her answers (asking, for example, why her kids couldn't take the bus or set up a car pool), Suzanne's reply was always the same: "I don't want to disappoint anyone." She spent no time building up her own self-esteem, having fun, or engaging in health-promoting activities because she was too busy shouldering everyone else's responsibilities.

Third-Chakra Pattern II: Tina

The second extreme persona with chronic third-chakra issues includes those who are incredibly focused on, and obsessed with, self-involved activities. In their attempt to elevate their own self-worth and self-esteem, they tend to neglect their responsibilities. For example, Tina, 26, had graduated from college and had moved right back into her bedroom at home as if nothing had changed. She had developed a variety of complex digestive issues at school that were diagnosed as irritable bowel syndrome, a third-chakra illness.

Although Tina found a great deal of joy being involved in local theater musicals, taking voice lessons, and working on her creative writing while she was home, her parents were pressuring her to get a job and start supporting herself. She was very good at finding activities that made her feel good about herself, but she wasn't very good at finding jobs that provided for her financially. She wasn't willing to take any entry-level positions because she said that would crush her self-esteem and spirit. Tina couldn't see how to balance her self-esteem with her responsibility to support herself.

●–●–●

If your personality style leans toward either extreme—feeling overly responsible for others, like Suzanne, or not being able to take full responsibility for yourself, like Tina—you'll tend to have third-chakra concerns such as weight, digestion, kidney, or addiction issues.

The Fourth Chakra/Energy Center

And then there are the fourth-chakra people, who tend to have problems with the heart, breasts, and lungs. They have to learn over time that their hypertension, chest pain, arrhythmias, coronary artery disease, breast cysts, and asthma are part of their intuitive guidance systems, alerting them to critical issues brewing in partnerships or in how they emotionally express themselves. And over time, people with health problems in this region also tend to lean toward two polar-opposite personality styles.

Fourth-Chakra Pattern I: Victor

On the one hand are the people who are so focused on partnerships, whether marriage or business, that they lose touch with how to nurture their own emotional needs or even how to be aware of them. This leads me to the case of Victor, 42, who was one of those guys I call a real sweet pea—a good guy, but someone who always seems to find himself in bad relationships. Victor had just gotten out of the coronary intensive care unit after having suffered his first heart attack and undergone open-heart surgery.

When I read Victor, I saw that his home life felt like a battle zone, with constant fighting and maneuvering for position and advantage. I saw that he was always sacrificing his mental and emotional sanity to keep his partnerships alive. Victor, in fact, had been married to an unstable woman who was emotionally and physically abusive, but had stayed in the marriage due to his wife's frequent suicide threats. This man was having a hard time balancing his emotional sanity with his partnership needs.

Fourth-Chakra Pattern II: Ursula

On the other hand are those individuals who are so marinated in their own feelings and in fulfilling their emotional needs that they have trouble making the energetic investment required to initiate

25

and nurture enduring partnerships. What's needed to maintain partnerships puts these folks over the deep end. For example, Ursula, 32, called me for a reading after having just gone to yet another family wedding. She was desperate to understand why she couldn't find a man, get married, and have kids like everybody else.

When I looked at her intuitively, I could see that Ursula had a very good heart, but her moods were a mess—up, down, sideways . . . all over the place. The slightest provocation could make this woman lose her temper to such a degree that I couldn't imagine how anyone could get along with her. Ursula admitted that she'd had a series of relationships with very sweet men, each of whom had bolted after about a year and a half. After the breakup, all of them had wanted absolutely no contact with her again, and they each said something vaguely similar to "It's not you—it's me." It was very clear to me that Ursula had to learn how to stabilize her emotions so that she could have a more long-term, steady relationship.

●–●–●

If you, like Victor or Ursula, are one of those people who tend to be closer to either polar opposite—those who nurture their relationships more than their own needs, or those who focus almost exclusively on themselves and their own emotions—you'll tend to have the same fourth-chakra health challenges, including heart disease, stroke, or breast or lung problems.

The Fifth Chakra/Energy Center

Rounding the bend of the energy centers, we next have folks with fifth-chakra concerns, who display issues with the thyroid, neck, mouth, and jaw. These people tend to learn over time that their health patterns get worse when they have difficulty speaking up for themselves—especially expressing their views to the right audience at the right time, with the correct amount of intensity. It probably won't surprise you by now to hear that after a while, those with fifth-chakra issues tend to split off into two polar opposites, like all the other energy centers.

Fifth-Chakra Pattern I: Wendy

First, you have individuals whom I refer to as your "Don't ask, don't tell" people. Their tendency is to under-assert their views in relationships in order to keep the peace and avoid conflict. They are all too willing to yield to the opinions of those around them.

For example, Wendy called me for a reading because all of her fifth-chakra problems were piling up. She suffered from temporo-mandibular joint syndrome (TMJ), hypothyroidism, painful arthritis in her neck, and chronic dental problems. Having survived a difficult childhood by learning how to shut her mouth and not make waves, this 53-year-old woman now found herself in both a business and a marriage with dominating, overassertive partners. Whenever a conflict arose, she'd try to do anything she could to avoid it, but the amount of energy it took to constantly walk on eggshells generated a host of problems in the areas of Wendy's body that had to do with having her say.

Fifth-Chakra Pattern II: Xena

The other extreme includes those overly assertive individuals who tend to dominate others with their views and willfully try to drown out other people's voices. For example, Xena, 23, had worked with me over the course of several medical-intuitive readings for her chronic fifth-chakra communication problems. From an early age, Xena had trouble knowing when to speak her mind, and when offering her thoughts or opinions would ostracize her from others and get her into trouble.

Xena's neck problems began in high school around the time she turned in some classmates for smoking. She found herself treated like an outcast and ended up changing schools. But her social-adjustment and neck problems followed her to her next school. In addition to chronic neck pain, for which she received chiropractic and acupuncture treatment, Xena continued to struggle with her need to let people know what was on her mind. She told herself that if they didn't want to hear the truth, it was *their* problem.

•—•—•

If you are closer to either extreme—like Wendy (under-assertive and excessively willing to please people), or Xena (overly assertive and willfully dominating others)—you'll tend to have fifth-chakra health concerns, including issues with your neck, thyroid, mouth, or jaw.

The Sixth Chakra/Energy Center

How about those sixth-chakra people with brain, eye, and ear problems? Those afflicted by these disorders learn over time that their symptoms are a key intuitive sign that they need to reevaluate how they perceive the world and also how flexibly and adaptively their minds function. Again, there tend to be two opposing groups of people who have sixth-chakra health issues.

Sixth-Chakra Pattern I: Zoë

On one side are the tidier, conservative thinkers who have a more inflexible, hypermoral, overly ethical way of looking at things and ordering their thoughts. For example, Zoë had a brain like a calculator. While she was a brilliant computer scientist, she had a very difficult time getting along with people or finding a job or stable housing situation.

Although Zoë was only 24 and appeared to be the typical carefree college student, she was actually very rigid in how she managed her life. Most of the time, she only contacted friends through chat rooms and computer games, and when the dormitory social life of college ended, so did her capacity to have any enduring relationship with friends or potential boyfriends. Zoë suffered from typical sixth-chakra problems, such as obsessive-compulsive disorder and Asperger's syndrome—brain styles with an unyielding, rule-centered way of approaching life and trying to fit everyone else into one's world.

Sixth-Chakra Pattern II: Yvonne

The other sixth-chakra extreme includes those whose thinking is so excessively unstructured, free-form, and wishy-washy that you can't nail them down to any specific viewpoints. This brings us to Yvonne, 34, who floated into her scheduled reading like she flitted about her life, calling 20 minutes late with a host of vague and confusing excuses for her tardiness. To me, this woman's mind felt like a popcorn popper going from one idea to another. Her thoughts were as disorganized as her life.

Yvonne dropped out of high school because she hated taking the required classes. She also dropped out of art school after only a few semesters because she thought that its teaching methods cramped her creative style. Unable to support herself as a freelance artist, Yvonne chose waitressing because its very flexible, open-ended scheduling made her feel independent. But after several years, she hit a wall of depression.

My client's sixth-chakra problem—her need for freedom and her excessively flexible, unstructured mind-set—had given her difficulty conforming to the structured world. Yvonne's mind had creativity without discipline. She had lots of content without the benefit of education, structure, or foundation. Yvonne couldn't thrive in the world, no matter how flexible she was, because her mind needed a more balanced sixth chakra.

•–•–•

If you see yourself nearer to one of two extreme personality styles—unyielding and rule centered, like Zoë, or unstructured and overly wishy-washy, like Yvonne—you'll tend to develop sixth-chakra illnesses such as headaches and eye and ear problems.

The Seventh Chakra/Energy Center

Finally, what about the seventh-chakra people, who have life-threatening health concerns? Once again, these folks tend to be in one of two opposite camps.

Seventh-Chakra Pattern I: Abby

The first extreme consists of those who have no idea what their purpose in life is supposed to be. After either a partner or spouse has died, these individuals go through life trying to keep busy, marking time with hobbies, the occasional volunteer activity, golf, tennis, or card games.

Abby was a good example of this. At the age of 63, Abby had suffered a stroke and a broken hip, and she called me for a reading only after much prodding by her family. It seemed that the previous seven years had presented her with many, many losses: the last of seven children had moved out of state three years previously, a grandchild had died of sudden infant death syndrome, a sister and a brother had died of heart disease, and most recently, Abby's husband had died of a massive heart attack.

Every aspect of Abby's identity was falling away: wife, mother, grandmother, and sibling. She felt as if nothing was left that could give her daily existence meaning and purpose. I tried to explain to her that having a strong sense of purpose in life tends to *extend* it, especially for those with life-threatening illnesses, but Abby seemed confused by the whole concept.

Seventh-Chakra Pattern II: Bill

The other seventh-chakra extreme includes those whose whole lives revolve around some single core identity, whether it's being a professional athlete, an actor or performer, a lawyer, a doctor, or a teacher. Once their identity comes to a close at retirement, these people's lives become meaningless.

Bill, 28, was a childhood actor who had been in many movies, but unfortunately, his career plummeted once he entered his 20s. After going from audition to audition without a single callback, Bill had quit his acting career three years earlier and had started doing voice-overs for commercials. After a few months of fatigue and flu-like symptoms, Bill was diagnosed with lymphoma.

With show business having been his sole focus since the age of three, Bill told me that once his acting career had ended, his life started to feel empty and meaningless. Although such a crisis for a child actor isn't unusual, we all can develop a seventh-chakra (potentially fatal) illness when our lifelong core identity has died.

●–●–●

If you find yourself lacking the benefit of an inner compass that gives your life direction, and you feel as though you tend to be closer to one extreme, like Abby (with no life purpose); or at the other, like Bill (needing to redefine your reason for living), you may tend to develop a seventh-chakra, life-threatening health problem signaling your need for a new sense of purpose.

Introducing the Seven Rules for Intuitive Health

After 20 years as a medical-intuitive advisor, I realized that teaching people how to listen for the intuitive message behind the disease wasn't enough to help them create true and lasting health. Even if clients grasped the intuitive chakra map of symptoms in their bodies and the intuitive language behind the outward manifestation of their health problems, a third vital step was missing—namely, how to effectively *respond* to what their intuition was advising, and how they could learn to heal their lives and assist in healing those around them.

That's when I came to the realization that the health of each of the seven energy centers of the body depends on following a rule that involves balancing two seemingly opposite or contradictory qualities in our lives. I call this set of balancing acts the *Seven Rules for Intuitive*

Health. Just as harmonized brain function depends on having both the left and the right hemispheres in sync, healing body and mind in each of these seven energy centers or chakras involves following a rule to balance dual identities and engage two paradoxical mind-sets simultaneously.

Thus, learning the *Seven Rules for Intuitive Health* will help you create a healthy mind and body. Whenever you're in danger of dropping the ball somewhere, you'll intuitively understand the warning signs your body is sending you via your health—and you'll know how to get back on track.

1. For the health of the first chakra—your bones, joints, skin, blood, and immune system—you must balance the personal with the political and follow the **first rule** for intuitive health: *All for one, and one for all.* To maintain health in this energy center, you will need to be intuitively in touch with your individual needs as you simultaneously negotiate your way around those of the group, whether that group comprises your family, those you work with, or some other organization.

2. For the health of the second chakra—your lower back and your reproductive/sex organs—you need to balance money and love, following the **second rule** for intuitive health: *To be a lover, you need to be a fighter.* To maintain health in this energy center, you must develop the sometimes feisty, detached persona of an entrepreneur and balance it with the warm sensitivity needed in an intimate relationship.

3. To tackle those hard-to-treat weight, addiction, and digestive problems—which can compromise the health of the third chakra— you need to balance self-esteem and responsibility by following the **third rule** for intuitive health: *You can't always get what you want, but if you try, you'll get what you need.* To maintain health in this energy center, you have to balance feeding your cravings and desires in an attempt to boost your self-esteem . . . with fulfilling your duties and responsibilities in your personal life and your job.

4. If you are one of the millions of people who suffer from heart disease or breast or lung problems, you'll need to pay attention

primarily to the fourth chakra by balancing partnership with emotional wellness, following the **fourth rule** for intuitive health: *Got to love her madly.* (After all, as the Doors song implies, it may not be possible to be in a relationship without going at least a little mad.) To maintain health in this energy center, you have to be able to be in a partnership and simultaneously maintain your emotional sanity, balancing your emotional needs with those of the partnership.

5. For those unlucky people (and I am one of them) who tend to have fifth-chakra issues—highlighted by chronic problems in the neck, thyroid, and mouth—the best course of action is balancing assertiveness with a compliant communication style by following the **fifth rule** for intuitive health: *Sometimes you've got to be cruel to be kind.* Maintaining health in this energy center involves knowing when to be boldly assertive and stick to your position, and when to be more compliant and yield to another's point of view.

6. For the health of the sixth chakra—eyes, ears, and brain—you must balance a more structured, detail-oriented mind-set with broader, more outside-of-the-box views by following the **sixth rule** for intuitive health: *I know I'm different, but from now on I want to try to be the same (as other people).* To maintain the health of this energy center, you need to cultivate a flexible and adaptive mind-set. This means developing the capacity to hold strictly traditional, toe-the-line views sometimes, and more loose and free-ranging ones at other times. It also means knowing when to agree for the sake of keeping the peace (agreeing to disagree and tolerating the difference in mind-sets), and when it's critical to stick your neck out and disagree with everyone.

7. Finally, for the health of the seventh chakra—your longevity and connection to the universe—you must be willing when necessary to revise your life's purpose by following the **seventh rule** for intuitive health: *What doesn't kill you makes you stronger.* To maintain the health of this energy center (and possibly manage a life-threatening illness), you need to learn how, at any stage of your life, to pursue a life purpose in the face of potential death. You must be able to reconstitute your spirit and find a new focus and a new life goal.

The Seven Rules for Intuitive Health

Rule 1: All for one, and one for all (balancing the political and the personal). The health of the first chakra—the bones, joints, blood, immune system, and skin—involves attending to your individual needs while negotiating your way successfully in groups, whether they're your family members or people in other organizations.

Rule 2: To be a lover, you need to be a fighter (balancing money and love). The health of the second chakra—the lower back, reproductive areas, and sex organs—involves balancing finances and relationships. It also involves being able to develop the sometimes feisty and detached persona of an entrepreneur balanced with the sensitivity needed in an intimate relationship.

Rule 3: You can't always get what you want, but if you try, you'll get what you need (balancing self-esteem and responsibility). The health of the third chakra—digestive tract and weight—involves reconciling your tendency toward wanting to boost your self-esteem by feeding your cravings and desires . . . with fulfilling your duties and responsibilities at work and in your personal life.

Rule 4: Got to love her madly (balancing partnership and emotional health). The health of your fourth chakra— heart, breasts, and lungs—involves being able to be in a partnership while simultaneously maintaining your emotional sanity, balancing your emotional needs with those of the partnership.

Rule 5: Sometimes you've got to be cruel to be kind (balancing assertive and compliant communication styles). The health of the fifth chakra—neck, thyroid, mouth, and teeth—involves developing a sense of when to be boldly assertive and stick to your position and when to be compliant and yield to another's will.

Rule 6: I know I'm different, but from now on I want to try to be the same (as other people) (balancing conservative and liberal mind-sets). The health of the sixth chakra—eyes, ears, and brain—involves developing a flexible and adaptive mind-set. This means having the capacity to sometimes hold structured, traditional views and at other times have a broader, less structured approach—occasionally agreeing for the sake of peacefully agreeing (and tolerating the difference in mind-sets by agreeing to disagree); and at other moments when necessary, sticking your neck out and disagreeing with all others.

Rule 7: What doesn't kill you makes you stronger (balancing life-threatening illnesses and revising your life's purpose). The health of your seventh chakra—your longevity and your capacity to survive a life-threatening illness—involves learning how, at each stage of your life, to be able to pursue your individual purpose, as well as how, when faced with potential death, to reconstitute your spirit and realign yourself with a new focus and a new life goal.

So there you have it: the Seven Rules for Intuitive Health. Now join me as a fly on the wall of my medical-intuitive advisor practice as we move on to use intuition to create health by doing the "intuitive intervention," as well as tackling the mind-body makeover. In the next chapter, you'll not only read stories about people's health problems, but you'll also see how they were able to use intuition to actually make changes in their lives to overcome their challenges.

* * * * *

Chapter Two

The Intuitive Intervention:
Tackling the Mind-Body Makeover

Once I've explained both the health problems in a client's body and the specific emotional situations in his or her life that are associated with the symptoms observed, nine times out of ten that person says, "I know that. I've worked on those issues in therapy for years. How come I'm not better yet? Why am I still depressed/in pain/overweight? Why do I still have the same problems?"

Understanding an emotional issue won't create true healing unless you also make an obvious change in how you conduct your life. Intuition can have an amazingly transformative effect—but in order for the effect to take hold, you must be able to use its messages to make over your life, mind, and body.

Nothing illustrates this concept better than *my* story of when I personally didn't follow my intuitive advice and paid for it. Recently, I developed a nagging cough lasting 12 weeks. No matter what I did, it wouldn't go away. One of my dear friends, Lisa, who is very intuitive, kept telling me that she was very anxious about my cough, but I'd been avoiding acting on it even though I'd been trying to figure out what emotional issue was underlying all the coughing. I just kept stuffing cough drops in my mouth. I thought that it really couldn't be anything too serious, because the drops seemed to have a calming effect, especially if I used up to 36 of them a day!

One afternoon, Lisa and I were trying on shoes in the middle of L.L.Bean when she said in her Queens, New York, accent, "I think that cough is something serious. I think you need an inhaler. Don't you want to go to the doctor and get one?"

In the middle of trying on some very sleek leather flip-flops, I screamed, "Inhalers are for weenies!" Everyone in the entire shoe department turned and looked at me as I launched into my diatribe: "Kids these days are weenies! Everyone needs an inhaler. Everyone needs ear tubes. When I went to school, *no one* had an inhaler, and *no one* had ear tubes, and no one ever died. I'm not getting an inhaler! Can I have this in a size 9, please?"

This ended Lisa's medical-intuitive reading of my pulmonary problem in the middle of L.L.Bean. The next day, my coughing escalated, and my breathing became shallower. Lisa was leaving for a vacation in the Caribbean, and she called me on her way to the airport. When she heard my voice, that was it—she went into intuition-intervention mode and called for reinforcements, knowing that this would be as gentle as a cattle prod in encouraging me to go to a local emergency room. And when I did, guess what they gave me that finally stopped my coughing? You got it—an inhaler.

So how, then, do I get other people to start to listen to intuition and be able to make the appropriate changes in their lives so they can get healthy? Well, we start with the following . . .

Mapping the Intuitive Mind-Body Makeover

When I do readings, I immediately try to help my clients use intuition to help themselves heal their minds and bodies. But a reading is like driver's ed, which has two parts: There's the classroom instruction, which is directed at gaining knowledge. But to really understand how to apply what they've learned there, the students also need the practical part of the process—learning to operate their vehicles on the road. And like a good instructor, I do both.

First, I teach clients how intuition flows through their right brain, left brain, and body. Then I walk them (or sometimes *push* them) through the mind-body makeover. In this way, they learn how to take their right-brain intuition and emotions and effectively respond to them with their left brains so that these things don't have to be converted into medical-intuitive health problems in their bodies.

TWO ROUTES TO INTUITIVE ADVICE

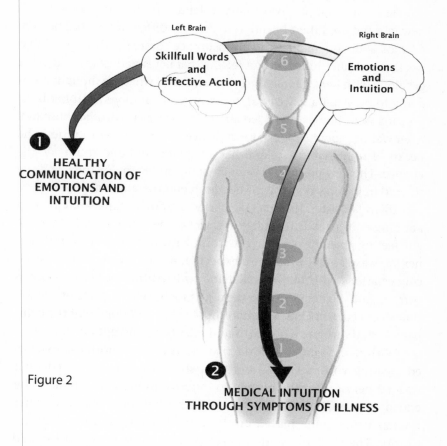

Figure 2

Figure 2 shows the layout of an intuitive mind-body makeover. First, look at the circle on the right, your right brain, which is where intuition begins. It is also, not so coincidentally, the part of your mind that's responsible for emotions such as fear, anger, sadness, love, and joy, which often underlie intuition. When your left brain responds to these emotions by creating effective strategies for change, it provides a healthy route through which you can express your intuition using skillful words and appropriate action. The more painful alternative? If the left brain doesn't respond effectively to your right-brain intuition and emotions, those feelings travel down to your body. There, they are eventually transformed into symptoms of illness, which become medical intuition.

Here's an example: Two sisters, Yolanda and Katrina, both started new jobs but used their intuition to get very different results. Yolanda, 47, took a job as a manager in an insurance company. During her first week, she got an immediate gut feeling that her supervisor would never get along with her and that the job wasn't at all what she thought it was going to be. After a few casual, tentative conversations with her boss, Yolanda went home and talked about her concerns with her husband. After waiting about a month for evidence to confirm her intuition, she began secretly looking for another job. She found one and made the change. The new position was much better suited for Yolanda, and she thrived in it. All was well with her, both emotionally and physically.

Yolanda's sister, Katrina, 45, started a similar managerial job in a banking company. During her first week, she also got an immediate gut feeling that she'd never get along with her supervisor and that her job wasn't at all what she'd expected. After a few tentative, casual conversations with her boss, Katrina realized that her intuition was correct. But she decided that she'd just focus on the parts of the job that she liked, work extra hard in those areas, and hope that the company would recognize her skills and talents and accept her.

Within a month, Katrina had a very uncomfortable extended meeting with her boss, and then she got a detailed e-mail that warned her of what she needed to improve in her performance. She ended up going into therapy to deal with what she thought were her mother issues being played out in a problematic situation with authority. Then Katrina started developing panic attacks and irritable bowel syndrome, causing her to miss a day or two of work. Within two months, out of the blue, Katrina was stunned when her boss let her go. She couldn't believe that the company would actually fire someone because she was such a diligent worker and tried so hard.

All of us have been in Katrina's shoes at one time or another. Like her sister, Yolanda, she had an immediate and accurate intuitive hit on day one that her job wouldn't work out. Even though her gut feeling told her that she and her boss would never get along and the job wasn't at all what she'd imagined, Katrina chose to ignore her intuition and instead tried to "fix" the situation, impose her will on her surroundings, and ignore the needs (or not-so-subtle requests) of the company. Katrina didn't convey her right-brain intuition and feelings into her left brain for effective words and actions. The emotion and intuition were transformed instead into her body, and her gut feelings quite literally became medical intuition in the form of gut *problems* (irritable bowel syndrome), while her job anxiety was transformed into physical panic attacks.

●–●–●

Sometimes your intuition gets converted into a medical problem even if you're able to translate your right-brain intuition into left-brain words and actions, because the words you choose aren't exactly skillful and the action is inappropriate. When it comes to delivering your message, if the volume is turned up too high with yelling and screaming or threatening; if you repeat yourself too much with bitching, moaning, nagging, and haranguing; or if you're just plain pathetic by being overly apologetic, self-deprecating, insecure, pleading, desperate, and shaming, then the process of communicating your intuition will backfire. It will instead show up in your body as illness.

Then again, your health will also fail if your way of dealing with intuitive information about your life is either under- or overresponsive. If you tend to be underresponsive to your intuition, you usually choose to ignore your gut feelings. You probably tend to run away, avoiding what makes you afraid. You fear rejection or loss of approval or acceptance, as well as a loss of monetary or financial security. You consequently spend a lot of time feeling worthless, powerless, hopeless, or helpless. You have trouble letting go of a dead or dying relationship, not wanting to accept what is or hoping to change reality. Because when you're in the midst of a personal crisis you tend to ignore the problem until it's too late, you're likely to also put off listening to your intuition until it's barreling down on your body in the form of symptoms of illness.

On the other hand, maybe you're overly responsive, too impulsive, or "trigger-happy" when it comes to mounting an appropriate response to intuition. If so, you're likely to try to fix every situation you encounter. You're way too intuitively keyed in and responsive to your life—and everyone else's as well. When you sense that something is about to go wrong, you try to prevent the "bad" things from happening. In doing so, you're creating an interpersonal judicial system, thinking, *I'm right—this is wrong,* or *Things should be different,* or *This is unfair.* You need to be in control, not wanting to acknowledge that you're not in a position ethically or spiritually to make these calls.

Keep in mind that it's possible to seesaw back and forth between being intuitively blind in our own lives and being intuitive busybodies in those of everyone around us. In fact, the usual scenario is that we're all far more capable of intuitively seeing the crises of our loved ones than we are of having an accurate read on our own lives, which is why our *emotional* intuition has to be converted into *medical* intuition—symptoms in our bodies that ultimately scream to get our attention.

Keeping a Lid on Intuition

When clients can't see the roadblocks keeping them from transforming intuition that could transform their health and their lives, I use a diagram that illustrates why they're keeping a lid on their intuition. I have them draw a circle and then place a horizontal line through the middle of it (see Figure 3), labeling the lower semicircle "Temporal lobe" and the upper one "Frontal lobe."

This little circle is a minimodel of how the mind processes intuition. Like the right brain, the temporal-lobe system is critical for emotion and intuition. So I have my clients write "Intuition that senses problems and change" in the lower semicircle. The frontal lobe, the upper semicircle, is important for censoring emotions and intuition or putting a lid on certain feelings and hunches in order to survive in the workplace, fit into society, or maintain peace and harmony in day-to-day relationships. So I have my clients write "Thoughts that censor intuition" in the upper semicircle.

Here's how this works: Let's say you have an intuitive feeling that your boss is cheating on his wife, but your socially savvy frontal lobe helps you keep your intuition under wraps and your mouth zipped so

KEEPING A LID ON INTUITION:
UNBRIDLED OR CENSORED INTUITION

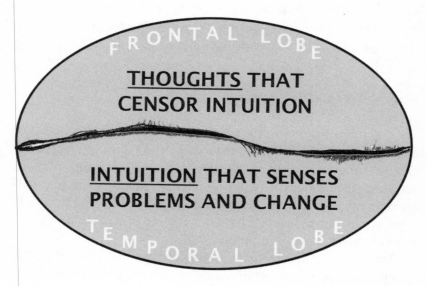

Figure 3

that your job will be safe. That frontal-lobe capacity to keep a lid on intuition gets loose when you experience PMS, enter perimenopause, have ADHD or ADD, or have a variety of other conditions that cause you to become "unhinged." In these more highly charged, impulsive, hormonally driven emotional intervals in your life, you're more likely to blurt out your intuitive hunches in a way that's not necessarily productive.

At the other extreme are the people who are so focused on keeping their lives the same that their frontal lobes block out any intuition that would help them make positive changes in their families, relationships, finances, or jobs. Thought patterns like *What would my family think? . . . I don't want to be alone . . . I'm too old to start a new career . . .* and a host of others prevent these folks from acting on their intuition.

If your intuition can't make its way out from under the weight of all those real-world requirements to keep everything the same, you're more likely to relegate your hunches to the realm of an existential and spiritual exercise. If you can't act on your intuition, you don't consciously acknowledge it, and then your body has no other option but to alert you through signs of illness and disease that something critical in your life needs to change.

Blowing the Lid Off Intuition

If you want to learn how to enhance your intuitive abilities, it's critical that you identify the roadblocks you've put up to prevent change. Intuition always warns that some type of change is necessary; and when certain areas of your relationships, finances, and work are open to examination and revision, you can hear intuition in its subtlest early forms before it has been allowed to escalate into symptoms of illness (medical intuition).

Sometimes, helping clients learn how to avoid censoring their intuition is a gentle procedure—a loving, subtle nudge or tap. In extreme cases, occasionally a less-delicate jackhammer approach is required. Remember, the title of this chapter refers to "Tackling the Mind-Body Makeover," because getting people to change how they think and act is really never easy. I chose the word *tackling* because it helps you envision a football team's defensive lineman, who tries to block a player's progress by seizing him suddenly and stopping him if necessary.

I've never performed a medical-intuitive reading that didn't involve some tackling. And I myself have had unhealthy thought processes that blocked my intuitive insight about my own life (in a not-so-subtle fashion, I might add). The intuitive intervention, however, is the best process I know of to make people see how they're blocking their own inner knowledge.

The Easy Intuitive Intervention

I think the easiest intervention is when someone doesn't need that much pushing. For example, I did a reading on Diana, 54, who'd spent several anxious years taking care of her alcoholic father, her drug-addicted brother, and then her alcoholic ex-husband before swearing that she would never have a problem with addiction in her relationships ever again.

After Diana's three children left the nest, she started dating a wonderful man and was thrilled to see that she was finally starting to lose those extra 40 pounds she'd had around her middle all her adult life. But after a while, Diana started noticing the same old anxiety returning, and the weight slowly began to climb back on. After one of her daughters was arrested twice for alcohol-related offenses, Diana called me for a reading. She asked how her weight was related to her past history with her loved ones and addiction. She wanted to know not only how to stop the weight gain, but also how to prevent herself from taking on those same old patterns of weight-bearing caretaking that she'd played out for most of her life.

I told Diana that she was on to something: her third-chakra weight gain was her body's intuition letting her know that someone near her was having a problem with both irresponsibility and addiction. And as the number on the scale went up, Diana's intuition was screaming at her that she was both carrying the responsibility for this loved one's life and trying to run interference for any fallout that would occur as a result of that person's reckless behavior.

Diana connected the dots between her anxiety, her intuition, and her weight gain. She understood that the extra 40 pounds were related to her concern about her daughter's recent arrests for driving while intoxicated. (This, by the way, was a daughter who was vehemently denying that she had any problems with addiction.) Diana learned that she was carrying the anxiety that her loved ones weren't able to feel because they were escaping responsibility in their lives through alcohol.

Diana immediately realized that she needed to attend to her own addictive pattern of eating to soothe her anxiety. She also saw that she would benefit from joining a 12-step group called Co-Dependents Anonymous so that she could find a way to respond more appropriately the next time a relative near her would invariably get caught up in his or her addiction.

There may be times when you've acted as an intuitive advisor for a friend or family member and have performed the easy intuitive intervention. Your pal approaches you and tells you that he just came back from the doctor after having a bad feeling, but the doctor wouldn't order the test he wanted and . . . blah, blah, blah. Before you know it, you have the same gut feeling your friend has, and then you become knee-deep in intuitive advocacy to get him to listen to his gut and follow up on the action it's trying to convey. You may even attend the next doctor's visit with him as an intuitive chaperone to make sure he follows through and acts on his intuition. In the easy intuitive intervention, all you have to do is nudge, and people quickly learn to stop ignoring their intuition and start to act immediately.

The Not-So-Subtle Intuitive Intervention

In the not-so-subtle or easy intuitive intervention, on the other hand, I use a variety of methods to help people hear their intuition. First, there's the irreverent-humor technique. They say you can always catch more flies with honey than with vinegar, and that also applies to medical intuition. Using exaggeration or hyperbole sometimes works to shock clients and get them to laugh about how stubborn they're being. (Then again, when the client doesn't get the humor, there's egg on my face.)

Esther, for example, had found herself in one bad relationship after another . . . and also in one life-threatening health crisis after another. After about 53 minutes of cajoling, prodding, and giving numerous examples of how these relationships would end up driving her to an early grave, I actually found myself blurting out in exasperation: "If you die, don't call me!"

After this ridiculous exclamation, a pregnant pause filled the phone line. I was absolutely horrified by what had come out of my mouth, but to my utter amazement, Esther started to laugh and laugh.

"Yes, my life is getting pretty ridiculous with all these dead-end boyfriends," she finally said when she could catch her breath again. It was an intuitive intervention—not so subtle, but effective.

Then there's the obituary technique. Although potent, this can be quite tricky to pull off. I discovered the obituary intervention technique accidentally one Saturday morning when I was starting a reading. I hardly ever do readings on Saturday mornings, so I was a little more casual in how I opened with Tiffany.

I said, "You're one of those people who does everything for everyone everywhere, and it's always done perfectly. Kind of like one of those women you read about in the obituaries—'Mary, 48, passed away peacefully last night after a long illness while in the loving company of her family and friends. A caring wife and mother, she homeschooled her children and volunteered for the local organic-farmers' collective, the National Audubon Society, the city homeless shelter, the rape crisis shelter,' and so on."

As I started to really pick up steam and get carried away, Tiffany interrupted me in midsentence, crying out, "That's me! That's exactly me! And lately I've even been obsessed with obituaries!" It turned out that Tiffany, a freelance writer, had just been diagnosed with stage II breast cancer.

This technique is a particularly effective type of intuitive intervention because it uses futuristic zeal in juxtaposing the concept of death and all of the client's unhealthy traits, crammed together for emphasis in the compressed literary style often seen in the obituary section of a newspaper. In the same vein, if I want to be even more direct in getting someone to see an intuitive message that she's been working very hard to avoid, I might use the tombstone technique— an exaggerated prediction of what her epitaph could be if she doesn't change course—because it uses fewer words and is actually more shocking.

The Mechanics of an Intuitive Mind-Body Makeover

So now we're almost at the part of the medical-intuitive reading that deals with the solution: the mind-body makeover. As you recall, the beginning of a reading involves pinpointing an intuitive message, an emotional situation in someone's life that's out of balance—one that, if left unattended, increases the person's chance of contracting an illness.

Then, in the second part of the reading, I scan the individual's body, looking for symptoms of illness. By having clients draw an intuitive mind-body map, I help them make the connection that their bodies' symptoms (the medical intuition) are part of their intuitive guidance system. If the individual doesn't see the connection, I may choose to do an intuitive intervention, subtle or not so subtle, depending upon the client's personality style.

Finally comes the point I'm trying to pull off, the intuitive mind-body makeover, which outlines how the person can support his body and mind while bringing about the appropriate life changes that his intuition is signaling.

The mechanics of how to succeed in your makeover first involve returning to the intuitive mind-body map that was constructed at the beginning of this chapter. Just like a hairstylist would show you how to fix your hair or a fashion stylist might illustrate how you could revamp your overall look, I outline a series of solutions as to how clients might want to fix their minds, bodies, and lives.

First, I address the client's body. Depending on the individual's physical disorders or the particular chakras or energy centers that are affected, I suggest a host of nutritional, herbal, medicinal, homeopathic, and other solutions that are available to help treat her physical ills. I also urge her to create a skilled team of physicians, nurse-practitioners, and other health-care professionals who can perform these treatments. In addition, I might suggest a variety of other solutions to consider, such as specific diets, certain exercises, yoga, acupuncture, light therapy, or osteopathic therapy, to name only a few. All of these may support the body while the mind makes its changes.

Next, I approach the client's mind, starting with the right brain. I outline options she can take to support her mood, soothe her anxiety and panic, or reduce her anger; and I suggest ways that she might obtain emotional support from others. I may recommend many healing treatments—medications, herbs, nutritional supplements, psychotherapy, art and music therapy, Eye Movement Desensitization and Reprocessing (EMDR), shamanism, animal therapy, as well as an endless supply of other therapies—to help support the right-brain emotions while the left brain brings about the important changes that intuition is promoting.

Finally, I move on to the client's left brain. To help it recognize and respond to intuition, I first must teach her to rewire the thought patterns that censored such information in the first place. To do that, I use affirmations, Cognitive Behavioral Therapy (CBT), or Dialectical Behavioral Therapy (DBT). Each of these techniques involves identifying negative thought patterns, the ones that most commonly prevent us from listening to our intuition and seeing what is possible in our lives. Examples of these thoughts include: *I need to be in control, I can't accept help*, or *I feel worthless or powerless*. (For more detailed explanations of these damaging thought patterns, read any book on affirmations, CBT, or DBT—or see my own affirmation card deck, *Mind/Body Makeover Oracle Cards*.)

Once the client identifies her negative, self-defeating, disempowering, or even willful thought patterns, affirmations help her replace those old patterns with more flexible, adaptive, and productive mindsets that allow other possibilities into her life, including the ones that the client's intuition suggests.

Speaking of possibilities, please join me in my intuitive advisory clinic, as we get an opportunity in the next part of the book to see what kind of healing is possible using medical intuition and the mind-body makeover.

•—•—•—•—•

PART II

Identifying and Resolving
Your Health Issues

Chapter Three

First Chakra: "Take Me Home"

(The Health of Your Blood, Immune System, Bones, Joints, and Skin)

Your first chakra—the area of your body that includes your blood, bones, joints, skin, and immune system—is the intuitive advisor that will let you know how safe you feel in the world. It reflects how much support you're receiving from any group and how stable, grounded, and rooted you are. Basically, the organs in the area covered by this chakra will start to act up if your survival is in any way threatened.

The first time your security is challenged is when you leave home and have to fit into a new group of people. Maybe you remember when you started kindergarten, middle school, or high school; when you went off to college; or the first day of any new job. You probably felt nervous or antsy, and then maybe your skin broke out or your immune system tanked. You became painfully aware of how you were different from the rest of the group, but you knew that you still needed to maintain harmony with them for your survival. In the midst of trying to balance being yourself while fitting in, you might have had problems with colds, flus, allergies, and fatigue; your joints and musculoskeletal system; or skin disorders such as acne, rashes, psoriasis, and eczema.

The first time I saw this first-chakra intuition in action was when I was a camp counselor back in 1978. The bus would drop off hundreds of screaming, shrieking kids between the ages of 5 and 15 every morning. Most of them were happy to be there, but I remember this one eight-year-old girl in a dress, black patent-leather shoes, and a hair bow who started to scream, "Take me home!" I looked up and saw her trying to hide behind a tree, so I went over to her and held her hand. Her name was Alexis.

Alexis stood out like a sore thumb. All the rest of the kids her age were sitting on the ground in a line in front of the office. When I told

Alexis to join them, she said that she couldn't because if she sat on the ground, she'd get a bladder infection. Her problem feeling safe enough to blend into camp routines continued when we went on to the kickball diamond. I assigned everyone a position on the team, and I symbolically put Alexis out in left field. When the other team kicked the ball, it sailed right over her head, but she appeared to be looking at a buttercup in the patch of grass by her feet. The rest of the team was very upset at Alexis for not paying attention and not being a team player. I yelled, "Hello! Earth to Alexis! *Earth to Alexis!* Come in, Alexis!"

By lunchtime, Alexis's first-chakra problems with fitting in escalated. The way her individual needs clashed with the group's was becoming much more apparent. As everyone grabbed a place at the picnic table, Alexis hesitated, pulling a plastic bag of carrot sticks out of her lunch. With a timid look, she tried to find a place to sit.

When I suggested she join the others at the picnic table, she told me she wouldn't sit there because there was no firm back support and the dirt and bugs made it unsanitary. All the rest of the girls started to view Alexis as a weirdo. I could see that we were going to need what I now would call a first-chakra intervention.

The next morning, Alexis's mother arrived dressed in a designer suit and heels. This time she brought a list of concerns, telling me that her daughter had come home tired and woke up achy, with joint pain everywhere; in addition, she'd seemed very nervous and had developed a faint rash. "Could it be poison ivy?" the mother asked, quite concerned. "You can never be too sure." She was also worried that Alexis might have the beginnings of a sore lower back and might have sprained her left ankle from too much running and playing kickball.

I quickly bid the mother adieu, and the first-chakra intervention began. No longer would Alexis be an outcast of the group. No longer would she believe that her body had to be hermetically sealed for safety from danger, germs, allergens, vermin, or chilled earth. I told all the kids to put on their bathing suits, the great equalizer. So off came the dress and patent-leather shoes, on went the bathing suit, and we headed to the beach. There, I announced to the group that we were going to have a "clean-and-dirty contest." Everyone had to get very wet and then roll in the sand. The person who became the dirtiest won a free soda at the end of the day. Within two hours, everyone in my group was standing in line coated with sand and seaweed, waiting to see if they would win the soda. Alexis received the "most improved" runner-up prize.

The next day, Alexis arrived at camp in shorts and flip-flops. By the end of the week, she was more or less mainstreamed with the rest of the campers. And although I'll never say that she was a normal outfielder (she remained more interested in horticulture than kickball), she seemed to have learned to balance her need for safety with her need to fit into the rest of the group.

• • •

Like Alexis and her mother, our 21st-century society has become obsessed with safety, antibiotics, vaccines, and all kinds of drugs designed to keep us out of harm's way. These medicines have become so commonplace that you can find antibacterials in hand soap, Kleenex, and even clothing. Everyone wears a helmet for every sport imaginable. Seat belts are mandatory in almost every vehicle. Take a stroll through your neighborhood Babies"R"Us store and you'll be amazed by the sheer number of safety devices designed to outfit homes that include children.

Moving on to the world arena, it's obvious that as a whole, people no longer trust each other. Children don't play outside unattended anymore like they used to do. There are pedophiles out there—haven't you watched the news lately? We need security systems, passwords, firewalls, and alarms for all our homes, offices, computers, e-mail accounts, and voice-mail messages. Even our identities can be stolen, for God's sake!

To enlighten ourselves, we seek information on how to remain safe, but that information keeps changing. First, we're told to use antibacterial soap to reduce the incidence of colds. Then we hear that doing so increases the cases of allergies and asthma. To lessen the chance of sudden infant death syndrome (SIDS), we're told to put babies to sleep on their sides. Then a few years later, we're told that to prevent SIDS, we need to put them to sleep on their *backs,* not their sides. The experts first advised us to eat margarine instead of artery-clogging butter. And sometime later, they proclaimed that the trans fats in margarine increase the chances of heart attack and stroke more than the saturated fat in butter. It's hard to know what information to trust anymore because the experts seem to be constantly changing their minds.

So if the more you learn, the more in the dark you feel . . . how, then, do you keep yourself and your loved ones safe? Simple. You can learn to tune in to the intuition available in your first-chakra immune system. Minute by minute, day by day, your first chakra monitors your life and simultaneously safeguards other people around you. It speaks to you through illnesses such as chronic fatigue syndrome, fibromyalgia, Epstein-Barr virus, hepatitis (A, B, or C), mononucleosis, Lyme disease, allergies, rashes, psoriasis, joint pain, fatigue, and autoimmune problems like lupus.

You can learn to use the intuition underlying these disorders to relieve your suffering by following the first rule for intuitive health: *All for one, and one for all* (balancing the personal with the political). You must be intuitively in touch with your individual needs, but simultaneously be able to successfully negotiate a way around those of a group of people, whether it's your family, co-workers, or members of some other organization.

People who have first-chakra health problems tend to fall somewhere in between four extreme categories: the *Pseudo–Social Worker*— those whose identity is so focused on supporting others that they neglect their own needs; the *Lone Wolf*—those whose individual needs are so great that groups overwhelm them; the *Pillar of the Community* —those who are so supportive of everyone and everything in the community that they become unnaturally rigid and inflexible; and finally, the *"Help! I've Fallen and I Can't Get Up!"* type—those who have become so destabilized and uprooted that they neither feel comfortable trusting others for support nor strong enough to stand alone.

The Pseudo–Social Worker

The first type of first-chakra extreme is the Pseudo–Social Worker, those who spend so much energy thinking and worrying about others that they could almost be Mother Teresa's replacements. Andrea, 17, is a prime example. Andrea's mother spent much of her time depressed and in bed, and her father wasn't around, so from the age of eight, the girl had to take care of her five younger siblings. Oblivious to any of her own personal needs, she made sure that all of her brothers and sisters were clean and fed and did their homework. If her brothers began to fight, Andrea disregarded her own safety and threw herself in the middle of the fray to break it up. When her sister was out all night with her boyfriend, Andrea went out in her robe and dragged her home screaming.

Because she didn't yet have the intellect to take on the complex role of being a surrogate mother, Andrea developed the intricate circuitry of intuition in her brain and body to help her take on that task. From an early age, she suffered from rashes, fatigue, joint pain, weight problems, and an autoimmune condition that had recently been diagnosed as lupus. Whenever some problem was brewing in the family, Andrea may not have known about it directly, but she'd become aware of it when the information began brewing in her body. Her immune system was hypervigilant, always looking for the next screwup or potential threat to her siblings.

Andrea's immune system, which was playing the role of her own mother and father to herself *and* all of her siblings, was living with stress similar to that of an air-traffic controller. Andrea's first chakra was intuitively signaling: "Hello! Can't the parents see what's going on? Earth to parents! Come in, parents!"

If you, like Andrea, are a Pseudo–Social Worker, you're the reliable team player in any group, the steadfast family member who is so grounded that everyone who needs to be anchored, organized, and stabilized depends on you for support. When you sense that a loved one is getting into trouble again, you become angry and nag or cajole her to change. If that doesn't work, you rush to support, rescue, or bail her out—one more time. Although you're the epitome of support for everyone else, you fail when it comes to safeguarding your own needs—and your immune system lets you know that through immune disorders, joint pain, and skin problems.

What I've learned from people like Andrea is that Pseudo–Social Workers become so intuitively keyed in to others' lives that they actually lose their own identities. Over time, the strategy of protecting others but not themselves warps their relationships in an unhealthy direction. Although our culture tries to push selflessness, there is a downside to being so *selfless,* in that you tend to attract people who are *selfish.* If you have trouble feeling lovable unless you're needed, you'll draw others to you who are needy and dependent.

What clues signal that you may be a Pseudo–Social Worker? Well, you're surrounded by relationships within which you fulfill the needs of others, but you yourself never have any, or you give more than you receive. You have trouble feeling loved by an independent person. You find it emotionally torturing to observe someone in pain without defending and rescuing that person. Watching reality shows such as *Survivor* drives you nuts because people who are supposed to be on the same team often double-cross each other. You've spent countless hours serving in established, grassroots organizations such as church or spiritual groups, political causes, volunteer associations, soup kitchens, hospital leagues, crisis shelters, and service clubs like Rotary International.

If you start to support everyone else but yourself, your immune system, bones, and joints will sound their first alarm through the subtle feelings of fatigue and achy, wobbly, unstable joints. The fatigue is the result of your white blood cells responding to potential danger by releasing inflammatory mediators that make you feel sleepy, tired, sore, and heavy. If your rescue missions and personal neglect continue long-term, your immune system's white blood cells will release more and more inflammatory mediators depending on your genetic, dietary, and environmental situations. You may develop full-blown caregiver burnout in the form of a more devastating first-chakra health problem that forces you to attend to your own physical survival needs.

All of us have a part of the Pseudo–Social Worker in us. Like Andrea, we all have a tendency to be oblivious to our own needs at one time or another when we're taking care of a loved one who seems to be in greater need. However, by immersing ourselves in others' lives to such a degree that we become intuitively disconnected from our own problems, we leave ourselves unprotected, and susceptible to one disaster after another. By learning to attend to our own needs and by balancing them with those of our family and friends, in the long run we'll guarantee *everyone's* survival.

Intuitive Advice for the Pseudo–Social Worker

Do you suffer from chronic health problems with your blood, immune system, bones, joints, or skin; and do you tend to have Pseudo–Social Worker issues? If so, fear not, for there is hope. You can learn to use mind-body medicine and medical intuition to manage and possibly eliminate your health problems. Your mind-body makeover begins by addressing your physical health, because if you don't support the needs of your body, your mind can't be in the place to make the critical life changes that are necessary.

You could have any first-chakra immune, autoimmune, or musculoskeletal health issue with Pseudo–Social Worker tendencies. But if, like Andrea, yours happens to be an autoimmune problem like lupus and you're already taking steroids or methotrexate to fight the resulting inflammation, consider supplements. A number of nutritional and herbal supplements can help counteract the toxic side effects that these potent drugs cause and can help reprogram your immune system. (For details on these supplements, see the extensive discussion on mood in the chapter on the fourth chakra.) You might also consider going on a macrobiotic healing diet, having acupuncture, and taking Chinese herbs.

The next step of the Pseudo–Social Workers' mind-body makeover is to address the emotional, intuitive right brain. Taking DHA (300–1,000 mg a day) will help the mind when it's in an immune brushfire. L-acetyl-carnitine (500 mg, two to three times a day) can be extremely helpful for the fatigue, attention, and memory problems that occur during the inflammation of an immune problem. And SAMe (800–1,200 mg a day, on an empty stomach) can be very effective for residual joint pain after chronic lupus as well as for the depression that can occur with immune and autoimmune problems. These supplements are particularly beneficial when taking methotrexate or steroids because both medications can cause moodiness, irritability, and depression—not to mention memory problems and "cotton-wool head" (the feeling that your mind is going in slow motion).

What follows is my seven-part program to rehabilitate Pseudo–Social Workers' compulsive rescuing of people in need so that they can protect their own interests as much as they safeguard everyone else around them:

1. **Identify** how when someone near you has a problem, you intuitively pick up on his pain and distress. Was it through a sense of dread? Anxiety? A dream or image? A gut feeling or a tightness in your chest? Or was it some other sensation in your mind and body?

2. **Recognize** that the person in need has other resources, including a higher power, which he can access for protection. Acknowledge that you are *not* his higher power (a sobering thought indeed). Join Co-Dependents Anonymous (CoDA), where you'll get support from compulsive rescuers who are also learning to resist the impulse to chronically attract and defend dependent people.

3. **Discern** whether helping this individual in the past has either strengthened or weakened him, making him more dependent. If your previous rescue missions have helped him learn to support himself, choose to intervene. However, if past efforts have done little to help him gain insight into the crises in his life (or worse yet, fostered more dependence), then sit on your hands. Learn to tolerate your anxiety as you watch the other person's life unravel, and learn to soothe the guilt you experience when he gets angry with you for refusing to play the rescuer yet again.

4. **Restrict** the amount of time you spend around people who depend on you. This doesn't refer to any young children, if you have them, but to that adult relative who's always calling you about his loser relationship and the friend who keeps asking for your advice on one emotional crisis after another. In the past, this may have helped you feel loved and needed, but now you can see that what it's really doing for you is draining your first-chakra health. As the saying goes, "Out of sight, out of mind" (and, I might add, out of intuitive field). Begin to develop relationships with more independent people who can love you even if they don't need you.

5. Know that *you* can be safe, even if certain loved ones' lives are in peril.

6. Change the unhealthy thought: *If I am needed, I feel loved, appreciated, and accepted . . .* to the healthy affirmation: *I am lovable even when I am not needed.*

7. Follow the first rule for intuitive health—*All for one, and one for all*—by emphasizing that your individual need for support and survival is as important as all the rest of the needs of all the other people in your life.

The Lone Wolf

The second pattern of first-chakra extremes is the Lone Wolf, those who are so focused on individual survival that the needs of groups and organizations feel very threatening to them. For example, Larry, 32, was always an outsider, feeling shy and awkward. Even his own brothers called him "weirdo." He suffered from lifelong problems of anxiety, asthma, and allergies—what I call the three *A*'s. His brothers entered into the family construction business right after graduation, but Larry chose to attend art school and try his hand at being a freelance artist. When his dream didn't materialize, he reluctantly began working in the family business. His asthma, anxiety, and allergies kicked in again—but when he also developed extreme exhaustion, achiness in his muscles and joints, a low-grade fever, and insomnia, his doctor diagnosed him with mononucleosis and the Epstein-Barr virus.

Larry's first-chakra immune-system intuition was signaling to him that ever since he'd started working in the family business, he hadn't felt safe. He was sure that his brothers, his father, and the other employees disliked him; were criticizing him behind his back; and, quite frankly, thought that he was odd. Larry was so focused on seeing these people as a threat that he was unable to key in to his job requirements or discern what the company needed from him: getting to work on time, meeting deadlines, and basically being a team player. His lifelong asthma, anxiety, and allergies had always signaled that he didn't fit in. However, the tension and anxiety he experienced after going from being a freelance artist to a company employee flooded Larry's capacity to balance his personal needs with the political dynamics of the family business.

If you, like Larry, are a Lone Wolf, you're very good at intuitively safeguarding your needs, but when it comes to reading those of your family or an organization (such as sensing the political undercurrents at work), you fail miserably. If you usually end up the scapegoat, chances are that you suffered some type of abuse growing up. If you're different, unique, or unusual in some way, your tendency to stand out from the crowd unfortunately makes you a more visible target for someone else's anger and violent temper. However, if you have resilience and the ability to develop social savvy, you can learn to protect yourself in potentially abusive situations and boost your first-chakra health.

This is an important ability, because even if you're a Lone Wolf, you need a place in society—the absence of human contact is biochemical poison to the immune system. So if you think you're going to handle your problems by running away and living isolated and alone in a tepee somewhere, think again. Your immune system will respond to the withdrawal from society by getting weaker. The allergy can eventually hit every organ and chakra in your body, whether it's skin rashes, eczema, or psoriasis (first chakra); being allergic to your partner's sperm, thus setting the scene for infertility (second chakra); food allergies causing digestive trouble (third chakra); asthma (fourth chakra); bronchitis (fifth chakra); middle-ear problems or sinusitis (sixth chakra); or a life-threatening illness (seventh chakra).

What I've learned from people like Larry is that some Lone Wolves are naturally solitary, yet others acquire the persona due to trauma in their families or other groups. Like Napoléon on Elba, they live their lives in exile, pining to reconnect to the rest of their homeland. They may say that they always want to be outside of any organized group, yet in reality they desperately need their individuality to be recognized by their families, co-workers, or some other organization in order to feel accepted and safe. After all, a Lone Wolf is not a safe wolf.

For first-chakra health, everyone needs stability—a home, a family, and roots.

What are the signs that you're a Lone Wolf? You're always on the run, trying to avoid dealing with painful family trauma, unsupportive marriages, or a series of failed jobs. You have trouble understanding the value of schmoozing, networking, or working the system to accomplish your long-term career goals. You tend to sit on the sidelines because you're comfortable only at the perimeter of the pack. You believe that conforming to what everyone else is doing would seriously threaten your individuality. You obsess about injustice between individuals and society. You have trouble handling office, church, or family politics. You tend to shy away from work situations that require partnership or group participation rather than individual achievement.

If this sounds like you, then you may be a Lone Wolf. You'll perceive so much danger around you that your first-chakra immune system will heed the call and come to your rescue, working overtime. The first alarm that will sound is usually allergy and joint inflammation, as your immune system begins to defend your body against things you perceive as dangerous that most people would find really quite innocuous—such as food, pollen, cat or dog hair, and so on. If you don't heed the initial allergic warnings, your immune system may respond with an even louder and more deafening message of more serious autoimmune disease that may force you out of the environment that you find so threatening.

If we look closely at Larry's story, we'll realize that we can all find somewhere within ourselves a Lone Wolf, a part of us that's awkward and shy and feels like an outsider in specific groups, such as the family we grew up in or the gang at school, work, church, or the exercise club. Whether we like it or not, all humans need such groups to survive. But it isn't necessary to have everything in common with every member of a group in order to feel safe or to feel like we fit in and belong. Sometimes being able to find the most basic commonalities with someone else (even if it's only that we're both mammals) gives us enough of a sense of connectedness to truly enhance our physical and emotional survival.

Intuitive Advice for the Lone Wolf

Do you suffer from chronic health problems with your blood, immune system, bones, joints, or skin; and do you tend to have some aspects of the Lone Wolf pattern? If so, you can learn to use mind-body medicine and medical intuition to get relief from your specific immune problems and musculoskeletal disorders, and your mind-body makeover begins by addressing your physical health. You could have any first-chakra health issue with Lone Wolf tendencies. But if, like Larry, you happen to suffer from the three *A*'s (allergy, asthma, and anxiety), you can go to an internal-medicine doctor and get a steroid inhaler as well as a leukotriene inhibitor. You can also take several asthma and seasonal respiratory-allergy medicines like Benadryl and Claritin (see the chapter on the fourth chakra for more details).

The next step is usually to find the item triggering the allergy and eliminate it. Yet rarely (and I cannot overstate this point) does this solve the immune-system dysfunction once and for all. If the allergen is eliminated for about a month or so, allergy symptoms abate, but then they return in the most insidious fashion, only to be followed by a more persistent search for more and more new categories of environmental allergens or food intolerances (a phrase I prefer to *allergies*)—usually noticeable around a certain family member, a significant other, or a specific job.

I've met people who have performed great feats of elimination—ridding themselves of every source of wheat, dairy, oats, peanuts, tomatoes, chicken, eggs, food dye, petrochemicals, cadmium, and mercury . . . not to mention even selling their houses and moving to rid themselves of environmental irritants. However, these same people never even considered that they could have developed an allergy or intolerance to a personal relationship or an organization. Medical science is now leaning away from allergy eliminations and toward creating toleration in the immune system by injecting minute quantities of the allergen into the person's blood to successfully neutralize the allergy—thus making patients able to freely roam among the rest of their pack.

You may also want to consider trying a treatment called Nambud-ripad's Allergy Elimination Techniques (NAET), which uses acupuncture to electromagnetically remove certain allergy patterns from your diet. A skilled practitioner in traditional Chinese medicine and acupuncture may also suggest the Chinese herbs lian qiao (forsythia), zhi zi (*Gardenia jasminoidis*), huang qin, scutellaria, or shou wu (*Polygoni multiflori*).

The mind-body makeover next moves to the Lone Wolves' emotional problems. If you often feel anxious, angry, bitter, and indignant when you perceive that you're being attacked, abused, and scapegoated for being different, you must learn to change the mental tapes you play over and over. Having your mind and body fester in the thoughts *I'm right; they're wrong* and *Things should be different* sets up an intuitive immune barrier that increases the setting for allergy and intolerance.

Similarly, having your mind and body constantly sounding the panic alarm that you're not safe from the people around you also sets your intuitive immune system into the attack mode. By first transforming your innate tendency toward anxiety and knee-jerk emotional irritability, reactivity, and intolerance to groups in general, you'll be able to make the appropriate mental changes necessary to balance your individuality with being a team player—without feeling like an outcast.

There are few truly effective nonpharmacological treatments for anxiety, which is why many Lone Wolves turn to certain street drugs, especially alcohol and marijuana. Although alcohol may initially have an antianxiety effect, over time it may hamper the ability to assume responsibility, hold on to a job, or maintain a relationship. Marijuana, if used longer than ten years, has a negative effect on the brain's memory center as well as its initiation and motivation center (not to mention what it does to the lungs).

If you haven't had a problem being addicted to alcohol or prescription medicines, you might try Klonopin (0.25 mg, twice a day), which works to both soothe anxiety and stabilize irritability. Supplements like kava kava (70 mg, three times a day) or valerian (400 mg, taken at night) may help initially, but they're not long-term solutions because after two weeks, the brain and body build up a tolerance to them and they stop working. For more mild cases of nervousness, consider chamomile (3 g in a half cup of water, three times a day) or passion flower (2 g in a half cup of water, three times a day). (For more information, see the advice for anxiety in the chapter on the fourth chakra.)

If you do have a history of addiction, I'd recommend you avoid both medications and supplements and instead address your anxiety by some means other than putting something in your mouth. Technically, there are medications—including a variety of antidepressants, such as Zoloft and Serzone, and other nonaddictive antianxiety drugs, like BuSpar—that may have some minimal effect on anxiety problems complicated by other kinds of mood issues. However, when a person has a serious anxiety or panic problem, these medications tend not to work. (For additional specific information on addressing anxiety, read chapters 6, 7, and 8 in my book *The New Feminine Brain*.)

Once you've supported your emotions and mood, you need to learn how to be both intuitively keyed in to others' individual needs and also appreciate the unique needs of the group as a whole. You must change the perception that you'll always be betrayed, attacked, or abused in groups to the understanding that organizations are an opportunity for gaining safety in numbers—something you can't get if you're constantly alone. You also have to learn to see that justice for the individual and justice for the group not only can, but *must* coexist if everyone is going to survive. By always fighting for your individual rights, you stand to alienate yourself from organization after organization, burning one bridge to safety after another.

Here, then, is my seven-step program to help rehabilitate the Lone Wolves' tendency to always run solo, feeling alienated from the safety and stability available in families, groups, and organizations:

1. Identify how, when you begin to feel rejected, criticized, judged, or treated unfairly, your intuition signals your fears of attack from the group in your mind or body.

2. Recognize the emotions and separate them from the message. Set aside your anxiety about rejection and your anger in response to being criticized, and understand what the group is saying it needs from you. See how you can respect your own values and needs and still be accountable to the group for what it is actually asking of you.

3. Discern which places in your life you simply need to go it alone, and keep in mind that in other places, you can't accomplish certain goals in a vacuum. People actually *need* groups and families.

4. Restrict your tendency to isolate, falling into your usual Lone Wolf pattern every day. Force yourself to be involved with at least two group activities a week, whether with family, friends, co-workers, church members, spiritual groups, or recreational clubs. Isolate your isolation!

5. Know that you can be safe and secure even if people appear to be different from you, disagree with you, or go so far as to make demands that may feel initially like they are impinging on your individual freedom.

6. Change the negative thought pattern: *People tend to control me—I easily get scapegoated in families and other groups . . .* to the following affirmation: *I skillfully act on my ideas and visions, and I free myself from emotionally distracting influences around me. I can still feel good about myself, even if someone is different from or angry with me.*

7. Follow the first rule for intuitive health—*All for one, and one for all*—by striking a healthy balance between your unique and often quirky form of individuality and finding your healthy place in society.

The Pillar of the Community

The next pattern of first-chakra extreme is the Pillar of the Community, those whom everyone else comes to for support. There's no better example of this than Carl, 70, a solid family man and the CEO of a local bank. Grounded and reliable, he was seen at every city event, bar mitzvah, ribbon-cutting ceremony, and election. Stalwart old Carl had been on the school board and on the town council, and he'd even been the mayor for three terms.

Carl was so solid and unwavering in his support that some people thought he was a little too rigid. People in his family and community loved how he was rock solid and dependable, but at the same time they noted that he was suspicious of innovation and change. Although Carl had created a stable life for himself, his family members, and his corporate structure, he was having trouble accepting an inevitable shift of leadership for the future. He struggled in his company as the board of directors imported a fresh viewpoint.

Carl was also having difficulty accepting the changes in his body that occurred as he got older. Upon awakening, he felt achiness and stiffness all over his body, especially in his back, neck, hips, and knees. Like an old car, it took him longer and longer to get himself started in the morning. Then he found that he was running out of gas and wanted to go to bed earlier and earlier in the evening. Eventually, Carl went to a neurologist to find out why he was moving so slowly and what to do about it. The doctor suggested he start by cutting back on his highly structured regimen of seven-mile daily runs and weight lifting.

If you, like Carl, are a Pillar of the Community, you're very good at being a rock of stability for those around you, maintaining the traditions and helping set an even course of action for everyone and everything. But by upholding this overly zealous mission of safety, security, and support for all, you run the risk of preventing growth and change. When you see signs of rebuilding, renovation, and reorganization, you may flip out, trying to hold on to old, outdated structures. You view any semblance of a break in tradition with suspicion, finding it disorienting, worrisome, and sometimes even terrifying.

What I've learned about people like Carl is that although Pillars of the Community can appear quite stoic and aloof on the outside, on the inside they're terrified about growing old and being left behind in the dust. They try desperately to hold on to times gone by, often keeping to outmoded, unproductive ways of doing things. But their communities inevitably move forward, growing and changing, leaving them feeling quite alone because they *haven't* changed along with the times. They fail to understand that life is in essence a combination of order and chaos, change and stability.

What clues signal that you may be a Pillar of the Community? It's difficult for you to discard worn-out, older objects that those around you think you're hoarding. You like to go to garage sales because you see value in other people's discarded junk. You've been accused of being a micromanager because it's hard for you to delegate a task to someone else. You love rules, order, details, and organization. You hate confusion, chaos, frenzy, or unruly behavior. You may try ball-room dancing or even the jitterbug or tango, but not hip-hop. You'd never drop in to see a friend without calling. You always write thank-you notes (or at least you have your partner or secretary do it for you). You rarely swear. You tend to avoid movies where the characters fling four-letter words around; and you think the current culture is much too rude or crude, lacking in morals, ethics, finesse, or etiquette.

If this sounds like you, then you may be a Pillar of the Community. You're unable to balance stability and order with change in your life and in those of everyone around you. Your intuitive guidance system will likely sound its first alarm through extreme tightness in your spine and whole musculoskeletal system, as well as the occasional slip and fall that will begin to make you feel like you're getting old. Your vulnerability to the passage of time will cause you to wonder if you're losing control over both time and aging.

If your response is to try to manage the process with more details, order, rigidity, and control, then beware, because your body is asking you to do just the opposite—to become more flexible and more adaptive. Trying to dig in your heels and keep your body and everything around you the same is *not* the issue. Your goal instead should be to try to accept how your body—and the world around you—is changing and to learn how to go with the flow.

All of us have a bit of the Pillar of the Community within us. Like Carl, we all like at least some stability and shy away from change at times, occasionally even coming completely unraveled when it happens. But like it or not, change is a part of life. Families and other organizations can provide a safe harbor for us, but to survive, we must learn to accommodate the ever-changing world we live in. By learning how to feel safe and secure during both stable and shifting times, we'll not only survive but *thrive*.

Intuitive Advice for the Pillar of the Community

Do you suffer from chronic health problems with your blood, immune system, bones, joints, or skin; and do you tend to have Pillar of the Community issues? If so, you can learn to use mind-body medicine and medical intuition to blend your naturally stabilizing nature with a healthier brand of flexibility so that you can grow old gracefully and painlessly. Your mind-body makeover first addresses your body's physical problems. You could have any first-chakra health concern with Pillar of the Community tendencies. But if, like Carl, you have such a regimented lifestyle that your joints and spine have become fossilized into a position as solid and unwavering as your mind-set, you need to ease up on the strength training. Concentrate instead on flexibility with programs such as yoga, tai chi, or any form of dancing (you get extra points for trying a type that's outside of what's usually acceptable for your age-group). The Feldenkrais Method or the Alexander Technique are also excellent for keeping your spine supple and stable.

In addition, working with a massage therapist who knows neuromuscular therapy is helpful because this decreases the tension and tightness in your tendons as they hold your muscles to your skeleton. An aspirin a day is good for decreasing inflammation in your blood vessels; and a variety of other antioxidant, anti-inflammatory medicines can improve not only your cardiovascular system but also any neurological issues that are causing slow, rigid movements.

Next, the mind-body makeover addresses the tendency you as a Pillar of the Community have toward an anxious and change-resistant emotional mind-set. First, identify the fear you experience when change occurs—whether you call it "anxiety," "jumpiness," "tension," "nervousness," "apprehension," or something else. Understand that you can't avoid change, which is a natural part of life, and that you can feel safe and secure even when you're not trying to organize, structure, and control things by making lists; straightening up your desk; and maintaining perfect order in the people, places, and things around you.

Cognitive Behavioral Therapy (CBT) is very helpful for this because it loosens up your mind-set. Learning how to balance a sense of stability with new ideas can also be helpful. Because youthful creativity is almost always a little disorderly, unruly, tumultuous, and disorganized, volunteering as a camp counselor or an athletic team coach of middle-school-aged or adolescent students will immediately throw you into a pool of people who will exceed your capacity to control, order, and organize to perfection. This will force you to establish a new set point of tolerance for chaos, confusion, imperfection, and spontaneity; and you may well begin to experience a newfound feeling of youthfulness, too.

The following is my seven-part program to help the Pillars of the Community rehabilitate their tendency to establish and maintain inflexible lockstep order:

1. Identify those moments when you feel edgy, jumpy, nervous, tense, uneasy, or worried about change of any kind in your life or in those of people around you—change that you frequently experience as disorienting, disorganizing, and destabilizing to the established order you've so carefully built.

2. Recognize how feeling like an anchor in your family or community helps you have a sense that you're keeping everything the same, constantly maintaining traditions and buffering everyone around you from fleeting fads and fickle trends. Also see the anxiety you feel when you can't keep things from changing.

3. Discern where in your life you can lend your skills in order to create a stable structure—for example, maintaining a secure financial foundation for a business or nonprofit organization. Then identify the places in your life where you're willing to import change and loosen the reins of control, allowing a breath of fresh air and permitting evolution to take its natural course.

4. Restrict your impulse to conform to the same routines every day, keeping to nearly the identical weekly schedule and even going on the same types of vacations each year. Break up the order and import some spontaneity into your life. Try a new flavor of ice cream. Buy a different type of bread. Change your hairstyle. You might consider hiring a coach to help you with this.

5. Know that you can be a strong pillar of the community, upholding valuable traditions and maintaining stability, yet at the same time embracing evolution. Realize that keeping any society alive involves not only maintaining stable roots but also planting new seeds of change and embracing the natural order of the universe, which is a tenuous balance of chaos and control, entropy and order.

6. Change the negative thought pattern: *I must be in control because I am responsible for holding everything up for everyone; when things around me go wrong, it's my fault* . . . to the healthier affirmation: *Everything around me is happening as it should.*

7. Follow the first rule for intuitive health—*All for one, and one for all*—by understanding that an individual's needs for control and stability are just as vital as the group's consistent need for evolution and change.

The "Help! I've Fallen and I Can't Get Up!" Type

The final pattern of first-chakra extreme is the "Help! I've Fallen and I Can't Get Up!" type, who don't have many innate skills for supporting themselves or maintaining stable ties to a community in a crisis. Denise is a good example of this: having moved 12 times during her childhood, her home life growing up was as unstable as her health. Her father was a gambling addict, and every time his debts caught up with him, the family would have to move.

Now age 53, Denise had to contend with musculoskeletal problems that began when she was 5 and fell out of a jungle gym and broke her arm. This was followed by a broken finger when she was 7; scoliosis at 14; broken ribs in a car accident at age 17; and, finally, a nearly broken neck from a suspicious fall during a fight with a boyfriend at age 28. Because of the scoliosis and the fall, Denise had frequently suffered from spine pain throughout her life.

Denise had worked hard to try to ignore the pain, but escalating weight problems and a variety of chronic disk diseases caused her to go on disability in midlife. The stress of being a single parent with three children and holding down two jobs for 18 years finally caught up with her. One day, Denise couldn't get out of bed because something went out in her back. She felt old and utterly helpless, unable to pull herself up from the pain in her spine and her hopeless life in general. Denise felt just like the old woman in that television commercial who falls and then pushes the medical-alert button, calling out: "Help! I've fallen and I can't get up!" She felt like she was screaming for support, but absolutely no one was there who had her back.

If you, like Denise, are a "Help! I've Fallen and I Can't Get Up!" type, you often feel like an outcast, abandoned and deserted or helpless and hopeless. You might have fallen out of favor with your family and may even have gone through so many traumatic relationships that you've finally thrown in the relationship towel. In addition to having multiple immune-system problems because the world feels like a dangerous and abusive environment, you tend to be accident-prone and suffer from a variety of orthopedic calamities as a result. The precarious nature and chaotic instability of your life is reflected in multiple automobile accidents, fractures, sprains, contusions, whiplashes, and other dramatic musculoskeletal issues.

What I've learned from people like Denise is that Can't Get Up types tend to be very emotionally porous, which makes them extremely intuitively keyed in to others' lives. As a result, they tend to have unstable emotional and physical health that reflects not just their chaotic roots but also the turbulent problems of anyone around them. In addition, their relationships and moods seem to be as unsteady as their bones and joints.

Some develop *Post-traumatic Stress Disorder* (PTSD), which causes them to reenact their unstable family environment in a string of abusive, neglectful, and violent relationships. Others have been labeled with the term *Bipolar II* or the pejoratively overused *Borderline Personality Disorder*. Although they might yield a reimbursement from a health-insurance company, these three labels rarely provide people with the skills they need to help them move forward in their lives with hope and pride. Their unstable moods are often reactions to difficult, traumatic lives that are so tumultuous that perhaps the only reliable thing these individuals can depend on is that the next disaster or mood shift will occur sooner rather than later. After decades of these ups and downs, multiple falls occur physically and emotional-ly—and they take their toll on these people, through chronic depression, hopelessness, helplessness, or just plain exhaustion.

What signals that you might be a "Help! I've Fallen and I Can't Get Up!" type? Well, you've severed all ties with at least one significant person in your life after a falling-out. In fact, you've burned so many bridges that when you leave a school, job, or town, you tend to never see the folks you left behind again. You're the black sheep of the family; and your siblings and other family members tend to in-validate, ignore, or deny what you remember about your childhood. In other groups, you always feel like an outsider looking in. People never seem to take your side or see your point of view, and you've had several arguments with neighbors that have escalated either to illegal action or cold silence. You frequently feel abandoned, betrayed, or rejected by your peers; and you've been suicidal more than two times in your life.

If this sounds familiar, you may be a Can't Get Up type. If you don't learn how to support yourself or how to *get* enough support from other people, the first alarm that your first-chakra intuitive ad-visor will sound will be a fall—a plummeting mood; a physical acci-dent; or a lowered immune system, with increased colds, flus, viruses, or bacterial infections. If you fall flat because you have no support in the world, you won't be able to get up again until you learn how to balance supporting yourself with getting backing from others.

If we look closely, we'll see a part of this first-chakra extreme in all of us from time to time. Although our tendency may not be *as* extreme as Denise's, most of us have been through times when we feel that some aspect of our lives is chaotic and unstable no matter what we do. Having structure and stability grounds us and gives us a sense of permanence, but if we allow ourselves to remain in the same place forever, like a pot-bound plant, we limit our growth. Allowing ourselves to uproot, change, and transplant a part of ourselves may at first feel extremely physically and emotionally disconcerting. But after a while, when the chaos and instability goes away and the dust settles, we will discover new, wide-open, and previously uncharted terrain in which to grow and explore.

Intuitive Advice for the "Help! I've Fallen and I Can't Get Up!" Type

Do you suffer from chronic health problems with your blood, immune system, bones, joints, or skin; and do you tend to have some aspects of the "Help! I've Fallen and I Can't Get Up!" pattern? If so, you can learn to break this cycle through mind-body medicine and medical intuition, and your mind-body makeover starts by addressing your physical health. You could have any first-chakra health problems with Can't Get Up tendencies. But if, like Denise, your problem happens to be that you've suffered from numerous falls and related injuries, you first need to stabilize your bones, joints, and spine so that they can mend.

But when you support a broken bone with a cast or a sprained neck with a brace, at the same time you need to help strengthen the other muscles in the area so that they'll be able to support a stronger posture. So to stabilize the bones and joints that have been previously injured, you may want to take a pharmaceutical-grade mega-antioxidant, a magnesium and calcium supplement, a high dose of vitamin C (up to 3,000 mg a day), grape-seed extract (360 mg a day), and glucosamine or chondroitin sulfate (200 mg a day).

In addition, you need to structure your life around a daily exercise routine that involves at least 30 minutes of vigorous aerobic exercise and another 30 minutes of vigorous walking. The operative word here is *structure*. This schedule must not endure for weeks or months, but *years*. Limited episodes of binge-like exercise or occasional periods of rehabilitation won't do the trick. The only way you can build a stable physical foundation for yourself is to construct your life around an almost compulsive daily exercise routine, as if you were in the military.

No type of supplement, medicine, alternative treatment, or surgery can give you the same sense of powerful confidence and resilience established by a regular schedule of exercise. And if you still slip, fall, fracture something, or blow a disk, then your systematic routine will ensure that you've built into your physical and emotional foundation the structured and disciplined sense of security that you'll inevitably bounce back from the injury.

You'll also find it helpful to have a team of neurosurgeons and orthopedic surgeons who can follow you through life, helping relieve your pain by rebuilding your body—both literally and figuratively. But take it from someone who had a spinal fusion for scoliosis at the age of 12 and who then had to have her spine rebuilt at the age of 40 after a series of blown disks in the neck and lower back—surgery can be very helpful, but only as a last resort.

Less surgery is always better. Despite surgical repair, there is always a chance that you'll be left with chronic pain, even if you had the most brilliant, gifted surgeon. Always obtain a second or third surgical opinion from a nearby major teaching hospital, preferably in another city or part of the country, to get a wide range of viewpoints about how to approach your condition.

Next, the mind-body makeover moves to supporting the Can't Get Up types' emotional, intuitive right brain. Examine your tendency to suffer from depression, grief, and sadness and see if you can't relate it to a lifelong pattern of losing people whom you thought you could depend on, as well as not having a stable home. Although it's pure folly to think that an antidepressant is going to erase a lifetime of family disappointment, certain medicines, supplements, and herbs will be critical for splinting your brain into place as you learn to reconstitute your first-chakra support with a reliable family of people who will finally make you feel rooted.

Unless you have classical Bipolar I Disorder, in which case antidepressants may not be good for you, you'll need a variety of mood splints (such as those outlined in the chapter on the fourth chakra). However, please consult with your physician before you start taking any medicine or supplement. In addition, please consider taking SAMe (800–1,200 mg a day, on an empty stomach), which is also good for joint pain.

Please do not think that taking an antidepressant medicine like Lexapro, Effexor, Zoloft, or Prozac makes you a weakling. You need to know that it isn't a moral failure to take pharmaceutical support for a broken mood that needs to mend. (After all, if you fractured your leg, you wouldn't blink an eye at getting a cast. The same applies with prescription mood stabilizers.)

Similarly, you're going to need very structured psychotherapy to help you learn the skills necessary in order to relate to people in a family again. Having had an abusive family may have left you with post-traumatic relationship disorder—shell shock from a variety of explosive relationships. You may consequently have a warped, overly submissive, or otherwise messed-up style of relating; or you may simply want to avoid relationships entirely.

Either way, years of unstructured psychotherapy (spilling your guts about all your emotional traumas and tragedies) are likely to make you even more depressed and give you further health problems. Instead, try a one- or two-year course of structured treatment like Cognitive Behavioral Therapy (CBT) or Dialectical Behavioral Therapy (DBT) that can teach you how to trust the right people and stand up for yourself in an appropriate way. DBT was originally used with people who suffered incest, sexual abuse, and trauma. Then it was used for people diagnosed with borderline personality disorder. Now anyone, including me, can use this form of CBT based on Tibetan Buddhism and mindfulness to learn how to skillfully voice and respond to emotions and intuition so they don't end up registering in the body. (For more information on DBT, see **www.behavioraltech.com**.)

The following is my seven-part program to beef up the "Help! I've Fallen and I Can't Get Up!" types' capacity to support themselves and accept support from a reliable family of other people whom they can trust:

1. Identify those times when you started a relationship that ended badly. Note how you emotionally and intuitively knew at the beginning that this individual wasn't going to be a safe, secure, and supportive person to be involved with. Pinpoint the moment when you chose to ignore your inner knowing. Then identify others in your world whom you intuitively sense are very solid, stable, grounded, and loving but whom you've somehow discounted as being unsuitable because they aren't your type, you aren't attracted to them, or they're boring.

2. Recognize that during times when you've had an immune-system disorder or some sort of fall, accident, or other orthopedic or musculoskeletal calamity, you were occupied with chaotic, precarious relationships and family dramas. Then look back at the most peaceful, least chaotic, or stablest periods in your life when you had no immune-system, skin, or musculoskeletal problems, and count the many individuals who backed you up during that time.

3. Discern your need to return to the people who are enduring and stabilizing so you can establish roots. Understand that your body and mind do bear the battle scars of an unstable life that could act up with a recurrence of pain, intuitively signaling you that someone's life near you needs to settle down.

4. Restrict your impulses to marinate in sadness. When a relationship has a momentary disappointment, resist the desire to pack it in and bolt. You may notice that you're seeing current relationships through the lens of your chaotic ones of the past. So be careful. Use CBT and DBT to coach yourself on relationship skills.

5. Know that even if you had a ridiculously difficult childhood, your painful past can allow you to acquire the necessary skills to have stable relationships, roots, and everything one can get from a healthy family. Find a place that you can call home (where people aren't necessarily relatives, incidentally) and start to refer to these people as family. You can have others in your life who are reliable, supportive team players who hold you up as much as you do them.

6. Change the negative thought pattern: *I feel rejected by my family and friends* . . . to the more positive affirmation: *I now have a wealth of family and friends who make me feel as though I belong.*

7. Follow the first rule for intuitive health—*All for one, and one for all*—by solidly supporting yourself in the world as much as you support a variety of families (whether it's your family of origin; one you marry into; a partnership; or an educational, vocational, spiritual, or recreational family) to create a wide network of alliances.

•—•—•

To create health in your first chakra, you have to *take yourself home*—make yourself feel comfortable, safe, secure, and at home in every group and every family in your life. To accomplish this, follow the first rule for intuitive health—*All for one, and one for all*—by successfully negotiating the delicate balance between your personal needs and each group's "political" ones, whether that group is the family you grew up in, your office- or classmates, a gang of friends, or any other, for that matter.

How well you maintain this equilibrium between your needs and theirs determines the health of your immune system, blood, bones, joints, and skin. But remember that even when your first-chakra intuitive advisor is speaking to you through signs of illness in these areas of the body, it's always on your side, reminding you that at any time, you have the ability to take yourself to a place that feels like home.

•—•—•—•—•

Chapter Four

Second Chakra: "I Got You Babe"

(The Health of Your Lower Back, Urinary Tract, and Reproductive Organs)

The health of the second chakra—the area of your body that includes the lower back, hips, urinary tract, and reproductive organs—depends on how well you balance love and money. Sound simple? Not on your life! The number one illness that causes disability in the United States is actually a second-chakra affliction: lower-back pain. Balancing relationships and finances—your heart in one hand, your wallet in the other—is never easy. People who are innately good at this are few and far between.

Who doesn't remember that famous married duo from the '60s, Sonny and Cher, singing, "I Got You Babe," a song about the struggles of a young couple learning to balance love and money? You know the story: when two teenagers leave home and move into an apartment together, they soon find out that their love doesn't pay the rent, but at least they have each other. I know, I know: Sonny and Cher ended up getting a divorce, with their show-business career overwhelming, even eclipsing, their marriage. Even so, their relationship (and their theme song) illustrates the point that love and money are intimately intertwined.

I saw this for the first time when I was eight years old while eating out with my family in a seafood restaurant. This was one of those places where the decor consisted of plain tables without tablecloths, and a bunch of fishing paraphernalia, like netting and buoys, hanging from the walls for atmosphere. Being a kid, I used to eat my dinner fast and then look around the room at the other diners while my family finished up.

On this evening, as our dessert arrived, I was watching an older couple with their kids having coffee after their meal. The waitress came by to refill their cups and, as was the tradition, plopped the black vinyl folder containing the check in front of the husband.

My aunt caught me spying and said, "Mona Lisa, why can't you mind your own business for once?"

So I turned my attention back to the vanilla parfait melting in front of me. But out of the corner of my eye, I kept watching, and what I saw transpire next fascinated me. From my vantage point, I could clearly see the wife take some money out of her purse and hand it under the table to her husband. After he sheepishly took the cash, he then placed it in the vinyl check folder with this odd, formal flourish.

So I turned to my aunt and asked, "Did you see that? That lady just handed her husband money under the table to pay the check! Why did she do that? Why didn't she just ask the waitress for the check herself if she was going to pay?"

My aunt, in her traditional educational tone, answered, "Because that's the way they do it. The check goes to the man."

"Well, then," I asked, "why can't she just give him the money on top of the table?"

My aunt, still with the patient tone intended to instruct me in the ways of the world, answered, "Because she doesn't want to hurt her husband's feelings."

Having now polished off my parfait, I continued my line of questioning. "But if she didn't want to hurt his feelings," I pressed, "why doesn't he have his own money so he doesn't have to ask her for hers under the table?"

The educational tone vanished from my aunt's voice as she sternly replied, "Mind your own business! Focus on what's going on at *this* table!" That's when I realized that money and love do not always make good bedfellows, and when there are problems, a lot of the conflict goes on underneath the table, below the surface.

●–●–●

Whenever the delicate balance between love and money becomes upset, second-chakra illnesses tend to follow. These include: chronic acne; lower-back pain and sciatica; hip pain; bladder, urinary, or vaginal infections; menstrual-cycle irregularities; PMS; fibroids; endometriosis; ovarian cysts; polycystic ovary syndrome (PCOS); infertility;

vulvodynia; vulvovestibulitis; prostate problems; testicular pain; and several other pelvic-organ disorders.

But no matter what second-chakra health problem you have, you can increase your chance of relieving your pain and suffering by following the second rule for intuitive health: *To be a lover, you need to be a fighter* (balancing love and money). You must develop the feisty, detached persona of an entrepreneur and balance it with the warm sensitivity that's needed to sustain an intimate relationship.

Most people who have second-chakra health problems tend to fall somewhere in between four extreme categories: the *"I Live for Love"* type—those who lead relationship-centered lives, but fail at financial matters; the *Real Go-Getter* type—those whose near turbo-powered drive for financial success eclipses whatever relationships they might have; the *Having It All* type—those who are so driven to achieve a near-impossible list of financial, marital, and reproductive goals that they spread themselves too thin; and finally, the *Bankrupt and Bereft* type—those who have become so handicapped and ultimately traumatized trying to acquire stable relationships and financial security that they've almost given up trying.

The "I Live for Love" Type

The first second-chakra extreme is the "I Live for Love" type, and an example is Elise, 55, who had never been truly happy until she met her husband when she was 26 years old. Up to that point, she'd searched for her passion by going from career to career, finishing a four-year program in business, taking art classes at night, and making a good living as a bookkeeper. Nothing really gave her true joy until the moment she laid eyes on Gerald, who soon afterward became her husband.

From then on, it was bliss. She became a stay-at-home mother to their four children, leaving the financial responsibilities to Gerald. It was utopia. The problem? When Elise's children had grown up and were about to leave the nest, her husband got laid off from his job at the automotive plant. The bliss went bust.

Gerald easily took to the idea of semipermanent retirement, so Elise had to go back to work as a bookkeeper to stabilize the household finances. Just as she was trying to hunker down in an office routine again—a routine she hadn't had to deal with in years—her health started acting up. Elise developed bladder infections (always burning pain with urination) that recurred despite antibiotic treatment. She also had terrible bloating around her lower abdomen and heavy periods, and her doctor eventually diagnosed her with a huge fibroid in her uterus.

Up to this point, Elise had experienced happiness only through marriage and through being a stay-at-home mom. Although her bookkeeping experience demonstrated that she had an innate capacity for business and numbers, Elise found that she was miserable unless she could be a wife and homemaker whose husband took care of all the money. She even told me, "I think I live for love. Now that my children have grown up and I have to work outside the home, I'm miserable." Clearly, Elise had problems balancing her desire to have a family and relationship with the need for a stable financial life.

If you, like Elise, are the "I Live for Love" type, you have great compassion and tenderness, and you're very good at creating love and passionate relationships in your life. While dating is probably very easy for you, the idea of getting in touch with your inner entrepreneurial nature makes you feel like a fish out of water. Money and finances, creating and following a budget, acquiring property, and all the other trappings of someone driven by power are matters you'd rather marry for, not handle yourself. You lack the ferocity and single-minded tenacity necessary for financial wheeling and dealing.

Why? In the pursuit of the deal, you have problems balancing a personal need for power and gain with your greater desire to preserve the relationship between you and the person you're negotiating with. You feel that profiting from someone you have a relationship with, or even immense compassion for, would be taking advantage of that person. For you, relationships reign supreme, over profit or gain. So you undersell yourself and give away earnings (or as they say, give away the store) so that people will love you. Unable to keep your overblown emotional sensitivity and compassion for others in check, you find it difficult to focus on your own financial needs.

What I've learned from people like Elise is that by clinging to the safety of relationships, Live for Love types ultimately promote their own financial dependency. As a result, they tend to attract partners who initially say, "That's okay. I'll take care of everything (financially, that is)." However, turning such a blind eye to finances backfires, because in the end, their trusted partners end up controlling all the money. This can set them up for abusive and dominating relationships, or at the very least, ones where they're taken advantage of.

What clues signal that you might be one of these folks? Well, you've lent a loved one money and either had a very hard time charging interest or let the person talk you into converting the loan into a gift. You've quit a job and uprooted your life entirely, moving for someone you're in love with, at least once. You're the type who would have fun rubbing it in if you won a bet with a friend but wouldn't dream of actually collecting your winnings. You go into a lot of debt every year for various family holidays.

If this sounds like you, then congratulations: you're probably the "I Live for Love" type. If you're always mortgaging your own future financial security to preserve a current relationship, your second-chakra organs will start to warn you through symptoms of illness. The first alarm you're likely to get is a burning or itchiness. Whether you experience the hot, searing pain of lower-back sciatica; the itching and burning of bladder infections; or discomfort in other pelvic organs, your body's second-chakra intuitive advisor is letting you know you're investing all of your energy in your love relationship, but you aren't taking care of your wallet or your bank account . . . if you even have one. For second-chakra health, you need to develop the capacity to stand firmly on your own two feet, focusing equally on your relationships as well as on managing your money.

If we look closely at Elise's story, we'll probably recognize parts of ourselves—including the one that sometimes secretly thinks we can be happy only if we're in a relationship. It's important to realize that if our happiness is dependent on the presence of another person, we are indeed living on a tightrope. Our chances of having any sense of stability and contentment will be narrowed down to those intervals of time when our partner is present, is in a good mood, or chooses to be with us. We're also opening ourselves up to being both controlled and abused. In that case, we're better off having our sense of joy and individual power derived from a variety of different types of relationships and personal and professional activities, not just a simple intimate relationship.

Intuitive Advice for the "I Live for Love" Type

Do you suffer from chronic health problems in your lower back, hips, urinary tract, and reproductive organs; and do you tend to have Live for Love–type issues? If so, you can learn to use mind-body medicine and medical intuition to discover how to support yourself both physically and emotionally, and your mind-body makeover begins by addressing your body's physical health. You could have any second-chakra health problem with Live for Love–type tendencies. But if, like Elise, your second-chakra issue happens to be chronic bladder problems that keep coming back despite taking antibiotics, you'll need to increase your immune-system resistance. Drinking cranberry juice and taking vitamin C (up to 2,000 mg a day) can help support your immune system. Eating yogurt with acidophilus or taking other products on the market designed to repopulate the healthy bacterial population of the urinary tract is also helpful.

If you're a woman, you may also want to address the fact that at midlife, changing estrogen, progesterone, and testosterone levels influence your bladder. When estrogen levels fall, for example, you may experience a sensation like urinary urgency (feeling as though you have to go to the bathroom) that may seem like a bladder infection, but it's not. This symptom may be relieved by seeing a gynecologist who can give you estriol cream that you can apply directly to your urethral opening (where you pee from).

A traditional Chinese acupuncturist or herbalist can further help you by giving you such herbs as *Andrographis paniculata* or *Desmodium styracifolium,* which work to prevent urinary-tract infections. The acupuncturist can also treat any abdominal bloating, distension, and heavy periods you might be having with Chinese herbs such as herba leonuri, heterophylia, angelica, and paeoniae, which promote energetic circulation in your pelvis and reduce abdominal distension.

Next, the mind-body makeover addresses this type's emotional health. The first order of business is creating new ways to pump up your opiates—chemicals your body manufactures that make you feel bliss and ecstasy—all by yourself. Your body naturally produces opiates, as well as the bonding neurochemical *oxytocin,* when you're around the people you love. Normally, that's not a big problem, but if you're a Live for Love type, you become dependent on those people as much as a heroin addict does on his drug of choice. Your mood will plummet if they don't call, write, or stop by; or if they express some disapproval. Then your mood soars when they show up again or otherwise let you know that you're back in their good graces. For the health of your second chakra, you must instead learn to acquire a positive mood (and maybe even attempt bliss or ecstasy) all by yourself.

One way to do this is to start an aerobic-exercise routine (whether it's dancing, working out on an elliptical trainer, or running), because exercise pumps up opiates and oxytocin. Consider getting a pet, too, because the presence of any other living thing that can give you love also provides you with the same neurochemical boost. Another option is to start gardening or filling your apartment with plants. Both animals and plants can elevate your mood and make you feel happy, breaking the emotional dependency you've had on specific other people.

Here, then, is my seven-part program to rehabilitate the "I Live for Love" types' tendency to deep-six financial power in order to feel lovable:

1. Identify a situation where you were so utterly devoted to a relationship that you didn't pay attention to your bills or your credit cards, and as a result, your expenses skyrocketed.

2. Recognize the many people around you who have loving mates and simultaneously have real financial prowess and a powerful zeal for monetary success.

3. Discern that it's possible to be in love with someone and simultaneously love *yourself* enough to be financially empowered and go after what you want in the world. You can be a nurturing, caring, empathetic person and still have money in the bank.

4. Restrict your impulse to have anyone else take care of your money because that person is "just better at it." Have a hand in the financial workings of every aspect of your life, including managing your income, understanding how your investments work, and learning how to go into an auto dealership and bargain for a better price. Inhibit your desire to escape into the relationship comfort zone, and force yourself to start developing and flexing your inner entrepreneurial biceps.

5. Know that money is *not* evil (nor is it the root of all evil); and becoming a financial success is a step toward maturity, not a sign that you're shallow or materialistic. Enlist the help of a tough-ass cognitive behavioral therapist or coach who can help you unleash your second-chakra financial power drive.

6. Change the unhealthy thought pattern: *One of the most important parts of a loving relationship is that someone gives me what I need; when I love someone, that person is my better half . . .* to the healthier affirmation: *If I cannot get my needs met in a relationship, I am able to get them satisfied in some other way. I am a whole person whether I am alone or with someone else.*

7. Follow the second rule for intuitive health—*To be a lover, you need to be a fighter*—by learning how to be a compassionate, loving person who can also take care of him- or herself financially.

The Real Go-Getter

The next type of second-chakra extreme are the Real Go-Getters, those who consistently place financial power ahead of relationships. Fiona, 59, perfectly fits this pattern. From an early age, she wanted to model herself after her father, who was a self-made multimillionaire real-estate developer. After buying and selling a few investment properties in her early 20s, Fiona quickly put the earnings into a series of Laundromats and storage-unit franchises, which made her a millionaire by the time she reached 30.

Although Fiona accomplished one financial goal after another (in the intimate company of her laptop, cell phone, and administrative team), she was entirely baffled about how to seal the deal when it came to creating an intimate relationship of the heart. She'd also suffered from serious migraine headaches and premenstrual mood swings since she'd started getting periods. When she went to her ob-gyn for chronic pelvic pain, the doctor diagnosed Fiona with endometriosis and suggested that the only solution for her would be to get pregnant.

Fiona's second-chakra health problem, endometriosis, was part of her intuitive guidance system, letting her know she was doing a poor job balancing money and love. The imbalance was apparently handed down from her father, Frank, who had spent decades away from his family while building his financial portfolio, thereby neglecting his intimate relationships. His original second-chakra wake-up call came in his late 40s in the form of a lower-back disk problem. But it wasn't until his second-chakra issues evolved to prostate cancer that Frank was able to consider how his drive for business and power had snuffed out the rest of his life, especially his marriage and family.

If you, like Fiona and her father, are a Real Go-Getter, you're very good at running after a new financial challenge, job, or business opportunity. But when it comes to handling up-close and long-term personal intimate relationships, you may run away and hide behind your calendar of schedules and meetings. You might keep yourself busy with the details of running a business or other financial endeavor to avoid the sense of ineptitude you feel when it comes to maintaining a healthy relationship.

What I've learned from people like Fiona and Frank is that Real Go-Getters often have huge hearts under that seemingly brusque, blunt, and often calculating businesslike persona. Even though they can cut to the bone of any deal or tease out any fluff in a budget and make a lot of money in the process, Real Go-Getters will often give away much of their profits to charity, sometimes anonymously. Philanthropy is often their only way of sharing love and giving in relationships.

What clues indicate that you may be a Real Go-Getter? Well, you don't buy gifts until the week or even the day before the special date. You've forgotten a mate's birthday or spaced out on an anniversary more than once. You know what NYSE and NASDAQ mean. You read the business section in the newspaper every day, and you always know if the Dow Jones average is up or down and what the current prime-lending interest rate is. You also know what percentage of your investments are in stocks, bonds, gold, or silver at any one time. You've bought and sold several real-estate properties and made a veritable killing on at least 25 percent of them. You pay off all of your credit-card balances in full by their due dates (but not more than a day or so before). When you play *Monopoly,* the other players find you a little scary because you make a point of buying all the railroads and utilities and always seem to end up owning a hotel on Boardwalk—or even an entire side of the game board.

Sound familiar? If so, then you may be one of these folks, whose intense need for financial wheeling and dealing is in overdrive. The first alarm your body sounds to notify you that your business isn't balanced with intimate relationships (and your second-chakra health is in jeopardy) is intense, crampy pain in your lower back, hips, or abdomen.

All of us have a part of the Real Go-Getter in us. Like Fiona, we all have a tendency to sometimes allow financial issues to dominate our lives so much that relationships are put on the back burner. But always remember that money will never, ever be more important than love. Think about the movie *Hello, Dolly!* in which Barbra Streisand's character was very angry with Walter Matthau's—a money-centric tightwad businessman—because he wasn't interested in marrying her. In her big scene, when she's screaming and singing a sarcastic good-bye song to him, one line pretty much sums up the limits to being a Real Go-Getter. She tells him that on cold winter nights, he can just snuggle up to his cash register. She was saying: Go ahead, focus on your money. But wait until you hit a dark patch and you need emotional support. You're not ever going to get any love from money.

Intuitive Advice for the Real Go-Getter

Do you suffer from chronic health problems in your lower back, hips, urinary tract, and reproductive organs; and do you tend to have aspects of the Real Go-Getter pattern? If so, mind-body medicine and medical intuition can help you learn how to better balance your focus between love and money, and your mind-body makeover begins by looking at your physical health. You could have any second-chakra medical problem with Real Go-Getter tendencies. But if, like Fiona, you happen to have endometriosis, your gynecologist may prescribe birth-control pills; high-dose hormones; or Synarel, Lupron, or other drugs that act on the pituitary gland. However, if you're uncomfortable with the potential long-term implications of being on high-dose synthetic estrogens or the discomfort of being temporarily menopausal using Synarel or Lupron, you may instead opt for laser surgery.

Even though this will initially relieve your endometriosis, it won't prevent it from returning. To reduce the chances of an endometriosis encore, follow a diet plan that reduces the estrogen content in your body by eating equal amounts of carbohydrates and protein. Consume more broccoli, cabbage, turnips, kale, and dark green leafy vegetables; and increase your fiber intake with whole oats, brown rice, or whole-wheat bread. (See the chapter on the third chakra for more information.) Acupuncture and Chinese herbs can also give you tremendous relief from endometriosis and painful menstrual cycles.

If you're a man with the Real Go-Getter pattern, testosterone imbalances—coupled with a variety of genetic, nutritional, and environmental issues—can set the scene for prostate problems. For this reason, reducing levels of testosterone, either with drugs like Proscar or other related anti-testosterone medicine or with nutritional supplements such as saw palmetto, can be helpful. Again, acupuncture and traditional Chinese medicine can further balance male reproductive hormones.

For both men and women with hormonally mediated second-chakra problems, a good multivitamin that balances levels of B vitamins is critical. Taking DHA omega-3 fatty acids (at least 100–300 mg, three times a day) can help mediate inflammation, pain, and swelling in pelvic disorders. One of the greatest ways to regulate hormone levels in your body is aerobic exercise, so try working out for 30 minutes a day, five to seven days a week. Reducing total body fat also reduces hormone levels, which will not only decrease your risk of endometriosis or prostate problems but will also lower the risk of breast cancer in both men and women.

The mind-body makeover next addresses the Real Go-Getters' emotional patterns. As a Go-Getter, you're drawn, almost addicted, to the thrill of chasing financial power, which causes a biochemical opiate rush. This rush becomes addictive as you begin to crave the next deal and the next deal and the next deal, and with it, more and more money, success, and power—all of which eclipse any relationship opportunities that could net love, passion, and affection. Anyone you're in partnership with is going to have to come to grips with the fact that your first love is the thrill of business. But for long-term health, you're going to have to diversify, regulate, and balance how you find your bliss, hopefully not spreading yourself too thinly between work and love.

Map out periods of time when you're focused 100 percent on business. That will be the easy part for you. Now take the more difficult step of setting aside two hours at the end of every weekday that will be 100 percent business free. Turn off your cell phone, your computer, your BlackBerry, or any other form of electronic communication that you use for work. During these two hours, you have to relate to *someone*. You can go for a walk, play tennis or some other sport, or have a bite to eat together as long as it's not for business, networking, or some other profit-related motivation. Preferably, the person you're relating to will be someone you're in an intimate relationship with, or at least a very close friend.

The idea is to start to import the kind of joy, pleasure, bliss, ecstasy, affection, love, kindness, and tenderness that you're never going to get through work. I warn you, though, that if you're a dyed-in-the-wool Go-Getter, your addiction to power and achievement may be so ingrained that you're going to need help accomplishing this two-hour moratorium on business. Enlist a sponsor or a trusted friend to support you. Offer this person a deal she can't refuse.

Once you've achieved a more balanced business-to-love ratio, you'll see that intimate relationships don't necessarily hold you back, weigh you down, or paralyze your progress in the business world. After all, any car that has only DRIVE—all gas and no brakes—is dangerous. Maturing involves developing a more balanced approach to second-chakra endeavors, knowing when it's appropriate to step on the accelerator and when it's better to apply the parking brake.

Here is my seven-part program to rehabilitate the Real Go-Getters' tendency to invest only in the market or in business and not in personal relationships:

1. Identify the physical euphoria that finances bring you, the thrills you experience during the process of cutting a business deal. Distinguish how the adrenaline feels as it flows through your blood vessels, rushing through your body—making you feel bouncy, bubbly, powerful, and invincible.

2. Recognize how the love and passion you experience in relationships can make you feel warm and sensitive, trusting but vulnerable, and out of control—a state you find a little uncomfortable at times.

3. Discern that although you'll never be the warmest, fuzziest nest-featherer, you cannot live by finances or monetary success alone. You ultimately want and need close intimates to share your life and your money with, especially if your turbo-powered business escapades have caused you to blow out your health.

4. Restrict your impulse to spend most of your time in business or other power-centric activities that give you a sense of being in control. Challenge yourself to think and act outside of your comfort zone. Although being in a loving relationship will make you feel more vulnerable, it will also cause you to make a broader investment in a more stable future.

5. Know that intimate relationships can coexist with and even promote the core persona of the mega–power broker.

6. Change the unhealthy thought pattern: *Intimate relationships interfere with my freedom . . .* to the healthier affirmation: *It's possible to maintain my individual aspirations for power and financial success and also be in an intimate, committed relationship.*

7. Follow the second rule for intuitive health—*To be a lover, you need to be a fighter*—by learning how to balance your feisty, detached, entrepreneurial persona with the vulnerable warmth needed for intimate relationships.

The Having It All Type

The third second-chakra extreme are the Having It All types, those who make Superman look like an underachiever. Geeta illustrates this pattern well: this 29-year-old woman had always been very organized and intent on what she wanted in life. At the ripe old age of seven, she knew that she'd grow up and have it all—get married, live in New York City, have both a girl and a boy, own an apartment, run an art gallery, buy and sell real estate, and make a lot of money. While all of her friends were reading fairy tales, Geeta disdained the vagueness behind the nebulous ending "They all lived happily every after." She preferred an itemized list.

When Geeta was in school, she had a part-time job at a restaurant, was on the debating team, belonged to the Future Business Leaders of America, edited both the school newspaper and the yearbook, and had an active social life, to boot. And the years she was the president of her junior and then her senior class were the only times her class actually turned a profit during their fund-raisers.

In college, Geeta's social, academic, and work schedules were equally exhausting. She rushed a sorority, declared a double major, and worked at least ten hours a week in the school cafeteria (not to mention ending up running a flower-delivery business on campus).

After graduating from her four-year program in only three years, Geeta married another college student who was still finishing up his senior year. When he graduated and started medical school, she was already in grad school, going for an MBA.

That's when Geeta's Having It All persona hit the wall. Once she tried to get pregnant, she was shocked to find that she had stopped ovulating and was infertile. Despite the fact that Geeta had what seemed on paper to be the perfectly well-planned life, her body was letting her know that it was, in reality, a mess. Having burned the candle at both ends since she was a young child, Geeta was about to see some of her goals go up in smoke.

If you, like Geeta, are the Having It All type, you are truly a force of nature, a real powerhouse. You rush, schedule, motivate, plan, organize, and drive yourself through life in an awe-inspiring fashion to accomplish in a decade what most people wouldn't even dream of doing in a lifetime. But in your zeal to achieve everything all at once, you don't know how to pace yourself. You have trouble synchronizing your long-range financial and relationship agenda with what plans and innate time schedule your body may have. In your missionary fervor to accomplish financial goals, find the right mate, and produce children, you give your body orders and expect it to immediately accommodate the next item on your agenda.

What I've learned from people like Geeta is that the reason Having It Alls have preprogrammed their lives with goal after goal is to give themselves a sense of control over their destinies. But guess what? They're *not* in control. None of us has that much ultra-micromanaged power over the future (at least not in the highly pressured way that Having It Alls tend to want). In fact, underneath all of our plans, degrees, business endeavors, and relationships, we have to come to terms with our human frailty and vulnerability—something that Having It All types have spent most of their lives anxiously running away from. They must realize that their bodies have needs and limits, and they can't escape their fears around that or medicate them by immersing themselves in the excess thrills and victories of love and money.

What clues signal that you may be a Having It All type? In your high-school class, you were voted "Most Likely to Succeed." You're never bored, but if you start to feel understimulated, you have a whole host of projects that you could engross yourself in at any given time. If you have children (or pets, for that matter), you've scheduled their afternoons with activities that are both socially and intellectually enriching. You're involved in sports that require intense training and extensive workout schedules, such as gymnastics, long-distance or competitive running, cycling, swimming, crew, figure skating, or the like.

If you gain a few pounds, you go ballistic. In the elevator, you tend to press the buttons repeatedly to speed up the closing of the door, even though it never seems to work. When you're driving in the left lane, you hate it when slow cars are in front of you. In fact, you can't stand to have cars in front of you at all, and you're always complaining about incompetent drivers who go too slow—meaning that they're actually driving the speed limit.

If this sounds familiar, you may be the Having It All type, but in reality, you probably don't *actually* have it all. You're used to getting exactly what you want because you aren't afraid to do what's necessary to make that happen, but all your pushing won't help you when your second chakra sends out its first alarm—you will quite literally lose it. You'll lose something vital in your second-chakra region, such as your fertility, a disk in your lower back, or the cartilage in your hip. Whatever it is, the effect is the same: everything comes to a grinding halt. To regain health in the second chakra, you'll need to learn how to honor your body the same as you would any other partner in your business or love life.

If we look closely at Geeta's story, we'll realize that each of us can find within ourselves a Having It All type, an aspect of our personality that wants everything—the money *and* the relationship—and that tries to burn the candle at both ends to get it. But the process ultimately hurts our bodies. Most of us can remember when we were children and wanted four desserts or maybe even four different main courses all at once. Our teachers and parents told us that a part of growing up was learning how to make choices. *Yeah, sure,* we thought back then. But as soon as we became adults, we tried to get everything we wanted anyway, because there was no parent around to say no.

Actually, there *is* an authority around to tell us to limit our choices: *our bodies,* whose health does set limits on what we can humanly accomplish during any amount of time. When we burn the candle at both ends, there won't be any candle left—we'll have burned ourselves out in the process of over-acquisition. The truth, we'll then realize, is that we really *can't* have it all, or at least not all at once.

Intuitive Advice for the Having It All Type

Do you suffer from chronic health problems in your lower back, hips, urinary tract, and reproductive organs; and do you tend to have Having It All–type issues? If so, you can still be your enthusiastic, optimistic, successful self if you use mind-body medicine and medical intuition to help you live your life at a healthier pace. First, your mind-body makeover addresses the physical challenges that have caused your body to go on strike. You could have any second-chakra health problem with Having It All–type tendencies. But if, like Geeta, your issue happens to be infertility, you must learn to work in partnership with your body so that your plans and its needs are more in sync.

If you've already gone to several physicians who couldn't find an obvious reason for your infertility, try a board-certified acupuncturist and Chinese herbalist who can help you replenish your body with the physical and energetic nutrients that have been skimmed off from years and years of overdoing. In addition, take a pharmaceutical-grade multivitamin that includes vitamin C, zinc, and folate and the other B vitamins. Eating enough to maintain an adequate body-fat percentage is also critical because body fat produces estrogen, and if your levels of this hormone aren't high enough, you won't ovulate. Finally, if you're smoking, drinking alcohol, or ingesting massive amounts of caffeine, *stop.* It's not helping you get pregnant, nor could you maintain a pregnancy to ultimately give birth to a healthy baby.

Next, the Having It All types' mind-body makeover focuses on the emotional intuitive brain. Find a spiritual advisor or ask a trusted friend to help you sit for a while, slow down, and come to grips with the fact that you're mortal and have physical limits . . . even if you don't want to believe in emotional and economic ones. And as you re-adjust your life to the time and intensity that your body needs, I warn you—you *will* go into second-chakra withdrawal. You'll crave the adrenaline rush, the opiates of success, and you'll get antsy and impatient for the oxytocin induced in intense relationships. Rest assured that this is an emotional-maturity exercise that will create growth in your mind and your body. It is critical to both healing your pain and health problems and to preventing them from recurring that you dial down the intensity in which you drive yourself in relationships and finances.

You must learn to have faith that at any moment, if you focus on one area—say, money and finances—your supportive partner and family can do their part. Similarly, if it's time for you to focus on love, relationships, and children, you need to trust that your partner will take care of the business end and that the finances won't go up in smoke. By transforming the concept that you have to do everything intensely, burning the candle at both ends and maintaining control at all times, you'll not only improve your second-chakra health, but you'll actually end up with a life that's more fulfilling than you ever imagined.

What follows is my seven-part program to help rehabilitate the Having It All types' tendency to get stuck in overdrive:

1. Identify your tendency for perfection and your drive to achieve the pinnacle of success in everything you do. See how you try to master some utopian ideal of both relationships and financial success in order to feel competent and in control of your life.

2. Recognize that when you aren't experiencing the constant, unending thrill of financial success and the intense pursuit of passionate relationships, not only do you feel like a miserable failure— defeated and dejected—but you also feel empty, useless, and guilty, as though you've lost control of your life in general.

3. Discern that the most important partnership, business, or intimate relationship you'll ever have is with your physical body, and that in order for you to be successful in both love and money, you and your physical self need to strike a deal. In your schedule of financial and relationship activities, you must also attend to your body's needs, factoring those requirements into the equation. By slowing down the timeline on some of your business, marital, and reproductive goals and making the choice not to do *everything* (or at least not to do it all at once), you'll be attending to your health proactively.

4. Restrict the number of relationships you have with other Having It All types, because being with such like-minded, power-driven individuals will only rev you up again. Instead, diversify the kinds of people you surround yourself with to reflect a more full spectrum of initiative and motivation.

5. Know that those other, more laid-back folks with a Zen-like approach to life achieve a different type of power. Realize that thinking that any of us can truly have it all is a ridiculous concept. It's the essence of the human condition to have at least some parts of us that are weakened or flawed. This gives us the ability to partner with others so we can create something new.

6. Change the unhealthy thought pattern: *If I achieve financial success, I won't be able to have a good relationship, and if I focus on an excellent marriage, I won't be able to achieve true financial success; therefore, I have to go full throttle at both so I know for sure I can have it all, all the time* . . . to the healthier affirmation: *True love and partnership allow timely and unlimited expression of financial growth in a mature and balanced way.*

7. Follow the second rule for intuitive health—*To be a lover, you need to be a fighter*—by learning that if you stop trying to have it all, all the time, you'll actually end up with *more,* starting with more second-chakra health.

The Bankrupt and Bereft Type

The final second-chakra extreme includes the Bankrupt and Bereft types, those who seem to always fail in matters of love and money, regardless of what they do. Consider Helen, 32, whose parents and extended family pushed her to call me because she was having trouble getting launched in the world. Helen had gone to all the right schools and had done well academically, but when it came to learning how to fly solo in the world, she crashed every time. After graduating from a four-year state university with a business degree, Helen began a series of jobs—in sales, marketing, secretarial work, and even waitressing—but something always went wrong.

Thinking that she didn't need the confinement of working under someone, Helen started a business with a couple of relatives—a coffee shop that failed after three years due to personality conflicts and problems managing money. As if her financial issues weren't bad enough, Helen was always complaining about her love life. All men were bums, she said. One after another came and went through her life. No matter how good her initial impression was of the guy she was dating, Helen always found something wrong—he didn't understand her, he didn't listen, he wasn't emotional enough, or he wasn't there when she needed him.

Helen was becoming anxious, frustrated, and despondent. She watched all of her siblings and friends move on with their lives—they got married, had kids, and progressed up the ladder of prosperity. Yet Helen herself seemed to be stuck, nearly bankrupt and bereft, going from one failed job and relationship to another, with no idea of what she was doing wrong. She did, however, enjoy the support of a family who cared about her and would always lend her a hand, helping her get by with the bare necessities. A never-ending list of aunts, uncles, and cousins was available—on a Friday or Saturday night to go out to a movie or dinner, for instance, or even to accompany her to a wedding—so my client never had to feel lonely.

Financially, Helen always seemed to have some relatives on some branch of her family tree who could extend a helping hand and offer her a job, tiding her over until she could figure out what she was finally going to do with her life. Even so, she just couldn't seem to make a go of relationships and financial success outside of the safety network of the family.

Helen had also long endured multiple gynecological problems. In addition to polycystic ovary syndrome (PCOS), she suffered from hormonally mediated moodiness, skin eruptions that doctors called inflammatory acne, and a painful condition affecting her bladder and vagina known as vulvovestibulitis or vulvodynia. She was also 60 pounds overweight, a trend that started in her teens when she turned to fried dough and chocolate-chip cookies for solace whenever she felt upset. Her body was intuitively signaling to her through chronic pelvic and hormonal reproductive-system problems that her second-chakra money and relationship skills were sorely lacking.

If you, like Helen, are the Bankrupt and Bereft type, you're very good at networking within your extended family to try to get your social and financial needs met, but when it comes to using the same skills to forge your way in the world, something always goes wrong. Although relatives are good places to start to achieve stability and receive support, if you become dependent on them and can't stand alone or partner with other people you're not related to, your family roots become shackles.

What I've learned from people like Helen is that Bankrupt and Bereft types blame their past problems on the inept performance of those around them. They assume more and more control and avoid working with others to prevent any further "errors" by people. They also apply the same faulty response to relationships. Rather than try-ing to learn the intricate skills behind the mechanics of a coopera-tive, intimate relationship, they seize control there, too. They either become very vocal and domineering in an attempt to preempt prob-lems, assuring that nothing that has gone wrong before will repeat itself, or they choose to be totally submissive, shutting up and saying nothing to avoid confrontations like they've had in the past. Ironi-cally, after each loss, they try harder and harder to seize even more control, rather than adopting the more skillful, effective approach that could actually help them—learning a more cooperative stance in which those involved are able to speak their minds in a mutual, sensitive, and well-timed fashion.

What clues indicate that you may be a Bankrupt and Bereft type? Well, your résumé shows frequent career changes, including positions lasting less than two years. You often rely on family members who have an "in" at a company to help you get a job. Your last supervisor was younger than you, was incompetent, and wasn't interested in your brilliant ideas about how you thought things could be better organized. Your income level and financial success is much less than what others would expect from someone with your intelligence and skill set.

You've found that working for businesses or corporations is not for you—and yet working as a freelance consultant or creating your own solo business isn't making the money roll in, either. You have trouble breaking in to the market or making connections outside of your family and friends, so you've begun to supplement your finances with part-time work at a job you absolutely hate. Moreover, your relationship résumé shows the same sort of frequent shifts, and family members frequently step in to fix you up with a new partner. You often wonder why many of your friends who aren't nearly as attractive as you are can make a relationship last longer.

If these scenarios sound familiar, then you may be a Bankrupt and Bereft type. As you try desperately to dig yourself out of this difficult, painful, second-chakra slump, the first alarm that your body will sound is that not-so-subtle feeling of the bottom falling out of your life. You get hit simultaneously with unrelenting catastrophes relating to money, relationships, and health.

It starts one morning with an achiness in your lower back that signals it's about to go out again. You go to the bathroom, and you notice that when you try to urinate it feels a little funny. Could it be another yeast infection? It's too soon to tell. You look in the mirror and note a blemish about to erupt in the middle of your face.

But you ignore these signs and go on with your day until all second-chakra-issue hell breaks loose after lunch. You receive two overdue notices from the bank. You can't get money out of the ATM. You have a major blowup with your partner. By the time you get home, you're doubled over in lower-back pain. The next day, you wake up with some strange, rip-roaring bladder and vaginal infection. Not to mention the Mount Vesuvius–shaped zit on your nose, which has doubled in size from earlier in the day.

All of us have periods in our lives when we feel like the Bankrupt and Bereft type. We can all remember times when, like Helen, no matter how hard we tried, we had one failure after another in love and in finances. We've all had the bottom fall out of a relationship or out of our bank account, and at that moment things truly seemed bleak. However, if we allow ourselves to continue to feel hopeless and helpless, that mind-set will sap all our strength—strength we need to fight our way out of this pit of despair. Instead, we must try to remember those other times when, in the midst of some other relationship or financial blowup, a miraculous turn of events saved us and helped us survive to succeed again. Just as we made it through that time, we'll make it through the next one—if we remember never to give in to our feelings of failure.

Intuitive Advice for the Bankrupt and Bereft Type

Do you suffer from chronic health problems in your lower back, hips, urinary tract, and reproductive organs; and do you tend to have some aspects of the Bankrupt and Bereft pattern? If so, mind-body medicine and medical intuition can teach you another way to approach the madness, and your mind-body makeover begins with your physical self. You could have any second-chakra health problem with Bankrupt and Bereft tendencies. But if, like Helen, your second-chakra health problems seem widespread and diverse (lower-back pain, recurring bladder infections, infertility, chronic acne), the truth is that they're actually all related. Each of them is exacerbated by problems with mood and mood-sensitive hormones like serotonin.

You've probably known since an early age that eating carbohydrates helps soothe you when you get irritable and moody. Carbohydrate "mood medicines" work, but their side effects can include dramatic, unrelenting weight gain. This extra weight becomes stored in estrone, a bad form of estrogen that causes all kinds of health problems, including ovarian cysts (polycystic ovary disease) and too much oil production in the skin (acne). The weight also causes back problems like sciatica (a form of lower-back pain).

If you then get depressed and angry about your health problems and appearance, the volatility of your mood swings only increases. This further disrupts your serotonin levels and increases your risk of acquiring a host of complex immune-system pain disorders, including conditions such as vulvodynia and vulvovestibulitis—chronic bladder and vagina pain.

To stop this chain of pain, rather than going from one doctor to another for each separate problem, it's best to address everything together. Assemble and rely upon a health-care team made up of an ob-gyn or nurse-practitioner who specializes in weight and mood problems, a psychiatrist, and a pain specialist who together will treat the intricacies of your hormones, mood, and pain. This is a tall order, but it's essential to approach it this way so you can minimize surgeries and narcotics, take antidepressants that won't make you gain weight, and create a meal plan that will balance your hormones and your mood.

Your nutritionist may recommend a low-oxalate diet if you have vulvodynia, suggesting you eat more rhubarb, celery, chocolate, strawberries, and spinach; as well as taking calcium citrate and grape-seed extract. You may also need interferon treatment or other more radical approaches for this chronic bladder pain. For vulvovestibulitis, you might require a small amount of estrogen locally in the urinary area.

Working with an acupuncturist or Qigong master may also be beneficial because it will not only help you control your pain but also create a more energetically balanced approach to conflict. Qigong teaches the benefits of balancing pushing with pulling, driving with yielding—metaphors that you will eventually be able to apply to the idiosyncrasies of partnership, love, and money.

The Bankrupt and Bereft types' mind-body makeover next moves to the emotional, intuitive right brain to address hormonally induced moodiness. Learning how to attend to your financial and emotional needs while also being cognizant of other people's points of view is a skill that's hard to learn with a hair-trigger reactive brain. A combination of mood stabilizers such as DHA (100–300 mg, three times a day) and prescription medications like Topamax or Lamictal (which both help with migraines and bipolar disorder) may slow down your right-brain emotionality and responsiveness so you can learn how to use new partnership, relationship, and financial skills to get a mate and be stable emotionally in a business situation.

On top of the mood stabilizers, taking a variety of serotonin agents such as SAMe (800–1,600 mg a day, on an empty stomach) or bigger guns like the prescription medications Prozac, Zoloft, or Effexor will ease both your mood as well as your chronic lower-back and vulvovestibulitis pain. (For additional specific information on stabilizing mood, see Part II of my book *The New Feminine Brain*.)

For help learning how to nurture and maintain healthy relationships founded on mutual respect, start by developing the technique of mindfulness, which teaches you how to observe and describe—but not judge—when you're experiencing emotion. Mindfulness, revolutionized in the modern world by the famous Buddhist monk Thich Nhat Hanh, can help you take hold of your mind—all the right-brain emotions and intuition and all the left-brain thoughts—and become conscious of them. By nailing down what feelings and thoughts are going through your head right now, you'll ultimately know what's affecting the physical reality in your body: your health.

You can practice mindfulness anywhere, anytime. You don't need to be in a spiritual sanctuary, meditation hall, or even a silent room. You could do mindfulness exercises in a bus station or your favorite fast-food restaurant, for heaven's sake! Wherever you are when you start to feel unbalanced, do the following:

1. Observe, sense, and identify every thought or feeling that wells up within you—whether it's *fear* or its cousins anxiety, fright, panic, worry, or edginess; *anger* and its relatives aggravation, frustration, resentment, or irritation; *sadness* and its subsidiaries gloom, despair, hurt, or agony; *shame* and its associates guilt, humiliation, regret, and remorse; *love* and its cohorts affection, kindness, lust, warmth, and tenderness; or *joy* and its partners bliss, ecstasy, hope, pleasure, and pride.

2. Pay attention to the physical sensations of your breathing as the air goes into your lungs and again as it leaves them. By being aware of your thoughts and feelings as you pay attention to your inhalation and your exhalation, you're uniting your mind with your body, increasing your awareness of both.

3. Don't try to analyze your feelings and thoughts as they arise, because if you judge them, hate them, worry about them, become frightened by them, or even try to push them away, they'll go into

your body and eventually create physical symptoms. Simply acknowledge their presence.

Once you've practiced this technique a bit, then, when you're with another person, you can detach from your feelings and learn how to simply observe and describe his or her emotions—also without any judgment. This allows you to not only attend to your own needs, but also to separate yourself from your emotions so that you can key in to what's going on with someone else, too.

(For information on combining mindfulness training with Cognitive Behavioral Therapy [CBT], see your local mental-health center, as well as the book *Skills Training Manual for Treating Borderline Personality Disorder,* by Marsha M. Linehan [Guilford Press, New York, 1993], pages 109–113. Many people use this book, not just those with borderline personality disorder, because it can be helpful for anyone who wants to learn how to manage moods and assertiveness.)

Knowing both what *your* feelings are as well as what the other person's are is the first critical step in a relationship. I call it maintaining your "dance space," an important concept in ballroom dancing that you might also remember from the movie *Dirty Dancing.* It's crucial because it allows you to create boundaries in a relationship while simultaneously setting up mutuality in the space between you and the other person.

While you're practicing the metaphor of maintaining your dance space, you might as well go ahead and take a ballroom-dance class as well. Sign up as a single person—don't go with a friend or a partner—so that you can learn how to lead *and* follow. By learning both positions (and maintaining a sense of humor as you do so), you'll better understand how to give and take orders in business and how to support and be supported in intimate relationships. You'll also gain an appreciation for why both are necessary for optimal functioning.

So now, here's my seven-part program for rehabilitating the Bankrupt and Bereft types' tendency to bottom out on their careers, love lives, and health at the same time:

1. Identify how engaging in work situations or in relationships with potential mates has been at times more akin to a tug-of-war than a dance of harmony and partnership.

2. Recognize the irritability and volatility you begin to feel when others look like they may be taking control of you or veering off in a direction that seems frightening and foreign to your perspective.

3. Discern that you can be safe and secure and produce long-standing financial and intimate partnerships where sometimes you're the leader and sometimes you're the follower. You can't always do everything on your own or within the safety net of your family. By discovering the yin and yang, the push and pull, the bob and the weave of mutual relationships, you can learn to have true prosperity and intimacy.

4. Restrict the time you spend with family on Friday or Saturday evenings. Join church or spiritual groups, recreational clubs, educational or vocational environments, or other mating pools where you can practice engaging with people while maintaining an appropriate amount of give-and-take. Volunteer for some nonprofit organizations, and practice both leading teams *and* following orders.

5. Know that there is power in yielding in a relationship and vulnerability in taking the lead and being assertive when necessary. Recognize that at certain times you may need to be a driven leader, and at others you may have to be a more laid-back participant, working to support someone else's grand plan.

6. Change the unhealthy thought pattern: *No matter what I do, I always manage to have health and financial disasters . . .* to the healthier thought: *I now release worry about finances and relationships. I trust that through partnerships with others, I will lovingly and energetically create financial power and genuine intimacy in my life.*

7. Follow the second rule for intuitive health—*To be a lover, you need to be a fighter*—by learning that sometimes you follow and sometimes you lead, and understanding that smoothly transitioning between one mode and the other makes the dance infinitely more beautiful (and your second chakra infinitely healthier).

•-•-•

To create health in your second chakra (your lower back, hips, and reproductive system), you have to be in either personal or business relationships where each party can, when necessary, back the other in some financial or monetary way. To achieve this tricky balance between love and money, you must follow the second rule for intuitive health—*To be a lover, you need to be a fighter*. This requires that you have the warm sensitivity that it takes to be in an intimate relationship as well as the feisty, detached persona of a wheeler-dealer entrepreneur. If you manage to just get the babe (the partner, whether male or female) or to just get the bucks (financial security), know that your second-chakra intuitive advisor won't rest until it guides you, for richer or poorer, in sickness and in health, back onto the relationship track.

•-•-•-•-•

Chapter Five

Third Chakra: "Strong Enough"

(The Health of Your Digestive System, Plus Weight and Addiction Issues)

Your third chakra—which includes the digestive tract, liver, gall-bladder, and kidneys—is your intuitive advisor that lets you know whether or not you're strong enough to both fulfill your responsibility to others and fuel your self-esteem.

When you're in infancy, everyone indulges you and pumps up your confidence with praise. Everything you do gives you thrill and pleasure. It's all about you.

Then, starting around age three or four, we're all taught how to be responsible, reliable, and dependable—even if it's just by having to pick up our toys. We're given small responsibilities that teach us how to balance our need to gratify ourselves and pump up our self-esteem with the requirement that we work and become trustworthy and conscientious.

The first time I ever saw third-chakra intuition in action was with a relative I'll call Zelda. This beautiful little girl was the apple of her father's eye, and everyone in her family doted on her. She was a brilliant artist, an incredible poet, and wise beyond her years. At the age of five, she was put in the gifted and talented program. It seemed like Zelda had it all . . . until, at age seven, she developed juvenile diabetes.

You would think that Zelda's vast intellect could comprehend the dietary plan of this disorder—that she wasn't supposed to eat large amounts of sugar. However, she was used to having every need and request gratified, so she continued to feast upon ice cream and candy bars. By the time this girl was a teenager, her diabetes was as out of control as her behavior. Not only was she continuing to eat junk food, but she began to skip classes and use drugs. Her father thought that the high-school administration didn't know how to appropriately cater to his daughter's unique intellectual and creative abilities, so he removed her from school and encouraged her to get her general equivalency diploma (GED). With a lifelong pattern of having every inner whim satisfied and pumping up her self-worth and self-esteem, Zelda had never developed the third-chakra discipline and strength to be a responsible adult in the world, whether it required working on her education or being conscientious with her insulin and her diabetic dietary regime.

I'd love to say that this story ended well, but alas, Zelda became totally disabled in her 20s. After a decade of senseless, undisciplined, and irresponsible neglect of her health, she developed painful medical complications—diabetic neuropathy and blindness—and she died in her early 30s. I hope that the rest of us don't need a third-chakra intuitive guidance system to scream as loudly as Zelda's had in order for us to see that we're having trouble balancing our self-esteem with responsibility.

●—●—●

The U.S. is in the midst of an epidemic of third-chakra illnesses, including obesity, gastroesophageal reflux disease (GERD), ulcers, various digestive disorders, irritable bowel syndrome (IBS), constipation, Crohn's disease, ulcerative colitis, anorexia nervosa and other eating disorders, and a host of addictions. Minute by minute, day by day, our third chakra monitors our lives and notifies us via these illnesses when we're having difficulty either building ourselves up or holding down responsibility.

To maintain wellness in the third-chakra region of your body, you have to follow the third rule for intuitive health: *You can't always get what you want, but if you try, you'll get what you need* (balancing self-esteem and responsibility). This requires balancing the desire to feel good about yourself, boost your self-esteem, and satisfy your cravings with the ability to fulfill your duties and responsibilities at work and in your personal life.

Most people who have third-chakra health issues tend to fall somewhere in between four extreme categories: the *Rock of Dependability*—those who feel so responsible to others that they neglect their own self-image and self-esteem; the *Constantly Craving* type— those who work so hard at pumping themselves up that they have little energy left for work and other obligations; the *Pumped Up and Rocking Hard* type—those supremely competent and confident dynamos who need more and more to satisfy themselves; and finally, the *Broken-down, Burned-out* type—those who avoid grounded, earthbound activities and instead focus on nonmaterial, impractical, and often spiritual endeavors.

The Rock of Dependability

The first third-chakra extreme are the Rocks of Dependability, those who are forever responsible and reliable as far as others go, but who neglect their own self-image and self-esteem. Isadora, 28, illustrates this perfectly. She was always the dependable one, be it at work, in her church, or with her friends. The most conscientious and diligent person in her office, Isadora arrived ten minutes early every day and was always willing to stay late if necessary. She was a rock of reliability, there at all times to lend a hand or carry a load, meeting her (and everyone else's) responsibilities.

If you needed a ride, Isadora would soon be at your doorstep in her equally reliable vehicle. If you needed a bridge loan to cover your rent, you could count on her. She was the first one people usually went to in a community disaster. Rock of Dependability folks like Isadora always open their hearts, roll up their sleeves, and do what needs to be done—whether it's helping a family whose house burned down at Christmas or comforting a group of children who lost their parents in an auto accident.

Although Isadora was dependable when it came to the people around her, she was irresponsible about taking care of herself. She was very uncomfortable with any activity that boosted her own self-worth and self-respect in any way. Basically, she let her appearance go. Although she worked tirelessly behind the scenes doing hair and makeup for her two sisters, who were professional singers, Isadora paid no attention to her own hair, nails, makeup, or clothing. She was 50 pounds overweight and hid in a sweat suit with her hair stuffed up underneath a baseball cap. Isadora would always say that being the "unsung" sister was such satisfying and fulfilling work because when the fans remarked on how gorgeous her sisters were, *she* could beam with pride.

However, whenever this woman looked in the mirror, to quote another famous singer, she didn't "get no satisfaction." So she'd *import* satisfaction instead from the nearest bag of chips or M&M's and then wash them down with soda pop, telling herself she needed to do this to coat her "nervous stomach." She was addicted to the opiate-induced biochemical high from working and serving—and, unfortunately, from eating and drinking as well. As a result, her health was in shambles.

In addition to the compulsive eating and the weight gain, she suffered from IBS and a host of other vague digestive problems. Isadora's third chakra was signaling to her that she needed to learn how to balance responsibility toward others with her obligation to feel better about herself by working on her appearance, self-esteem, and self-worth.

If you, like Isadora, are a Rock of Dependability, your capacity to hold down any job is awe inspiring, but you think it's selfish, vain, and maybe even narcissistic to attend to your self-esteem, self-worth, or self-confidence. You'd spend more time cleaning a mirror than gazing at yourself in it, admiring your jawline or abdominal muscles. You're the very opposite of what we think Paris Hilton is like, with her hedonistic, extremely singular focus on fame, self-promotion, glamour, and the use of Chihuahuas as fashion accessories.

What I've learned from people like Isadora is that Rocks of Dependability tend to partner with those who are irresponsible, unemployed, or disabled; have addiction and dependency issues; or are trust-fund babies. Ironically, Rocks often marry individuals who seem quite delicate and are constantly craving the company of others to pump up their self-esteem or ego. During the course of their relationship, the Rocks will tend to gain weight as they carry more and more responsibility, and their mates will *lose* weight as they shed or avoid their concerns. This transfer of responsibility (and weight) demonstrates a dangerously unhealthy interdependency.

What clues signal that you might be a Rock of Dependability? In high school and college, you were the one your classmates copied notes from or called to get the assignments. People are always asking you for a ride. If you miss two days of work in a row, your office becomes chaotic and co-workers call you at home to ask where things are. People seek your advice, even though you're not a therapist. You're a tried-and-true friend who often goes on rescue missions, whether you're bailing others out financially, helping them through health crises, or just being there for them when they feel down. You'd give the shirt off of your back to a friend. In fact, you loan your clothes out *a lot.*

You'd rather have fudge than a facial. You'd choose pizza over a pedicure. When it comes to jeans, you're more likely to plunk down money for Levi's or Wranglers than True Religion or Rock & Republic. The mere thought of walking down a red carpet in an evening gown and heels makes you feel nauseated.

If this sounds like you, then you may be a Rock of Dependability. Who *wouldn't* want you on their team? But be careful, because over time your excessive devotion to everyone's needs but your own will take its toll on your third-chakra health. The first alarm will sound as a pang of guilt right in the center of your gut whenever you aren't able to come to a loved one's rescue.

When someone has a problem and you feel pity for him, you're actually intuitively experiencing his sorrow when you say, "I'm sorry." And when you can't do anything to eradicate the problem, not only are you left empathetically holding his sadness, but you also feel shame because you believe that bringing him relief from his suffering and making him happy is your responsibility. It doesn't occur to you that this person has some responsibility for taking care of his own pain. If you continue to carry the weight of everyone's suffering and feel guilty when you can't help others, you'll be sick to your stomach but still gain weight.

If we look deep enough, we'll find a part of ourselves that tends to have some elements of the Rock of Dependability. It shows up during those times when we, like Isadora, let ourselves go, neglect our appearance, and allow our exercise routine to fall by the wayside because we're immersed in responsibilities to others that we think are more important than our responsibility to ourselves. But beware. Veterinarians know that when a pet doesn't groom itself, it's always a telltale sign that the animal may be depressed or seriously ill. We can apply this concept to humans as well.

When we take time every day to buff, puff, and preen, it's not a sign that we're selfish and conceited any more than a cat or dog grooming itself indicates that it's self-absorbed or narcissistic. Grooming is a critical part of third-chakra behavior that enhances the health of our self-esteem, which is critical for our physical well-being. If we—animals and humans—have stopped grooming our fur or styling our hair, working our coats or attending to our clothes and fashion sense, or stretching our bodies and running around, it's not a sign that we're too busy. Rather, self-neglect signals that we're losing our capacity to experience joy by attending to our own needs; and it's a one-way, often nonstop, trip to depression and poor health.

Intuitive Advice for the Rock of Dependability

Do you suffer from chronic health problems in your digestive tract, liver, gallbladder, and kidneys; and do you tend to have Rock of Dependability issues? If so, you can learn to use mind-body medicine and medical intuition to successfully heal your life. You could have any third-chakra health problem with Rock of Dependability tendencies. But if, like Isadora, *yours* happens to be a combination of overeating, being overweight, and having low self-esteem, the intertwined nature of these issues requires a different type of mind-body makeover. You must address your physical health problems while *simultaneously* addressing your emotional intuitive brain.

Here's why: If you have weight issues, the chances are good that you often experience cravings or feel like you're starving. But we're not just talking about physical hunger here. Those feelings also apply to other third-chakra self-esteem needs, such as appearance, self-worth, self-confidence, and self-esteem. So when you feel as if you're starving, you're right: you *are*—but you're starving for self-esteem, not for Ben & Jerry's. The reason you want to go for the Cherry Garcia, or whatever your favorite flavor is, is that food temporarily increases the level of natural opiates in your body, tricking your brain into feeling good. Think of it as importing the biochemical equivalent of love and self-worth.

That's why you try to satiate your sense of inner emptiness by raiding the refrigerator or emptying the pantry—your nearest medical-clinic window. Yielding to the immediate hankering for something, anything, to fill up this emptiness, you reach for the Double Stuf Oreos or barbecue potato chips (serotonin plus opiates). In about 30 minutes, your mood *and* your self-esteem are elevated. The drug was indeed effective: you feel confident, strong, fulfilled, and gratified.

If you reach for a Coke, you get a little caffeine with your sugar rush—no extra charge. If you pour yourself an alcoholic drink, you'll get about two hours of therapeutic relief from anxiety, with an additional elevated capacity for social finesse, smoothness, and courage. But with all of these options, the cost is indeed steep, which you may realize the next time you step on a scale.

If you're a Rock of Dependability, you must begin the intuitive mind-body makeover by asking yourself, *Am I strong enough?* Can you finally attend to yourself as much as you attend to everyone else? If your self-worth is entirely based on carrying burdens for others to the point that you ignore taking care of yourself, your resulting weight problems will increase your risk of diabetes, heart disease, stroke, breast cancer, and other illnesses. In other words, you won't be able to help as many people as you'd like to, simply because you won't *live* long enough to do so. So if I may appeal to your codependent nature, let me point out that it behooves you to ration your efforts and to invest more in your self-worth, appearance, and pride.

To make the investment and lose the weight, I recommend that you follow a meal plan that balances seven elements: *protein, carbohydrates, vegetables, water, multivitamins, mineral supplements,* and *exercise.* Yes, water and exercise are part of your meal plan (I shun the word *diet*). Basically, you eat healthy food, drink water to help pump the nutrients through your digestive tract, and exercise to burn calories and facilitate eliminating waste out of your colon.

Here's how it typically works: When you get up in the morning, you drink about 26 ounces of plain water, and then you eat two egg whites or whole eggs (you pick), half an English muffin (with a reasonable amount of butter), and coffee or tea (with or without cream and sweetener). Then you exercise for a half hour to a disco-like or fast dance beat on an elliptical trainer or an exercise bike. The idea is to really whale away hard. At midmorning, have your second 26-ounce bottle of water along with half of some type of protein bar.

Lunch is your biggest meal of the day. Mentally divide your plate into thirds. Fill one third with protein (and you know this doesn't mean fried chicken or prime rib dripping with fat), another with carbs (including bread, pasta, rice, or potatoes), and the final third with vegetables (heavy on the greens and light on the carrots, corn, and other sugary vegetables that we all love but know are really candy). If you want dessert, which I highly recommend, take some (or all) of your carbohydrate away and have the equivalent portion for dessert. (See? I'm not an absolute nutritional Nazi.) Then, at midafternoon, eat the other half of that protein bar you started earlier in the day, downing it with your third and final 26 ounces of water.

Dinner is your tiniest meal of the day: a small piece of protein, a dark green leafy vegetable, and a small piece of fruit. (By the way, alcohol is a carbohydrate, so if you want a drink with dinner, you must limit yourself to one and forgo the dessert or carbohydrate at lunch. Choose your carbs wisely!) Then, if you can, walk or run after dinner.

At the same time you're addressing your body's needs by following your new meal plan, you must also address the needs of your intuitive emotional brain. Basically, you have to find a way to build self-esteem, import opiates, and improve self-worth with a biochemical side-effect profile that doesn't include weight gain or other health problems. How? Diversify! Input thrill, satisfaction, and fulfillment in every chakra category of your life:

- To add a little pizzazz to your **first** chakra (families), join spiritual, recreational, or educational groups.

- To spark your **second** chakra (relationships), take your partner out to a bowling league or some other recreational event. Have a couple of date nights. If you don't currently have a partner, do something creative, such as taking an art or dance class.

- For a little **third**-chakra zing, have a day when you dote on yourself. Go to a high-end clothing store or makeup counter and have one of the stylists give you a makeover, or spend a day exploring the nearest big city with some friends.

- To pamper your **fourth** chakra, go to a movie—a romantic comedy, a drama, or a tearjerker where you can have a good long cry. Or buy yourself some flowers. If you can tolerate a massage, get some friends together and go to a spa so that everyone can feel nurtured.

- For **fifth**-chakra thrills, join a theater group—but try out for a part this time; don't hide out backstage. Or join a chorus or singing group, but don't get involved with the support staff.

- To stroke your **sixth** chakra, take a class or finish that degree you've put off.

- And finally, to cultivate a little **seventh**-chakra bliss, go on a spiritual retreat that involves taking a sabbatical from responsibility (*not* the type where everyone has to pitch in to cook and do chores, which would probably be your first choice otherwise).

After you've increased your seven-chakra self-esteem-building activities and simultaneously given yourself firm guidelines for a food plan, you'll see your weight gradually start to melt off. If it doesn't, it's probably because part of you is still keyed in to, or meddling with, the affairs of people around you. You simply can't disengage your emotional intuition, your capacity to feel others' pain, and your subsequent sense of responsibility to fix their problems.

If this is the case, you're going to have to realize that even if you end up reducing your meal plan to braised celery and sautéed water, the stress of solving everyone else's problems and easing their pain and sorrow will make your body act like it's on steroids. Heavy steroids release insulin, and regardless of what you eat, they increase your weight. So put down the celery stick and call a 12-step-centered cognitive behavioral therapist who can help you break your compulsive codependence. You may just save your *own* life for a change.

What follows is my seven-step program for rehabilitating the terminal tendency of Rocks of Dependability to be devoted to everyone but themselves:

1. Identify that most of your self-esteem is based on being responsible, faithful, and dependable to others, but you're not conscientious about your own physical and emotional needs, especially when it comes to appearance, fashion, self-image, and general pride in yourself.

2. Recognize your belief that self-care, self-adornment, and working on your image and pride are self-absorbed, selfish, and narcissistic.

3. Discern the difference between healthy self-esteem (appropriately satisfying your need for a strong, beautiful, attractive, and competent self-image) and being selfish (developing the overblown, overindulged, self-centered persona that you fear). Further realize that by ignoring your need for self-worth in an attempt to avoid becoming narcissistic, you may actually end up attracting people who have narcissistic qualities.

4. Restrict the time that you're responsible and depended upon to work for others. Schedule an hour or two on a regular basis for a little indulgence that's not related to eating or drinking. Increase your daily quota of time spent on your personal appearance, including hair, nail, and skin care.

5. Know that you're lovable for who you are, not just how responsible, trustworthy, and faithful you can be.

6. Change the unhealthy thought pattern: *I am not lovable unless I am responsible, dependable, and working to take care of everyone's needs* . . . to the healthier affirmation: *I love with wisdom. I nurture and support others as much as I nurture and support myself.*

7. Follow the third rule for intuitive health—*You can't always get what you want, but if you try, you'll get what you need*—by feeling as good about yourself when you're fulfilling duties and responsibilities in your personal life as you do when you're helping others.

The Constantly Craving Type

The next of the third-chakra extremes are the Constantly Craving types, those who are more focused on indulging themselves with various feel-good activities and substances than they are on meeting their responsibilities in the world. Take Jackie, 37, who was always pursuing happiness and trying to find herself (as they used to say in the '60s). She spent the greater part of her 20s and 30s living in the Pacific Northwest in one alternative-living community after another. Jackie experienced a long list of occupations in the fine arts—not to mention illegal, mind-altering drugs—along the way.

First she lived in a spiritual community, following the teachings of a guru, while she learned how to make fine blown glassware. She also worked part-time canvassing the community for donations. After a while, though, the community environment got "a little too heavy" in asking for a greater job commitment from Jackie. She ended up leaving the confines of the ashram for a commune called Sunny Muffin Farm that was off the grid in the backwoods of Oregon.

During the next several years, Jackie worked on her physical, emotional, and spiritual health to purify herself, using a variety of exotic (and not-so-exotic) hallucinogenic drugs. While living in the commune and making pottery that was spiritually inspired, she had a series of arguments over chores around the farm. Jackie soon realized that her soul was telling her that she needed to move on. She craved another opportunity where she could further explore and cultivate her happiness and her art.

While celebrating with some old friends at a Rainbow Gathering during the summer, Jackie either smoked some bad weed or drank some bad water. She ended up at a nearby hospital's emergency room hallucinating and delusional, with profuse diarrhea. The doctor diagnosed her with amoebic dysentery and infectious diarrhea, a condition that caused her to have bowel problems lasting for more than a decade.

Jackie had a great capacity to work on herself and look for her self-worth. In fact, she'd been spending decades in an intense search to find herself, even using hallucinogens to make the exploration more successful. However, in the midst of her relentless pursuit of self, she wasn't very good at making herself available for any responsibilities or setting the discipline-grounded parameters that mature work requires.

Constantly Craving people like Jackie have a specific mind-body brain style that makes them so driven to fulfill personal and creative satisfaction, peace, and clarity that they don't find being answerable to others to be as rewarding or satisfying. Their brains and bodies are finely tuned to a constant drip of feel-good, opiate-boosting neurotransmitters released through satisfying their moment-by-moment desires. When they put off pursuing these activities and desires, however, they go into emotional and physical withdrawal.

If you, like Jackie, are a Constantly Craving type, you've spent a lifetime trying to find satisfaction and fulfillment in everything you do, minute to minute. You would find it very hard to delay momentary emotional and physical gratification for a long-term goal, such as developing a lucrative business or getting an education or undergoing training that takes years. Working in a quasi-mindless desk job would be almost impossible for you, especially if you had to do it to put a partner through medical school or otherwise help your significant other pursue his or her bliss. Consequently, you'd develop a series of digestive disorders (including constipation, diarrhea, or full-blown IBS) as your third-chakra intuitive advisor alerts you that you're having a hard time balancing personal satisfaction with interpersonal responsibilities.

What I've learned from people like Jackie is that when Constantly Craving types eventually run dry in their quest for self-discovery, they usually turn to a series of drugs such as marijuana, alcohol, LSD, or a host of others to give them a temporary sense that they've found themselves . . . not to mention that they absolutely love themselves! The delusionary quality of drugs fools them into thinking that they're better, tougher, more able-bodied, and more powerful than they really are. This is why, after all, these drugs are called *hallucinogens*.

However, when the substance wears off, Constantly Craving types have to face the fact that although they may feel high as a kite when they're on the drug, without it they don't like themselves very much at all. They don't feel dependable, reliable, strong, skilled, trustworthy, or even very useful to anyone. This is so traumatizing and leaves them feeling so empty that they're driven to take the drug again.

What they don't yet understand is that the only way to acquire the tough, able-bodied, powerful persona that they're seeking through a chemical compound is to stop hallucinating and escaping and instead to actually do work. They need to get busy by going to school; getting a job; or otherwise becoming responsible, reliable members of society. Although this responsibility truly does slowly drip opiates into their systems, it may not initially give them the intense high they've been craving all these years.

What clues signal that you may be the Constantly Craving type? You can sit for hours in a coffee shop in the middle of the week, reading or having a casual conversation with the person at the next table, without feeling guilty. Most of your friends know that you'll regularly be between 20 and 25 minutes late for whatever appointments you make . . . on those days when you don't miss the appointment completely. You've gotten in trouble with bosses for not being on time. It would be a very rare occasion for you to pick up a check for everyone at the table when you dine in a restaurant—you're more likely to ask for separate checks or to space out once the bill comes.

You can go to almost any city in the United States and be able to talk your way into a part-time job and a place to stay for free to tide you over until you decide if you want to live there or not. If you go to college, you're not likely to be pre-law, pre-med, pre-vet, or "pre" anything that involves years of unrewarding prerequisite classes before you get to work in the job of your dreams. Even if you buy your clothes at the thrift shop, your appearance is almost always dynamic, charming, intensely spiritual, sensitive, vulnerable, and draws people to take care of you. You tend to wear berets. You've had a Volkswagen at least once or twice in your life, and whatever you drive generally has a lot of bumper stickers on it. You've smoked marijuana before work twice, at minimum, and you know from memory the lines to at least two Grateful Dead songs.

If this sounds like you, then you may be the Constantly Craving type. If you don't come down from your perpetual high of self-stimulation and learn to take care of the daily business of life, you're likely to get a third-chakra wake-up call. The first alarm that the feeding of your self-esteem is outweighing your capacity to attend to your responsibilities is that your hankering for substances will get out of control—although you probably won't see it that way at first.

Let me give you some examples to help you recognize this: A mate (or two or three) may leave because he or she couldn't handle your drug or alcohol use. You start to avoid more and more people in your life because they're "judgmental" about your habits. You could even lose a job because you're repeatedly late or absent. And finally, your doctor might tell you to stop drinking, smoking, or snorting drugs because it's aggravating a health problem.

It's possible—no, *probable*—that the only time you'll recognize that your constant craving has gotten out of control is when that control is taken away from you because you've been arrested or hospitalized. Although these "hit bottom" events (to use 12-step parlance) are humiliating, they're actually opportunities to get the help you need in order to learn how to be more responsible about your life.

If we look closely at Jackie's story, we'll realize that all of us have a part of ourselves that has elements of the Constantly Craving type. We all have had our moments when we couldn't help but over-indulge. But when constantly giving in to temptation interferes with our job, costs us a relationship, drains our bank account, or affects our health, then we have to reevaluate our escalating consumption—be it of handbags, Beanie Babies, ice cream, chocolate, soap operas, or whatever we're addicted to—or our compulsive urge for a "fix" of eBay, QVC, **Zappos.com**, or **Amazon.com**.

Our pursuit of happiness and serenity via a therapeutic level of Jimmy Choo shoes or Häagen-Dazs ice cream is nothing more than an attempt to medicate a hankering inside ourselves. If we plan our day around getting our daily dose, we must look at the feeling our addiction helps us achieve—whether it be happiness, reduced anxiety, escape from anger, or an infusion of love and joy—and consult a life coach or other professional, depending upon the severity of the problem, to help us get that feeling without the use of our beloved fix.

Intuitive Advice for the Constantly Craving Type

Do you suffer from chronic health problems in your digestive tract, liver, gallbladder, and kidneys; and do you tend to have some aspects of the Constantly Craving pattern? If so, you can indeed use medical intuition and mind-body medicine to develop a more balanced approach to self-esteem and responsibility and get yourself out of your binges and sprees, and your mind-body makeover must first address the physical. You could have any third-chakra health concern with Constantly Craving tendencies, but if, like Jackie, your third-chakra issue happens to be bowel problems, look at your use of antibiotics. Taking frequent courses of antibiotics can kill off the normal bacterial flora of your bowel, so try repopulating it with healthy bacteria by eating yogurt with acidophilus. If your digestive distress has progressed to the abdominal bloating, distension, and severe pain of IBS, however, your physician may need to prescribe Bentyl, Levsin, Librax, or NuLev. If you have severe constipation, your doctor might prescribe Amitiza.

If, like Jackie, you also have addiction problems on top of bowel issues, you'll need to address both together because chronic, crampy pain and digestive stress can be aggravated biochemically by certain addictive substances. If you're still using and abusing marijuana, alcohol, or even pain meds, no treatment is likely to work on your health problem because these addictive drugs disrupt the various neurotransmitters (including serotonin, dopamine, norepinephrine, and acetylcholine) that line the bowel wall.

All these neurotransmitters that are related to addiction and emotions such as fear, anger, sadness, love, and joy are the building blocks of normal bowel function and, interestingly, of normal self-esteem. If chronic depression, rage, anxiety, and pain are underlying your self-esteem and responsibility problems, it's likely to disrupt the neurotransmitter soup that helps bowel motility and may in fact be the reason behind why you crave these substances in the first place.

An acupuncturist and Chinese herbalist can help remedy the complex biochemical interplay between IBS, depression, anxiety, and addiction. Also, try walking for half an hour a day to jiggle your colon and get the motility started. In addition, experiment with what I call the soccer-ball bowel technique (after checking with your doctor first): Buy a children's size-three soccer ball and inflate it until it's reasonably firm. Every morning, put the ball under your stomach and roll it from side to side and up and down, feeling the loops of your bowel and stomach rolling slowly under it. The direct massage of the ball against your bowel wall can be enough to get things moving again.

All this will be a cakewalk compared to reworking the chemical craving behind your addiction. This is not a time to go it alone, nor is it a time to go cold turkey. Attend the nearest Alcoholics Anonymous (AA) meeting, or call your local crisis line to ask how you might get more supportive help in a protective setting.

Next, the mind-body makeover deals with the Constantly Craving types' emotions, including any underlying chronic depression, anger, anxiety, or pain. Although a knee-jerk use of standard antidepressants, antianxiety medicines, or other herbal and alternative remedies may seem to be appropriate here, think twice. These aids are only useful to support mood and pain relief if you aggressively address your addiction at the same time. In some cases, your doctor will suggest that you be hospitalized. In any event, you'll need to be completely detoxed of all mood-altering substances for about a month before your physician will know how to properly address your depression and anxiety with nonaddictive medicines.

But beware! If you think that after the detox your doctor will hand you a prescription for a bottle of pills and send you on your merry way, you're in for a rude awakening. The process of recovery from your third-chakra self-worth and responsibility imbalance will take years of work in a variety of Cognitive Behavioral Therapy (CBT) groups that probably have a 12-step framework. These groups—such as AA and Narcotics Anonymous (NA)—help individuals reorient their mind-sets so they not only are able to rebuild an authentic chemical-free self-image but also find that doing responsible, trustworthy work for others can be a healthy source of self-esteem. You'll also soon learn that whenever you get a craving for something that you've previously been addicted to, it's your third-chakra intuitive advisor at work, letting you know that your desire to pump up your self-esteem is once more out of balance with your work and responsibilities.

Here is my seven-part program to rehabilitate the Constantly Craving types' need for perpetual self-stimulation to the detriment of meeting their obligations to their families and society:

1. Identify the feeling of emotional emptiness and the plummeting of your mood that occurs while you crave something. Notice those moments when you choose to pursue some activities that pump up your self-image rather than attending to your regular work or responsibilities.

2. Recognize how the cravings that you've satisfied over the years only temporarily elevated your self-respect and self-confidence. The alcohol and the drugs (or your shopping, eating, drinking, smoking, or whatever else you do to get a "high") do wear off eventually, and the energy required to obtain them in order to maintain a constant flow of self-satisfaction is emotionally and financially exhausting.

3. Discern that you may be able to feel good about yourself in a more permanent, enduring fashion by developing the capacity to be reliable and dependable at work. This more disciplined, tried-and-true conscientiousness that is required for attending to regular responsibility gives you a similar neurochemical opiate boost to the one you get from drugs. This boost may not be as potent or intense, but it ultimately lasts longer, and unlike the others, it has no negative side effects.

4. Restrict the number of activities you engage in that contain the words *self, creative,* or *artistic* to only one or two a day, unless these pursuits involve gainful, taxable employment. Volunteer at least once a week at a homeless shelter or other nonprofit organization. Befriend some of the other volunteers who are characteristically reliable, faithful, or selfless and find out what makes them happy and pumps up their feelings of worth.

5. Know that with practice and support from others (including 12-step groups), you can increase your capacity to satisfy your cravings for self-esteem and reward by being a responsible, trusty, and dependable worker. Experience how this ultimately feels better than abusing drugs or other substances.

6. Change the unhealthy thought pattern: *I need other people to take care of my responsibilities and practical details because I am more of a free-spirited and creative soul* . . . to the healthier affirmation: *I am strong enough to build my self-esteem and work to take care of my responsibilities every day.*

7. Follow the third rule for intuitive health—*You can't always get what you want, but if you try, you'll get what you need*—by balancing your responsibilities at work and in the world with your own personal desires and cravings.

The Pumped Up and Rocking Hard Type

Now we move to the next kind of third-chakra extreme—the Pumped Up and Rocking Hard types, those whose confidence and dynamism requires never-ending fulfillment. Ken, 27, was one of those people in the gym whom you don't want to exercise next to. As if powered by NASA, these people pound away so hard on the workout equipment that you just know you're going to look ridiculously anemic in comparison. Not surprisingly, Ken's motto was "Nothing succeeds like excess."

In high school, Ken was the captain of the tennis and track teams and president of the debating team. He could out-serve, outrun, or out-argue anyone in the state of New Jersey. Ken left college after two years because he realized that school was too confining for his business plans to be a clothing designer and fashion magnate. By the time his contemporaries were graduating, Ken was going national with his fashion line in major department stores.

With his house in the Hamptons, penthouse apartment in New York City, four sports cars, and too many lovers to count, Ken craved being pumped up by constant adoration from the public and by working full throttle to meet the demands for more and more of his brilliant fashions. In fact, he needed both the satisfaction his work and lifestyle brought him as well the hard-driving pace that made him so successful.

The Pumped Up and Rocking Hard type isn't uncommon in our culture because not only is this personality style very lucrative, but it also feels wonderful . . . at least for a while. However, if the ever-expanding bubble of success eventually *stops* expanding for these folks—or if they stop getting gold records, promotions, awards, raises, or other measures of success—their self-esteem bubbles pop. When their admiring publics desert them for the next phenomenon and their moments in the sun are over, they hit bottom.

In Ken's case, he wasn't getting any younger, so to rev up his metabolism and maintain his trim physique, he had to use a very expensive combination of steroid shots and cocaine. In addition, his Pumped Up and Rocking Hard persona was very expensive to support. The cost of keeping up his huge inventory of real estate and automobiles, not to mention his excessive spending on day-to-day luxuries, was now far exceeding what Ken was able to earn from his clothing line. Eventually, he developed a duodenal ulcer, and the emergency-room physician at the hospital gave him an additional diagnosis of anorexia nervosa.

If you, like Ken, are the Pumped Up and Rocking Hard type, you've been driven by a lifelong tendency toward excess. To quote Kimora Lee Simmons, the famous model, fashion designer, business mogul, and star of the Style Network's television show *Kimora: Life in the Fab Lane*, "More is more." (She once added to an employee, "If you think less is more, I'll remind you of that the next time I hand you your paycheck." Very funny.)

For Pumped Up and Rocking Hard types, more is always more because these people have a huge appetite for constantly escalating amounts of success and personal achievement, as well as a steady desire to pad their self-confidence, value . . . and yes, their *vanity*—let's put the word out on the table. Unlike Isadora and her fellow Rock of Dependability people, who tend to shun anything self-focused, the

Pumped Up types welcome pampering and adore activities that are focused on "me, me, me!"

But as much as they'd like to be the flavor of the month all the time, it's the nature of life that after a while they'll go through a series of downturns. Nobody is number one forever. Sooner or later, someone is going to come along and knock the Pumped Up people off their pedestals, and when that happens, watch out. These folks may be fun to be with when they're on the way *up* the ladder of success, and even when they're on the top. But when their stars start to burn out, their moods turn dark and they aren't so fun to be around anymore.

For one, Pumped Up people don't age well. The mottos "More is more" and "Nothing succeeds like excess" do not help the body and mind age gracefully. Nor do Pumped Up people really accept the process of growing older to begin with. They hate the sands of time as they flow through their mortality hourglass. They believe that aging is evil and should be destroyed by all methods possible—plastic surgery, Botox, Restylane . . . whatever it takes to turn back time and look, well, pumped up and rocking hard. Their overemphasis on perfect physical appearance instead of on true, long-lasting intimacy leads to either midlife adultery or divorce. After all, there's nothing like an affair (or even an anonymous one-night stand) to make you feel desirable and youthful again, especially if the person you're involved with is at least 20 to 30 years younger than you are.

What I've learned from people like Ken is that even though seriously competent and intense Pumped Up and Rocking Hard types appear capable of attaining anything and everything, they're driven by an emptiness inside. This void can never be filled, no matter how much success they achieve. I've heard stories of such individuals owning 17 Rolls-Royces and 75 Mercedes-Benzes. I ask you, will getting the 18th Rolls bump these folks over the edge into happiness? Can any of us really be satisfied deep down by acquiring more and more? The superficiality of the disco era and its hit song "More, More, More" by the Andrea True Connection can be pretty exciting on the dance floor, but when Pumped Up and Rocking Hard types go home alone (and everyone, no matter who they are, *always* has to eventually be alone), they feel the emptiness and do whatever they can to push it away.

What clues indicate that you might be a Pumped Up and Rocking Hard type? You have more than 12 mirrors in your house, and you check your appearance in them four to five times a day. You know exactly how much fat you have in your "love handle" or "muffin top" area (which is hardly anything because you would never let yourself go like that). If you went to your first plastic surgeon before the age of 30, you intend to get some "freshening-up work" in his office before you reach 40. By 50, you believe that people who care about themselves should fix their appearance before they go downhill.

You don't like others to know your age. You follow the careers of all those in your field and frequently lunch with them in the very best restaurants. You go to fund-raising events to schmooze, network, and be seen. When something good happens in your life, you immediately call your publicity people, tell all your friends, and update your Website and Facebook page. Whenever you get to a restaurant, you expect to be given the best table and to be served first. At the last several concerts you've attended, you've sat in the VIP section or expected star treatment. You don't think it's a big deal to get a laminated all-access backstage pass. (When you get home, you throw it away rather than enshrining it for all perpetuity.)

You expect people to give you their goods wholesale because it's great publicity for them if you use their products or services. You'll think nothing of having an extended conversation during dinner on a cell phone—even when you're not dining alone. You can't imagine being under a manager or having to ask for vacation or time off. You bring work home all the time. In fact, it doesn't matter *when* you work—if you're on a roll and the spirit moves you, you'll labor all day and all night. You've been motivated to work since you were in diapers.

If this describes you, then call your publicist and put out a press release, because you're the Pumped Up and Rocking Hard type. If you continue to feed your ego by expecting to be worshipped and admired by the mere mortals beneath you, then your third-chakra intuitive advisor will eventually sound the first alarm: the shock and just-slapped-in-the-face feeling of being yesterday's news. I doubt you've studied physics, but if you *had*, you'd know that on planet Earth, what goes up always comes down. People *love* to knock anyone off of a pedestal and bring the person down to their own level because, frankly, it makes them feel better and improves their mood. Suffice it to say that if your self-esteem is dependent on constantly flying at a higher altitude than others, your body will eventually bring you down from the clouds.

If we look deep enough, we can all find a little of the Pumped Up and Rocking Hard type in ourselves. Like Ken, no matter to what extent we work on ourselves, no matter how much we exercise or how successful our career becomes, sometimes it never seems to be enough. We always need more and more to feel satisfied. In the musical *A Chorus Line,* one of the characters asks himself who he is, wondering if *he* is his "résumé."

That pretty much sums up the issue of being defined by who we are and what we do. If we're basing too much of our self-worth and identity on our work and not enough on other parts of our lives, it's like trying to get a balanced diet by eating only eggs. We need to round out our self-esteem quotient and build a diversified portfolio with a whole list of satisfying non-work-related activities so that we'll have more than just our career to give us a sense of true fulfillment.

Intuitive Advice for the Pumped Up and Rocking Hard Type

Do you suffer from chronic health problems in your digestive tract, liver, gallbladder, and kidneys; and do you tend to have Pumped Up and Rocking Hard–type issues? If so, medical intuition and mind-body medicine can help you stabilize your descent to planet Earth and the level of the rest of us mere mortals, and your mind-body makeover will first attend to your physical self. You could have any third-chakra health concern with Pumped Up tendencies. But if, like Ken, you happen to have a little substance-abuse problem going on, even if you think you're using just to keep your weight down, you're probably going to need intensive treatment from a physician, possibly in a hospital.

Many people (it's not just women) are actually addicted to stimulants such as the drink Red Bull, diet pills, Ritalin, and amphetamines like Adderall that they take to decrease their weight. Addiction and eating-disorder problems work very closely together, and to maximize your success in fixing both, you'll need to treat them extensively and simultaneously. If you go into recovery just for addiction, you're going to miss the coinciding issue of body image and weight, and your third-chakra wake-up call will just go into snooze-alarm mode—it won't *really* turn off. You'll just find another stimulant to curb your appetite and keep your physique trim or to fuel your engine so that you can work, work, work at levels of superhuman capacity. (Triple-shot mochaccinos, anyone?)

You're going to have to get help bringing your body down slowly from the constant influx of stimulants that you depend on to give your self-esteem a boost and to fuel your illusion that you're all-powerful, tough as nails, and überstrong. Getting off caffeine, uppers, or cocaine will feel like the equivalent of taking away your car keys, but you'll eventually realize that your level of drive *without* chemical stimulants will still outpace that of most of us.

If you have a tendency to get high-powered gastroesophageal reflux disease (GERD) or duodenal or peptic ulcers, your doctor is probably going to prescribe such medicines as Prilosec, Nexium, Prevacid, Reglan, Zantac, Carafate, Pepcid, or Tagamet. Whether you use these or other antacids, you'll still have to reduce your consumption of alcohol, cigarettes, and caffeine because all of these vices tend to corrode the pipes of your digestive tract.

The mind-body makeover next moves on to address the Pumped Up and Rocking Hard types' emotional starvation. After failing to fill up a nameless inner hankering through achievement and goods, many Pumped Up types finally stumble upon spirituality. They find that communion with a higher power (the only thing they can find that indisputably ranks above themselves) fills them up and brings them higher than any Rolls-Royce or seven-figure contract ever could. It is no coincidence that most, if not all, of the many addiction programs (AA; NA; Cocaine Anonymous, CA; Co-Dependents Anonymous, CoDA; or Overeaters Anonymous, OA) have 12-step formats that recognize that a higher power exists that can help. Many people who get stuck at this higher-power step don't do well handling their addiction problems long-term.

A famous story goes around AA circles: One participant was having a problem accepting the fact that there might be a God or something greater than himself. As an agnostic, this individual had trouble with the notion that to do 12-step recovery work, he'd have to place his health and sobriety in the hands of a higher power and not rely solely on his own all-powerful self. When he admitted this, someone in the back of the room stood up and asked, "Well, if you don't know whether there is a higher power or not, can you at least admit that you ain't him?"

The part of all of us that gets trapped in the Pumped Up and Rocking Hard persona will eventually have to come to terms with the fact that we *don't* have all the power. We can't be omnipotent. There's always going to be another, mightier force outside of us, a *higher power*. The greatness we can achieve through our own efforts can only exist in concert with that higher power. And when we have the impulse to start pumping up and rocking hard, to go higher and higher and make ourselves look stronger and richer and all-powerful, then our third-chakra intuitive advisor will signal that we're experiencing an inner emptiness again. The message our advisor is sending through symptoms of illness is that we need to stop, take a step back, and come into communion with that higher power that is far greater than ourselves so that we can finally feel fully whole and complete.

What follows is my seven-part program to rehabilitate the Pumped Up and Rocking Hard types' constant hunger for more power and success:

1. Identify the constant high you need in order to acquire things that make you feel good, look good, and perform at your peak. Also identify the intense power you feel when you have to work at full throttle nearly 24 hours a day, seven days a week.

2. Recognize the immense boredom and emptiness you experience if you can't keep buying things, acquiring possessions, or building your self-image or career.

3. Discern the difference between continually aspiring to be more self-confident, powerful, and successful and actually fulfilling what you need to be truly satisfied. Do the things that you want really fulfill your inner needs? If not, reevaluate the difference between your addictive cravings and desires and what you actually *need* to achieve self-esteem and a successful career.

4. Restrict your rampant overconsumption of things in the outer world. For at least one day a week, don't buy anything, use credit cards, handle currency, or work with earnings. Your life will feel simple for that day. You'll be able to reset your experience of what can truly satisfy you—but be warned, you might go into withdrawal from constant achievement and the ring of the cash register. If this is the case, get help from a specialist who works with addiction and recovery.

5. Know that there are multiple forms of self-worth *and* net worth . . . and most of them have nothing to do with your material success. They can include spending time with family members, mates, and friends; building your intellect, artistic talent, or creativity; and increasing your capacity to communicate and connect with a spiritual power. All of these types of self-esteem can make you feel fulfilled and satisfied.

6. Change the unhealthy thought: *I feel happy only if I am busy, productive, and the best at everything* . . . to the healthier affirmation: *I can be happy whether I am busy with my own work and personal satisfaction or am focusing on and admiring others' gifts and talents. I can still feel fulfilled when I am in awe of other people's power.*

7. Follow the third rule for intuitive health—*You can't always get what you want, but if you try, you'll get what you need*—by balancing the power you feel within yourself with one far greater than you.

The Broken-down, Burned-out Type

The final kind of third-chakra extreme—the Broken-down, Burned-out type—refers to people who shy away from all things having to do with vanity and pride so that they can focus on creative, spiritual, and nonmaterial endeavors. Lorinda, 58, was one of them. She had a library filled with every kind of book on philosophy and spiritual traditions that you could think of. Ever since she was little, she'd shied away from the activities that other young girls were obsessed with. While they focused on how to apply the new shades of makeup, what clothes to buy at the upcoming back-to-school sale, whether the hemlines were going to be long or short this year, or which boys liked them, Lorinda couldn't have cared less.

As if she were off in her own world, Lorinda started reading about the various Eastern religions—such as Buddhism, Zen, and Taoism—as well as exploring the Christian mystics. While all the kids in high school were busy competing to get the highest SAT scores, the best grades, and the most acceptance letters from prestigious colleges, my client once again couldn't have cared less. Deciding to get out of the rat race entirely, she stayed closer to home and took courses at a local community college, thinking that all the big schools were only about drugs, sex, and drunken escapades anyway.

Decades passed. Lorinda married, had children, and lived a very simple life in the backcountry in a ramshackle house with a bunch of broken-down farm equipment in the backyard. When her husband was killed in an automobile accident, this woman was forced to raise four teenage children alone, relying on food stamps and what wages she could earn from several waitressing jobs. But she could never get back on her feet.

You couldn't really say that Lorinda let her appearance go because she'd never truly worked on it to begin with. All her life she'd shunned anything having to do with self-adornment or vanity—including hairstyles, makeup, or fashion—because she thought all of these were banal, trivial, weak, and self-indulgent. As far as a career went, Lorinda had no extensive experience, training, or expertise that could make her powerful or competitive in the job market. Her attitude that such worldly pursuits were materialistic and spiritually corrupt wasn't helping her turn her third-chakra deficit of self-esteem and responsibility around.

This was evident in Lorinda's health. After decades of denying her personal needs and avoiding the chance to develop basic job skills that could have made her life physically and emotionally less stressful, she found that her choices had taken their toll on the organs in her third chakra. The chronic anxiety of not knowing when the next economic shoe would drop put constant pressure on her pancreas to churn out insulin and on her adrenal glands to pump out cortisol, both of which led to obesity and diabetes.

If you, like Lorinda, are the Broken-down, Burned-out type, you tend to find your fulfillment and satisfaction through spirituality and philosophy. You avoid the sort of personally gratifying, self-focused activities that fuel vanity, such as being concerned with hairstyles, nails, weight training, clothing, and makeup. You're probably very good at learning advanced spiritual practices, but when it comes to advancing your career aspirations, you simply aren't motivated. Self-admiration, work, and real-world status are all akin to spiritual anthrax for you. You're more likely to achieve your neurotransmitter opiate high from working on your relationship with God than from trying to achieve status on this earthly plane.

Broken-down, Burned-out types like Lorinda work hard on Earth for a place in heaven, but unfortunately, their lives aren't grounded. By having a healthy self-esteem and a stronger capacity for work, they'd be in a better place to perform their spiritual responsibilities.

What I've learned from people like Lorinda is that the reason why Broken-down, Burned-out types tend to avoid any form of personal adornment and vanity is often because they believe that their bodies are flawed on some fundamental level. Assigning a level of self-worth to the size of a nose, the circumference of a breast, or the length of a penis sounds funny on paper, but it's all too common in our culture. In addition, people who have invested little in developing a career are often embarrassed about their lack of skill in living up to everyone's expectations in the real-world workplace. In addition to withdrawing due to not wanting to be seen, Broken-down, Burned-out types also tend to apologize a lot—almost to the point of apologizing for the space that they take up on the earth. They feel utterly unlovable.

What clues indicate that you might be the Broken-down, Burned-out type? You are in your 40s and haven't updated your résumé or CV (curriculum vitae) within the last two to three years. Actually, you don't even know what a CV is. You're familiar with the latest books about Kabbalah, astrology, archetypal psychology, and spirituality.

But when it comes to knowing which nail-polish colors are hot this year, whether hemlines are above or below the knee, or whether liquid eyeliner is in or out, you have no idea. When everyone else is watching the newest reality TV show emceed by a man with a British accent or is flocking to the latest blockbuster about Batman, Spider-Man, or Iron Man, you'd rather go to the nearest avant-garde movie theater and watch an art, cult, or foreign film. When someone gives you a gift certificate for a day at the spa, you're more likely to give it to a friend or to one of your children than use it for yourself. You don't know if an American size-8½ shoe is equivalent to a European size 19 or 39. You have no idea how many kids Angelina Jolie and Brad Pitt currently have, nor do you care.

If the preceding description rings true, then you may be the Broken-down, Burned-out type—and you have the health problems to prove it. With all the weight you've piled on over the years, you either already have diabetes or you'll soon be diagnosed with it. Your near-compulsive capacity to shun all things that feed self-image and power your career have almost reached martyrdom levels of self-sacrifice. That sounds good to you, though, because many of those Christian mystics you read about and admire were also martyrs who shunned real-world status, career fulfillment, and vanity. On the other hand, such Christian mystics never lived very long, because they had horrendous health problems (see the chapter on the sixth chakra). So at least you're in good company.

The first alarm that your third-chakra intuitive guidance system will sound is weight gain that begins to spiral out of control. After this goes on for a while, the metabolic cow will be let out of the barn and proceed to wreak havoc in the form of a seemingly unending list of serious health problems: elevated cholesterol, high blood pressure, and increased levels of blood sugar, which then progress to coronary artery disease, heart disease, and stroke. You might as well add renal failure, sleep apnea, peripheral neuropathy, chronic pain, and loss of limbs due to amputation to the list, too.

It's like a snowball rolling downhill. Ironically, while your sights are always set on heaven, it's usually the case that all hell is breaking loose in your body on Earth. If you don't learn to regain your third-chakra balance, your health won't allow you to concentrate on any real spiritual work.

If we look closely at Lorinda's story, we'll see that at one time or another, all of us have become the Broken-down, Burned-out type. We've all felt so bad about ourselves and our career at some point that the only thing that gave us any satisfaction was turning away from the material world and immersing ourselves in spirituality and philosophy. While taking such a sabbatical for self-improvement may inititally be critical to our healing, if our break becomes *too* extended, it's actually not very good for us (unless we're yogis, monks, or nuns).

Getting most of our self-worth and fulfillment from spirituality and philosophy isn't a balanced way to live. If we neglect the basic, fundamental aspects of caring for ourselves—such as our appearance, our physical strength, and our capacity to advance in our career—any spiritual endeavor we enjoy will have an unreal, ungrounded, impractical quality. Taking care of our business on Earth *is* caring for the heavens.

Intuitive Advice for the Broken-down, Burned-out Type

Do you suffer from chronic health problems in your digestive tract, liver, gallbladder, and kidneys; and do you tend to have some aspects of the Broken-down, Burned-out–type pattern? If so, mind-body medicine and medical intuition can help you put yourself back together—even if you don't think you're worthy of being helped—and your mind-body makeover starts with your physical body. You could have any third-chakra health problem with Broken-down, Burned-out tendencies. But if, like Lorinda, your third-chakra challenge happens to be weight and blood-sugar issues, you must first follow the meal plan outlined in the intuitive advice for the Rock of Dependability earlier in this chapter. In addition to balancing the carbohydrate and protein ratio of every meal you eat, doing 30 minutes of aerobic exercise in the morning and taking a walk after dinner are critical to returning your blood sugar and insulin to healthy levels. Don't take this advice lightly. I hate to say it, but there are deadly consequences to being overweight.

A board-certified acupuncturist and Chinese herbalist could readily help you drop the extra pounds and avoid many of the secondary issues that your weight causes (including the second-chakra lower-back problems and the first-chakra fatigue and immune-system dysfunction that seem to coexist in the Broken-down, Burned-out type). The Chinese herb ren shen feng wang jiang (ginseng with queen-bee royal jelly) is a good general nutritional supplement for the chronic exhaustion that you may experience from the many aftereffects of diabetes. Another herb, *Acanthopanax senticosus* (also called eleuthero, previously known as Siberian ginseng), also helps the inflammation underlying the multi-organ illnesses that result from being overweight and diabetic.

Next, the mind-body makeover moves to the Broken-down, Burned-out types' emotional intuitive mind, which is often filled with shame. You'll need a lot of support to rebuild your self-esteem and light a flame under your career. Setting up grounded first-chakra mentorship training programs, like the old-fashioned apprenticeship, will help build your job skills, pump up your self-confidence, and ignite passion in a real-world position that gives you recognition in your community. (Remind yourself that even Jesus was an apprentice carpenter.)

Similarly, you need to join a club that will enhance your appearance. If you're female, the women-only gym Curves or some other group where everyone is overhauling her appearance inside and out is great because it will prevent you from avoiding what you hate focusing on: yourself. If you're a man, you could get a bunch of other guys together to work toward achieving some group fitness goals in a supportive, team approach.

Either way, by being in a group of shame-based, Broken-down, Burned-out types who are all trying to rehabilitate their self-esteem, *you* won't feel so bad. Everyone will be embarrassed and mortified together. And when you start to climb the scale of self-respect again, you'll notice that the pounds will begin slowly falling off and your blood sugar will decrease. If the weight ever starts to creep back, don't panic—just recognize that it's your medical-intuitive advisor signaling that a little third-chakra self-esteem-building is once more in order.

And now, here is my seven-part program to rehabilitate the Broken-down, Burned-out types' perpetual-wallflower approach to life:

1. Identify how you never felt an emotional thrill from focusing on yourself, whether it's your appearance or working on developing your career. Also admit that you dread such pastimes as styling your hair, giving yourself a manicure or pedicure, and paying attention to clothing and fashion, categorizing them as trivial and spiritually bereft activities.

2. Recognize that you also have some insecurity and shame underlying the tendency to avoid physical adornment. Whether you believe that some part of you is too small, too big, too long, too short, or not the shape that's currently in vogue, you shy away from anything that highlights your insecurity. In your career, you feel strongly that you'll never be able to measure up to anybody else's expectations.

3. Discern that it is possible to attend to your physical appearance in a balanced way—and still have an active spiritual life. Similarly, realize that you can build a powerful career and create a level of skillful dependability without giving up the emotional depth necessary for a relationship with the divine.

4. Restrict your urge to avoid those elements that have anything to do with the self—including self-esteem, self-confidence, and self-image—because you think they are *self*-ish. Understand that the process of "de-selfing" yourself, although it may feel as if it makes you more spiritually tuned in, really makes you biochemically out of touch with your body to a degree that has become life threatening.

5. Know that you can be yourself and truly believe in spiritual teachings that say you're lovable and valuable. You *are* worthwhile; and therefore so is investing some of your time and energy in your appearance, physical fitness, and career development.

6. Change the unhealthy thought pattern: *If people really knew me, they wouldn't respect or love me . . .* to the more healthy affirmation: *My emotional fulfillment and satisfaction radiates to everyone around me.*

7. Follow the third rule for intuitive health—*You can't always get what you want, but if you try, you'll get what you need*—by emphasizing that you really deserve more than you think you do.

• • •

To create health in your third chakra, you have to make yourself strong enough—strong enough to pump up your self-worth, fulfill your responsibilities, and have the self-restraint when necessary to walk away from excessive self-indulgence. The key to successfully accomplishing that is following the third rule for intuitive health: *You can't always get what you want, but if you try, you'll get what you need.*

Balancing self-esteem with responsibility isn't easy, but when you're successful, it will be reflected in the health of your digestive system as well as your ability to maintain a healthy weight and freedom from addiction of all kinds. Rest assured that anytime you're being either consistently overly indulgent or overly responsible, your third-chakra intuitive advisor will have the guts (pardon the pun) to alert you to the imbalance, giving you the opportunity to do some much-needed "beefing up."

• • • • •

Chapter Six

Fourth Chakra: "A Different Kind of Love Song"

(The Health of Your Heart, Breasts, and Lungs)

The fourth-chakra area—your heart, breasts, and lungs—is the part of your body that intuitively advises you when you're having difficulty balancing partnerships and your emotional health. Whether the partnership is with a mate, a business colleague, or even a child or parent, you need to be able to attend to it while simultaneously maintaining an even keel in order for the relationship to be long lasting. Not easy! This requires that you not only be aware of your own feelings and reactions, but that you also be conscious of those of the other person at the same time.

If you don't have your emotional wits about you, which call for balancing the five basic emotions (fear, anger, sadness, love, and joy), you're likely to lose your emotional footing, and—*poof!*—the relationship unravels. On the other hand, if you've completely ignored your feelings and attended to the partnership instead, you're apt to suffer physical and emotional consequences as well.

My first experience in understanding the idiosyncrasies of balancing fourth-chakra emotional partnership came when I was a kid, watching soap operas with my aunt Edie. On most days, whenever the opening credits would roll and I'd hear the familiar "Like sands through the hourglass, so are the days of our lives," Aunt Edie would shoo all the kids out of her house, locking the door behind us. It was time for her to watch *her* story, her daytime soap opera. If I was lucky enough to have a cold, she let me stay inside and watch with her. Picture it: my aunt Edie, all 4'11" of her—a woman with a sixth-grade education who emigrated from Portugal via Ellis Island—and me. We'd sit together (she'd be wearing one of those housedresses with a blue flowered apron, a black hairnet, and stockings rolled down to her ankles) glued to *Days of our Lives,* essentially a fourth-chakra documentary on how well or poorly people balance their emotional health with their partnerships.

As I watched, I'd see how at one moment the lead character, scorned by her lover, would be consumed by a fit of rage and throw a vase across the room at him. Despite this woman's anger-management problem, it was obvious that the man she was in love with was also madly in love with *her,* because five seconds later their bodies would be lustfully intertwined in some sexually charged love scene. I might have assumed that this was normal behavior after seeing it played out again and again on the TV. But my aunt Edie would reorient my mind-set every time. She'd get up from her chair, shake her fist at the screen, and yell: "No! No! Don't fall for him! He's a no-good-dirty-dog!" (The way she spoke, that phrase was always hyphenated.) She'd end her tirade with: "All he will ever bring you is heartache and misery!"

Thus went my early training in how to recognize the nuances of balancing emotional health and partnership, courtesy of Aunt Edie, that quasi-psychologist from the old country. Notice the words she used: *all he will ever bring you is heartache and misery.* This was her way of warning the poor soap-opera leading lady that if she didn't make better partnership choices that truly honored her emotional health, not only would she suffer depression (also known as "misery"), but her poor decisions would end up hitting her in an organ in her fourth-chakra territory: the heart.

●–●–●

The domain of the fourth chakra registers the heartache, pain, and misery that we experience in partnerships all through our lives. Health problems associated with this region of the body include shortness of breath, a persistent cough, asthma, emphysema or chronic obstructive pulmonary disease (COPD), lung cancer, panic disorder, heart palpitations, elevated cholesterol, high blood pressure, heart attack, breast lumpiness, and breast cancer.

However, you can learn to use the intuition inherent in your fourth-chakra physical problems to determine if your mental health is shaky or if your partnerships are unstable. To maintain wellness in this region of your body, you need to follow the fourth rule for intuitive health: *Got to love her madly* (balancing partnership and emotional health). This involves the ability to be in mutually beneficial relationships while simultaneously maintaining your emotional sanity—in other words, being able to balance your emotional needs with those of the partnership.

Most people who have fourth-chakra problems tend to fall somewhere in between four extreme categories: the *Puddle Tsunami*—those who are extremely passionate and have trouble containing emotions enough to maintain stable relationships; the *Perpetual Partner*—those who conceal their emotions behind forever-happy façades in order to preserve their long list of stable partnerships; the *Helluva Bonder*—those who maintain firm emotional footing even amid tragedy, with a near-savant capacity to bond with even the most difficult people; and finally, the *Emotionally Alone Again (Naturally)* type—those who have trouble experiencing and expressing emotions directly and engaging in partnerships beyond a superficial level.

The Puddle Tsunami

The first category of fourth-chakra extreme is the ever-passionate yet emotionally incontinent Puddle Tsunami, who has difficulty containing feelings and sustaining partnerships. A 60-year-old client by the name of Mary was a good example of this. She was the most emotional and animated person you could ever meet.

Mary's voice always reverberated with the ups and downs of the latest dramatic episode of her life. She could be talking with deep joy and sentimentality about her high-school reunion, and then with great melancholy launch into how *miserable* it was meeting all those ex-boyfriends who'd broken her heart. On other occasions, her voice would shake and quiver as she spoke of her fears about some ailing family members . . . and then a minute later, she'd use an angry, terse tone to complain about yet another drama brewing at her workplace. Mary's emotions cycled so frequently from one intense state to another that she could have easily starred in her own soap opera.

For years this woman had been in therapy to explore why she was so emotionally intense. One therapist told her that she had a narcissistic mother. Another informed her that her rocky, unstable moods were due to Bipolar II or post-traumatic stress disorder. A boyfriend even accused her of having Borderline Personality Disorder when they were about to break up. (See the chapter on the first chakra for a further discussion of these diagnostic terms.) Nonetheless, my client was frustrated because she wanted nothing more than to get married and have a stable partnership. But every time she neared that goal, something went wrong.

Just when Mary would get close to the threshold of a more serious commitment—anywhere from a year and a half to three years into the relationship—the guy would always break up with her. She'd inevitably find out that these boyfriends had other girlfriends waiting in the wings whom they'd quickly marry once they dumped *her*. After another failed relationship, this time with a married man who for four years promised to leave his wife but never did, Mary lost it emotionally. She suffered a prolonged coughing fit that sent her to a doctor, who told her she had to stop smoking because she had asthma and the beginnings of emphysema and chronic obstructive pulmonary disease (COPD).

If you, like Mary, are a Puddle Tsunami, you're very good at being in touch with your own emotions (maybe a little *too* in touch, actually), whether you're enthralled in joy and love or languishing in fear, anger, and sadness. Your normal day consists of a roller coaster of intensely unstable mood swings, assuring that you're never boring to be around. On the one hand, your friends love you for your huge heart. Your deep kindness, caring, and tenderness make you a big puddle of emotional warmth. But then those same friends go running for the hills or freeze like scared bunny rabbits when you pitch a fit of rage about a seemingly innocuous event, such as a story in the news, the latest political scandal, or a new tax levy on cigarettes (and yes, you probably smoke, too). Not surprisingly, your health is likely to develop energetic whiplash from your near-tsunami ups and corresponding downs.

What I've learned from people like Mary is that the part of the Puddle Tsunamis' brains that creates emotion and intuition (the temporal-lobe limbic area) far dominates the one that censors that same emotion and intuition (the frontal lobe) so that a person can maintain a place in society, a job, or a relationship. These types are also very sensitive, emotionally porous sponges for other people's feelings—which is great if they want a career in the fields of acting, singing, or counseling, but it's not so good if they hope to maintain a long-term relationship.

With all the turmoil in their lives, those who fall into this fourth-chakra category can barely maintain their own emotional footing. But when these people spend much time with partners of any kind (be they mates or colleagues), they react to *their* emotional ups and downs as well. Overwhelmed by trying to balance their partners' feelings with their own, Puddle Tsunamis go over the edge. They lose it. Their emotional needs overwhelm their frontal lobes' capacity to censor their reactions for the sake of maintaining relationships. They can no longer hold their panic, fury, or despondency at bay to attend to their partners' feelings. Their own come spilling out like a tidal wave, a tsunami of emotions that knocks over any man, woman, or child who happens to be nearby. Even the pets of Puddle Tsunamis tend at times to be emotional wrecks.

What clues signal that you might be such a person? Well, in high school, you always got in trouble for talking in class. You regularly lose at poker or other types of card games because you can never bluff. Your friends seek you out whenever they want a little excitement. You read *People, In Touch Weekly, Star,* or the *National Enquirer* while in line at the supermarket. You gravitate to the phone when you have to make a decision or solve a problem, calling multiple friends and family members to vent and ask for their points of view. Your monthly cell-phone minutes run up into the thousands.

You love romantic films like *Sleepless in Seattle* and *Moonstruck,* while "serious" movies (particularly foreign ones with subtitles) put you to sleep. The history of your love life could be a script for a day-time soap, with dramatic breakups that have included angry text messages, nasty e-mails, or car chases. You've slammed doors, screamed, and maybe even slapped your partner out of deep frustration, pain, and grief.

You drive erratically because the way you handle a vehicle is disproportionately affected by your mood. You often tailgate or flash your bright lights at drivers in the left lane who won't move over and let you pass. If you're a woman, your PMS is murder, and when you reach perimenopause, your mood swings are even worse. You've been heard to utter, "I could just kill for a _____ [cigarette, drink, cookie, bowl of ice cream—fill in the vice of your choice]."

If this description applies to you, brace yourself, because you meet the criteria for a Puddle Tsunami. The first alarm that your fourth chakra will send is that you'll feel like you're boiling over with unbridled outrage and anger. But you can't see clearly through the steamy haze of your emotions to witness the immediate damage that you're inflicting on the people around you. After your anger has cooled and you notice the injured bystanders, you become paralyzed by shame and regret.

After a series of emotional blowups like these, you may find yourself sitting in a pit of emotional rejection and abandonment, the casualty of yet another relationship failure. You may try to medicate your resulting heartache by smoking, eventually resulting in asthma and COPD. In addition, your grief will always register in some fourth-chakra organ, letting you know that you need to better attend to the delicate balance between emotions and partnerships.

If we look closely at Mary's story, we'll realize that each of us can find a Puddle Tsunami somewhere within ourselves. At certain times, we've all felt that our emotions are an out-of-control roller coaster and we're about to lose it. It might be when someone does something that makes us want to pull our hair out. Or it could be one of those hormonal days when we feel so drained that if one more thing goes wrong, we just know we'll pop a gasket and make a fool of ourselves (and maybe even scare somebody).

The weather never stays the same, nor can our moods and feelings . . . or even the state of our relationships. The best we can hope for is managing to maintain our composure in both rocky and smooth times by learning how to ride the ups and downs of our feelings, thus helping preserve our partnerships and create stable emotional and physical health in the process.

Intuitive Advice for the Puddle Tsunami

Do you suffer from chronic health problems in your heart, breasts, and lungs; and do you tend to have Puddle Tsunami–like mood swings? If so, medical intuition and mind-body medicine can teach you how to calm the emotional waters of your relationships, and your mind-body makeover begins by addressing your physical well-being. You could have any fourth-chakra health problem with Puddle Tsunami tendencies. But if, like Mary, *your* concern happens to be asthma, your doctor may prescribe a steroid inhaler such as Advair or Pulmicort, in addition to oral steroids. These medications can calm the inflammation in your lungs and bronchial pathways that make it hard for you to breathe (although, unfortunately, they can also make you even moodier than usual). Your doctor may also prescribe a rescue inhaler containing the stimulant albuterol, as well as a nebulizer with Xopenex, which is less likely to make you edgy and panicky than the other inhalers.

You could elect to go to an acupuncturist and Chinese herbalist, who may give you herbs like fritillaria, polygalae, tenufoliae, schisandra, perilla, pinelliae, ternatae, or *Magnolia officinalis* to help eliminate the phlegm, the cough, and ultimately the shortness of breath experienced with asthma. Even more important, acupuncture can help you kick the cigarette habit, even if you've tried and been unable to do so before.

The next part of the mind-body makeover addresses your emotional state. As a Puddle Tsunami, you must learn how to buffer your highs and lows by training your frontal-lobe brain areas to better censor your emotions when you want to maintain a relationship. This will enable you to attend to your feelings and at that same time be present for your partner's emotional reactions, without becoming mentally unglued.

When I was training to be a lifeguard, we were shown a lifesaving video on what to do when caught in a marine plant called eelgrass. If you get tangled in it while swimming, the more you struggle and try to break free, the tighter your legs and arms will get snared, and you're likely to drown. The video suggested that you relax, get a grip on your emotions, monitor your thoughts, and calm yourself—but don't move and don't react. Just observe yourself and the events in your mind. Then, as the water and tide rushes by you, the eelgrass will magically untangle and you'll be free.

If you're a Puddle Tsunami, you can apply the same tactic when you find yourself getting stuck in the emotional spiral that occurs when *your* feelings get entangled with your partner's. By learning how to get a grip on them both and allowing them to flow around you, neither emotional tide will overwhelm you. You'll be able to swim away instead of getting caught and drowning. A special technique that helps you implement this fourth-chakra lifesaving approach is mindfulness. (See the chapter on the second chakra for information on mindfulness exercises.)

While you're learning these techniques, you might want to take DHA (100–300 mg, three times a day) for a little extra support. If you need additional help, consider talking to a health-care professional about the possibility of being prescribed a more potent mood stabilizer, such as Lamictal, Topamax, or Tegretol.

Although it may take a while for you to achieve the intricate balance necessary for maintaining both healthy emotional expression and functional partnerships, know that such balance is indeed within your reach. Remember what it was like when you learned to ride a bicycle for the first time or when you tried to master the clutch in a car with a standard transmission? In the beginning, it was hard to keep the bike from falling or the car from stalling out, and you may have felt as if you'd never get the hang of it. But once you finally succeeded a few times, your body memory took over, and that made it easier . . . to the point that you could eventually do it without thinking. The same is true with learning how to manage your emotional temperament in a relationship. And the payoff—health in the fourth chakra—is well worth the effort.

What follows is my seven-part program to rehabilitate the Puddle Tsunamis' tendency to experience emotional tidal waves:

1. Identify that to some degree you count on the daily highs and lows of your very dramatic life to keep things interesting. Next, understand that although you may feel that there's nothing like a good crisis to get your juices flowing, your reactions are actually so passionate that they can endanger your partnerships. Others find your emotional intensity simply too much to handle, so they back away.

2. Recognize that all the arguments in your relationships occur when you insist on sticking to your guns and fail to balance your emotional needs with those of the other person. Realize that, for the sake of the partnership, it may be necessary to set aside your own concerns for a short time (I repeat, *for a _short_ time*) and do what is required to keep the relationship functional. See how doing so doesn't mean giving up your own identity, but instead allows you to satisfy both your requirements *and* those of your partner.

3. Discern that it's possible to be internally present and conscious about a feeling you have but not talk about it until you can deliver your message in a more skillful way. By learning how to stabilize your emotional reactions around other people, not only do you preserve your sanity and your dignity, but you're also then able to take care of one of your long-term emotional needs—namely, being in a relationship.

4. Restrict the impulse to blow up, and instead attempt to stop the tsunami-like emotional-meltdown pathways in your brain by creating a place in your home or office for a "time-out." When you're about to blow up, politely excuse yourself and sit in the time-out spot until you're calmer, performing the mindfulness exercise (as outlined in the second-chakra chapter) to help the feeling pass over you. Don't judge; don't struggle; and when the emotional storm is over, return to the scene of the crime and apologize.

5. Know that with some education, supplements, and treatments, you can still delight and entertain your friends and family with your big heart without having to worry about driving away long-term partnerships.

6. Change the unhealthy thought pattern: *I am incapable of having long-term relationships in my life because they all seem to crash and* *burn eventually* . . . to the more positive affirmation: *I now have the opportunity to move through my fears and failures and give birth to satisfying relationships in which I balance both my emotional needs and those of others.*

7. Follow the fourth rule for intuitive health—*Got to love her madly*—by being able to maintain your sanity while balancing your emotional needs with the ones of partnership.

The Perpetual Partner

The second type of fourth-chakra extreme is the Perpetual Partner, those who always hide their emotions behind a happy face to maintain their partnerships at all costs. Take my client Nina, 33, who seemed so incredibly sweet and calm that being in her presence was always very soothing. Whatever was happening in someone's life, Nina would always know what to say to make the person feel better. She'd open her refrigerator and pull out some kind of meal, be it meat loaf, chicken soup, her famous peanut-butter cookies, or her celebrated chocolate-chip banana bread. Whatever she plopped in front of a loved one in pain, the person knew that in 20 minutes everything would be all right in the world again.

Nina was constantly nurturing everyone and everything. She volunteered at the nearest rape crisis center, delivered canned goods for the school food drive, and taught migrant workers how to read and write in English. Although she got herself into some fairly difficult situations at times, trying to deal with people who were pretty rough around the edges due to their traumatic lives, she never let down her pleasant façade. Always kind, caring, warm, and tender, this woman cheerfully approached even the most difficult situations without showing fear, the slightest bit of annoyance, disappointment, or tension.

Nina was still in touch with the same friends she had in grammar school, high school, and college. She married her high-school sweetheart, Ned, when she was 21, and they'd been happily married for more than a decade. Yet after having four children—three boys and a girl—my client was horrified to find that she'd gained 22 pounds. She was starting to get irritable and cranky for the first time, and she'd begun to get hot flashes and palpitations, as if she was entering perimenopause.

When her doctor found a lump in her left breast and diagnosed invasive breast cancer, Nina realized that she needed to begin to nurture herself as much as she nurtured everyone around her. Her fourth-chakra intuitive advisor was signaling to her that she was attending to her partnerships more than she was in touch with the full spectrum of her own emotions.

If you, like Nina, are a Perpetual Partner, you never bitch, moan, or complain. You're likely to be very happy swimming in the more positive emotional pool of feelings like love, adoration, kindness, joy, and happiness. But when it comes to fear, anxiety, anger, frustration, sadness, or loneliness, you're likely to shun these emotions completely, not willing to take the risk that you might hurt or offend someone. This censoring of negative emotions is a good short-term strategy to manage long-term relationships and your career until you can figure out a more skillful way to voice your feelings and tend to your intuitive messages. However, over the long haul, putting on a brave face, being stoic, and shunting your emotions into your fourth-chakra organs can have disastrous consequences for your health, including an increased chance of developing breast cancer (whether you're a man *or* a woman) or dying of a sudden heart attack.

What I've learned from people like Nina is that the lid that Perpetual Partners keep on their emotions starts to come undone in midlife. The frontal-lobe brain areas that have helped them censor their feelings are always under the control of estrogen and progesterone. When these hormones start to change at midlife, the frontal lobe can no longer contain the emotions. Perpetual Partners get irritable; and all the fear, anger, and sadness that they've been stuffing all these years starts spilling out. Afterward, they often say something like, "I just had to get that off of my chest."

What clues signal that you might be a Perpetual Partner? You find comedians such as Kathy Griffin (of *My Life on the D-List* fame), Joan Rivers, and Rosie O'Donnell impolite, unkind, and maybe even downright rude. You rarely honk your horn in traffic, and you wouldn't intentionally cut anyone off on the highway, no matter *how* poorly the person was driving. You've never given anyone an obscene gesture. You seldom swear, nor do you see why cursing is a necessary form of communication. You know what the saying "Feed a cold; starve a fever" means. Your freezer contains enough food for a family of four to survive on for at least three days. You love kids, whether you have any or not, and you always give out candy (usually full-size chocolate bars) on Halloween.

Sound familiar? Then you might be one of these folks. Everyone loves you because you're so nurturing, but watch out—the more out of balance your nurturing becomes, the more you'll be setting yourself up for a fourth-chakra health crisis. The first alarm you'll experience is what I call "pronoun fusion." Your use of the personal pronoun *I* will greatly decrease, and in its place you'll adopt the telltale partner-ship pronoun *we*.

For example, if someone asks how you are, you'll answer something like: "We're doing fine. The whole family is great. The children all had a touch of that flu that's going around, and Ned's very busy at work, but we can't complain. How are you?" You'd almost never answer by graphically complaining, "Crappy. I have diarrhea and a horrendous yeast infection, and yesterday I was up all night with the dry heaves." Yet if you don't start attending to your own emotional needs as much as you focus on your partnerships, your medical-intuitive advisor will let you know through a health problem in your fourth-chakra area.

All of us have a part of the Perpetual Partner somewhere within us. Like Nina, we all have a tendency to try to hide our anger, frustration, or disappointment behind a pleasant face to keep the peace in relationships and get people to love us. Although we may feel that avoiding revealing our negative feelings to others preserves our relationships long-term, the truth is that swallowing anger, sadness, and anxiety over time can end them for two different reasons:

1. Those negative feelings will fester until all of a sudden, when we least expect it and probably at the most inappropriate time, the emotional backlog will blow up in our faces (and our partners', too).

2. Because stuffing negative emotions into our bodies isn't good for our fourth-chakra organs (our heart, breasts, and lungs), sooner or later our health is likely to fail, making us unable to be truly present—or maybe even costing us our lives.

So even if it's uncomfortable in the short run, learning how to maintain a relationship by sharing our emotions—the good, the bad, and the ugly—in a timely manner is going to make our health and our partnerships thrive.

Intuitive Advice for the Perpetual Partner

Do you suffer from chronic health problems in your heart, breasts, and lungs; and do you tend to have some aspects of the Perpetual Partner pattern? If so, you can use medical intuition and mind-body medicine to thaw that frozen cheerful grin and loosen up a little more so that you're able to take care of yourself as well as you do others. Your mind-body makeover begins with your physical health problems. You could have any fourth-chakra health issue with Perpetual Partner tendencies. But if you, like Nina, happen to have breast cancer, and if your tumor is found to be estrogen sensitive, your doctor will begin to look at ways to block levels of this natural hormone in your body.

Your physician may prescribe tamoxifen or suggest that you shed any excess weight. Losing the extra pounds helps lower your levels of estrogen because body fat is converted readily to this hormone, so body-fat stores are like having constant supplies of bio-identical estrogen replacement. So estrogen, whether synthetic or bio-identical, can increase your chance of breast cancer. Needless to say, as a result, you may, then, want to drop your morning duty as a soup-kitchen volunteer and devote that time instead to working out. In addition to daily 30-minute aerobic exercise and evening walks, implement a meal plan that balances protein with carbohydrates (see the advice for the Rock of Dependability in the chapter on the third chakra). In addition, take protective supplements, including coenzyme Q_{10} (400–600 mg a day) and vitamin D, either orally or by stimulating your body to produce it naturally by going out for a walk in the sun for 30 minutes a day.

Attending to the emotional intuitive brain is the next part of the mind-body makeover. If you have a tendency to hide your feelings behind a smiling mask so that you can maintain every relationship at all costs, you must learn to communicate the fear, anger, and sadness that are critical parts of your intuitive guidance system. By censoring your negative emotions, you're also blocking your intuition, a key lifesaving skill.

For this healing step, you're going to need an emotional midwife. Find a friend or a therapist (preferably one who reminds you of a big, warm teddy bear) who can provide you with a safe, accepting area where you can test the relationship waters and say something negative without getting rejected. You'll soon find out that no one will think you're a "devil child" and run screaming from the room. By learning to skillfully voice fear, anger, and sadness in a trial partnership, you'll face and conquer your emotional phobia of rejection. With practice, you'll be able to get mad, grouchy, nervous, overwhelmed, lonely, depressed, and sad—and see that you can still be lovable, striking a healthier balance between your emotional and partnership needs.

Here, then, is my seven-part program for rehabilitating the Perpetual Partners' Pollyanna personas:

1. Identify how showing even a little irritation, grumpiness, and disappointment makes you very anxious and even causes you to feel guilty because you believe that you'll be rejected for not living up to the perfect person you think everyone needs you to be.

2. Recognize that many people in your life have no problems displaying the full range of human emotion and you still love and want to support them, especially when they're sad, frustrated, frightened or in pain. Realize that they probably feel the same way about *you*.

3. Discern the difference between expressing a negative *emotion* and having a negative *attitude*. Understand that eliminating all trace of negative emotions also disconnects you from a key source of intuition that could warn you when you may be about to experience a painful or threatening event. Swallowing such feelings might make you appear to be an absolute angel on Earth, but it will tend to leave you intuitively unprotected.

4. Restrict your tendency to gloss over disappointments, annoyances, and daily worries by employing your usual emotional-bypass procedure. In everyday situations where there is an adverse circumstance, begin to use a balance of both positive and negative emotions to describe the event. For example, instead of thinking up understandable excuses for why the technician from the telephone company didn't show up, also admit that the experience was exasperating.

5. Know that accepting support from other people is helpful for you *and* the partnership. The strongest relationships are those in which each person both gives and receives support at different times. After all, if you're always the giver, you rob the other person of the joy and deep satisfaction that come with that role.

6. Change the unhealthy thought pattern: *I won't be loved or accepted if I get angry or sad* . . . to the healthier affirmation: *I express all of my emotions openly, willingly, and skillfully.*

7. Follow the fourth rule for intuitive health—*Got to love her madly*—by expressing your full range of positive and negative emotions and realizing that you can still remain in mutually caring partnerships.

The Helluva Bonder

The next type of fourth-chakra extreme is the Helluva Bonder, who is very good at maintaining partnerships and a stable emotional footing in the face of even the most difficult of circumstances. My client Odette was just such a person. She was voted Miss Congeniality, "Most Likely to Succeed," and homecoming queen in her senior year in high school. In college, she earned the best grades and got along well with all of her professors. Now at the age of 53, Odette had it all—she was smart and gorgeous, and she had a wonderful partner.

Even if you wanted to despise her for seeming too perfect, you simply couldn't, because she really went out of her way to make you feel wonderful. You couldn't help but absolutely love Odette.

After college and law school, my client worked as an assistant district attorney for several years, putting some of the most violent offenders behind bars. When she hit her early 30s, Odette realized that she wanted to be a mother, so she gave up her job to start a family, a move that stunned her colleagues. Finally, after both of her daughters reached middle-school age, she created a law practice with two other men that was, of course, a raving success. But after a lifetime of perfect health, this active woman was shocked to find out during a routine annual exam that her blood pressure and cholesterol were beginning to rise.

If you, like Odette, are a Helluva Bonder, you may be an unbelievable parent, spouse, and business partner who has an almost genius capacity to express your feelings and simultaneously make other people feel completely understood. No wonder everyone loves you! But around the age of 50, chances are you'll start to feel exhausted; and health problems in your heart, breasts, and lungs will begin to appear for the first time. That's your medical-intuitive advisor letting you know that your fourth-chakra-centric life will need to be reevaluated, because at this stage both your emotional and your partnership needs are beginning to change.

What I've learned from people like Odette is that the immense capacity these types have to balance their own and everyone else's emotional needs, nurturing everything in sight, tends over time to act as a parasite to other forms of individual and spiritual development. With the midlife change in hormones, the intricate balance between expressing emotional intuition and censoring feelings and hunches shifts for the first time. As estrogen, progesterone, and testosterone decline, the frontal-lobe censor tends to become less operational. This hormonal decline facilitates access to an inner yearning for spiritual communion and creative expression that previously was completely repressed. If, however, these Bonders are completely immersed in their marathon lists of fourth-chakra responsibilities (car pools, church committees, work, date nights, and so on), the only alarm they may receive that some internal passion for another realm needs outlet is through a fourth-chakra physical warning sign.

What clues indicate that you may be a Helluva Bonder? Well, your children and all of their friends know that they can always go to you when they have a problem, because you just *know* how to help them feel better and find the solution. You've spent a lot of quality time driving your kids to school, to athletic events, and even on shopping excursions. You're privy to almost all of the gossip in their friends' lives.

Your kitchen cabinets, refrigerator, and freezer are filled with fun foods and treats that kids love. If you dig deep enough, you might find an old sippy cup or two in one of your cabinets. You make sure that your partner and children take nutritional supplements, eat breakfast, and have a sit-down dinner together almost every night of the week. If you leave your house for an extended period of time, things tend to spiral out of control: The milk, bread, eggs, and butter run out; and people eat a lot of takeout or drive-through meals. The living-room couch becomes disheveled, with the pillows all misplaced, and the laundry piles up.

You're not so sweet; at times you're feisty and don't mince words. If a cable technician is extremely rude to you, you tell your kid, "Honey, can you go in the other room while Mommy talks to the nice repair-man?" And then you wait until they're out of earshot before you chew the guy out, using enough choice words to immediately get what you want (although your language would shock even a longshoreman). When you play poker with friends, family, and even with your partner, you can win and take their money without batting an eyelash.

If these scenarios fit your experience, then you may be a Helluva Bonder. There's probably a long waiting list of people who want to hang out around you because you combine a loving, nurturing household (like the ones in *Little House on the Prairie* or *The Waltons*) with the girl-next-door charm of Mary Tyler Moore. But if your life-long emotional balancing act takes precedence over new interests and needs that are trying to emerge at midlife, the first alarm that gets your attention will be pressure building up in your chest. No matter what your particular symptoms are, no physical treatment will relieve this pressure until you simultaneously identify and express whatever inner drive needs to be released. This might be a spiritual yearning; a need for more passion in a partnership; or a hankering to express yourself through art, poetry, or some other creative activity.

If we look closely at the elements of Odette's story, we'll realize that we all have within us at least a little bit of the Helluva Bonder, because we aspire to this type's unsurpassed ability to get along with everyone. Part of us secretly admires those Miss Congeniality people and wishes we could be both homecoming-queen beautiful or homecoming-king handsome and most likely to succeed at emotional sanity—complete with sanitized emotions and well-preserved relationships. We all try to achieve this enviable state, with varying degrees of success.

But we must take care not to beat ourselves up if we fall short of that mark again and again. If we think about it, the people who win those Miss Congeniality contests are never postmenopausal. Whether we're male or female, when we're under the influence of hormones as younger adults, it's much easier for us to keep our cool, stay sane, and remain congenial to our partners. However, once midlife rolls around and those hormones start to change, not only does this emotional sanitizing and agreeable demeanor grow old, but it also becomes almost impossible to maintain. So we can certainly admire that rare person who is an absolute Helluva Bonder, but we can also understand that no one can maintain that pattern throughout a lifetime.

Intuitive Advice for the Helluva Bonder

Do you suffer from chronic health problems in your heart, breasts, and lungs; and do you tend to have Helluva Bonder issues? If so, mind-body medicine and medical intuition can help you heal your health problems . . . but get used to the fact that your life is going to be disrupted for a while because your usual expertise is no longer going to be as effective. Your mind-body makeover will first address your physical problems. You could have any fourth-chakra health issue with Helluva Bonder tendencies. But if, like Odette, your fourth-chakra problem happens to be high blood pressure and cholesterol, your physician will probably suggest Lipitor or one of the many statin drugs available that not only lower cholesterol but also decrease your risk for dementia and heart disease. However, if you take these drugs, you need to take coenzyme Q_{10} (400–600 mg a day) as well, because statins deplete this antioxidant. As a bonus, coenzyme Q_{10} protects against breast cancer, too.

While you're working with your physician to lower your cholesterol, you could also go to an acupuncturist and Chinese herbalist to address your increased risk for heart disease. Unlike Western medicine, which assigns a different drug for each cardiovascular symptom (one to lower blood pressure, another to lower cholesterol, and so on), Chinese medicine recognizes that all symptoms have a similar origin in your body and treats you accordingly. For example, the herbs *Prunella vulgaris, Scutellariae baicalensis,* lumbricus, and chrysanthemi, among others, treat the tendency toward high blood pressure, elevated cholesterol levels, and fragile blood vessels that could lead to stroke or other cardiovascular diseases.

If you elect to go to your ob-gyn, he or she would also be familiar with the cholesterol and blood-pressure problems that typically increase with perimenopause. Besides all the medicine the doctor is likely to suggest, taking extra magnesium (200–400 mg a day, on an empty stomach) on top of your regular calcium and magnesium supplement can lower your blood pressure as well as decrease the anxiety and insomnia that often occur at midlife. Likewise, herbal mood stabilizers such as black cohosh and soy may also lower your blood pressure. Finally, get 30 minutes of aerobic exercise a day to elevate your HDL (the "good") cholesterol and decrease your LDL (the "bad") cholesterol.

Next, your mind-body makeover moves to the right-brain emotions. Once midlife hits and new inner needs (be they spiritual yearnings or creative abilities) begin to build up inside of you, the resulting pressure will wreak havoc on your life until it can be expressed and released. The only way you'll be able to identify that nameless sensation is to withdraw from earthbound partnerships and nurturing responsibilities for extended periods of time in order to explore the emotional terrain and spiritual territory of a different love. This isn't the kind they talk about in songs on the radio, but a different sort of passion that involves getting in touch with love for creation and spirituality.

During this time, you may feel an irrational desire to run away, take a sabbatical, move to a monastery for a month, or learn meditation at a spiritual retreat or ashram. The act of sitting on a mat all day and directing your emotional and partnership drives inward and toward the heavens rather than outward and toward a relationship can help release this inner pressure and passion. Practices like meditation not only help you increase your emotional- and spiritual-partnership capabilities, but they also lower cholesterol and blood pressure. If meditation doesn't appeal to you, then attend a writing workshop, take a painting class, go on an outdoor-adventure trip, or sign up for a weekend spiritual conference. In short, follow your bliss.

Yes, the refrigerator will stop being constantly well stocked, and the laundry will begin to pile up. But in time, your family will learn to adjust and become more independent, evolving in their own capacity to take care of themselves.

What follows is my seven-part program to rehabilitate the Helluva Bonder types' emotional imbalance between relationships with the earthbound and the inner, spiritual realms:

1. Identify how much of your identity has been defined by being the emotionally stable person whom people go to when they need to be held, nurtured, and accepted.

2. Recognize an ever-expanding pressure within you to at least temporarily take a break from that omnipresent nurturing persona to explore something new—a more spiritually inward life or the creative expression of inner passions—without the distractions of day-to-day, grounded life.

3. Discern that temporarily disconnecting from earthbound partnerships and responsibilities isn't a sign that you're having a nervous breakdown or losing emotional touch with your loved ones. Understand that throughout life, your emotional health goes through developmental stages with ever-increasing requirements for growth. With the "changing of the guard" at midlife, additional emotional and spiritual needs must be addressed for complete physical and mental health.

4. Restrict your tendency to cling to the safety you've always known and been very good at—the juggling of the endless obligations for nurturing that have kept you stable up to this point in your life. Allow your loved ones to assume more of the responsibility for taking care of themselves than you've permitted them to do so far.

5. Know that you can let yourself experience a little turmoil, apprehension, and initial loss of emotional composure as you journey into new, uncharted creative and spiritual waters. Allow yourself to surrender emotional and mental control into this more vast inner territory, opening yourself up to a wellspring of passion that you've never before experienced.

6. Change the unhealthy thought pattern: *We live in a world of disorder and chaos, in which I create partnerships, nurture others, and experience emotional fulfillment . . .* to the healthier affirmation: *In this world of human chaos and divine order, I can experience a balance of earthly and spiritual fulfillment and passion, both personally and in partnerships.*

7. Follow the fourth rule for intuitive health—*Got to love her madly*—by balancing your need for emotional fulfillment on Earth and passion for spiritual and creative expression.

The Emotionally Alone Again (Naturally) Type

The last type of fourth-chakra extreme is the Emotionally Alone Again (Naturally) type. People with this pattern have great difficulty experiencing emotions and (like the sad fellow in the Gilbert O'Sullivan song with a similar name) engaging in partnerships beyond their superficial daily existence. For example, 23-year-old Paul was the apple of his mother's eye. He was always a bit of a homebody and very good with machines and electronics. He kept all the VCRs, cell phones, and computers in the house in working order. If the doorbell malfunctioned, Paul fixed it. If your motherboard wasn't talking to your mainframe, this young man would perform his technological magic and—*voilà!*—you'd be up and running again.

However, outside of his family, Paul had no way of easily relating to people. Girls found him odd and emotionally aloof. When he was in high school, unless his classmates needed help with their physics, chemistry, or math homework, he had no real contact with any friends. His widowed mother and his sisters were ever-protective of him, always making sure that he had somewhere to go on Friday and Saturday nights while they were off on their own dates or social events.

Soon, however, his sisters married and left the nest, and his mother became engaged to a man who had little patience for the way this young man perpetually hung around the house unless someone else orchestrated events for him. Just as his new stepfather was due to move in, Paul's lifelong problem with bronchial asthma and allergies kicked in to high gear, and he developed heart palpitations that a doctor diagnosed as panic attacks.

If you, like Paul, are the Alone Again type, you have trouble emotionally relating to people, especially those outside your family. The realm of relationships is truly a mystery to you. Usually, there are two causes for this pattern:

1. Being born with a very left-brain-centric mind with an incredible capacity for details, numbers, logic, and linear reasoning (see the chapter on the sixth chakra) but without the ability to encode right-brain emotion, which is critical in comprehending the subtle nuances underlying relationships

2. Having experienced such severe trauma due to injury or epilepsy that your brain has been rewired for emotions, causing you to experience them in a different, more detached manner

Either way, you don't easily bond or connect with others, and you're also more likely to have fourth-chakra health problems in your heart, lungs, and breasts (even if you're a man).

What I've learned from people like Paul is that even though Alone Again types may appear at times to be aloof, indifferent, or unconcerned, they have a huge backlog of bottled-up emotions inside them that are awaiting some route of expression. They don't often voice their feelings in a way most people can comprehend and instead use words and actions that are confusing to others. One moment they're calm—and then, in a manner that totally baffles those around them, they may suddenly flee and hide, become overwhelmed with anxiety, get tight-lipped or flushed, clench their teeth, break things in rage, or slam the door shut or the phone down. Afterward, feeling intense shame and embarrassment about their unskilled emotional carryings-on, they may apologize profusely and withdraw even further into their personal humiliation. This is ironic, because their intense emotional outbursts reveal that these individuals truly have big hearts overflowing with feelings and really do ache for understanding and some form of partnerships. But they simply don't have the skills to achieve their goal.

What signs indicate that you might be someone of this type? Well, you'd rather stay home and read a book than go to a cocktail party or on a dinner date. Noises and bright lights make you edgy and irritable. In high school, you did whatever you could to avoid any of the dances, and you never followed what was going on in the "in" crowd. You've always gotten along better with people who are 20 to 30 years older than you, even when you were a very young child. In fact, many of your parents' friends are now *your* friends. Your eyes wander during a conversation as you try to choose your words. People have often told you that although you seem shy, you're easier to get to know once they start talking to you.

You may feel much safer emotionally in your own protective world of spirituality or fantasy. You relate to God, nature, and objects more than you do with people, because here, no words are necessary to explain your feelings; and it's not possible to be misunderstood, criticized, or rejected. You can easily tolerate spiritually intense, emotionally ecstatic states, but handling other people's feelings or the more mundane daily crises drives you crazy.

You'd rather live in a pseudo-monastic existence, relating emotionally to spirituality and God far more than living close to people you'd have to relate to socially—with one exception. You have probably relied on one somewhat maternal person throughout your adult life who is your social chairperson. This could be your biological mother or sister (whom you may live with), or it could be a doting mate.

If this sounds somewhat like you (and do leave me some wiggle room here, because I know that everyone with this personality style has some detailed, left-brain perfectionism going on), then you may be the Emotionally Alone Again (Naturally) type. If you regularly keep your feelings at a distance, even from yourself, the first alarm that your fourth-chakra medical-intuitive advisor will sound is that you'll begin to have sudden, unexpected, panicked, and angry outbursts. You'll typically walk around with a relatively calm expression, but inside, undetected even by you, your emotions will begin to heat up until they reach the boiling point and finally blow. In time, if you continue to stifle your right-brain intuition and emotions instead of skillfully voicing them and acting appropriately *on* them, you may develop fourth-chakra health problems.

All of us have a bit of the Alone Again type in us. Like Paul, we all have those times in our lives when we're totally out of sync with our feelings and with other people. We might feel that we've lost our "mojo" or gotten into a funk, and there's a confusing backlog of emotions inside of us. All we know is that the only thing that feels right is spending time alone to process grief or tragedy or to figure out what's going on that's making us feel out of sorts, as well as alienated from those around us.

Removing ourselves from the distracting presence of other people's feelings always helps clarify our own—at least temporarily. But if we use our solitude as a form of sustained exile, we aren't healing our emotions; we're *escaping* them—and avoiding emotional intimacy with people in general. Learning how to be "upset" alone and intimately in the presence of other people is an emotional skill that, when acquired, will support our physical and mental health.

Intuitive Advice for the Emotionally Alone Again (Naturally) Type

Do you suffer from chronic health problems in your heart, breasts, and lungs; and do you tend to have some aspects of the Emotionally

Alone Again (Naturally)–type pattern? If so, you can learn to use mind-body medicine and medical intuition to help you gain access to and express your emotions so that you can develop and maintain healthy relationships. Your mind-body makeover begins by addressing your physical health problems. You could have any fourth-chakra concern with Alone Again–type tendencies. But if, like Paul, you happen to suffer from a panic disorder, you may experience shortness of breath, a sense of smothering, and the feeling that you're choking—aggravating any lung conditions like asthma or allergies, or heart problems such as palpitations, night sweats, chest pain, angina, or atrial fibrillation.

(For support with asthma and allergy problems, follow the advice given for the Puddle Tsunami earlier in this chapter and for the Lone Wolf in the chapter on the first chakra. For support with cardiovascular conditions, follow the advice given for the Helluva Bonder in the preceding section.)

The mind-body makeover next addresses the emotional right brain of the Alone Again types. If this is your pattern, the only way to soothe your earthbound emotions is to learn how to skillfully transform them into appropriate words and effective actions rather than reacting, retreating, or having a knee-jerk response that confuses people. This is a three-step process:

1. Use the mindfulness exercise earlier in this chapter, which will teach you to sit, observe, and allow yourself to describe the feeling you're experiencing without judging it.

2. Determine what event precipitated the emotion.

3. Discover which thought patterns are responsible for your getting stuck in that emotion or mood. I call these the "gum on your shoe" thought patterns, because they're so sticky that they tend to keep you stuck on your negative mood and prevent you from moving beyond whatever set you off.

Here is my list of the top-ten gum-on-your-shoe thought patterns that can provoke you to emotionally respond in a way that prevents healthy relationships:

- *This is hopeless.*
- *I'm helpless.*
- *I've failed.*
- *I'm a loser.*
- *I've lost control.*
- *I'm going to get hurt.*
- *I've gotten hurt.*
- *I'm going to die.*
- *This will be painful.*
- And everyone's all-time favorite: *This is unfair— things should be different; I'm right and they're wrong.*

With practice, you'll be able to experience an emotion, sit with it, name it, pinpoint what event caused it, and then identify the thought pattern behind it that causes your fear to escalate until your behavior gets out of control. This sequence reestablishes the connection between your right-brain emotion and your left-brain capacity to talk about it in a way people understand. Once you've done that, it will be easier for you to respond to the emotion by taking appropriate action that won't damage your relationships. And yes, you *do* need relationships in your life if you're to be healthy and truly happy.

Here, then, is my seven-part program to rehabilitate the Emotionally Alone Again (Naturally) types' pattern of ignoring their emotions and intuition until they erupt in a display of socially inappropriate behavior:

1. Identify that your tendency to stick to the rational details in life and avoid intimate, emotional situations may help you feel more in control. Further see that your attempts at aloofness and detachment let your true feelings get bottled up inside—a condition that, if allowed to fester, will eventually blow up in your face (or someone else's) at the most inconvenient times.

2. Recognize that by learning a more flexible way of translating your inner feelings into words, other people will be able to "get" you, and in the end, your world will become more stable and nurturing.

3. Discern that you may feel more comfortable emotionally relating to the spiritual realm, your religious practice, and your lifelong connection to God or your higher power. However, understand that to move about in the world and have stable emotional health, you also need to have fulfilling contact with humankind.

4. Restrict your tendency to withdraw into your monastic life of people-free intervals for days on end. Instead, interact with others to force your brain to sprout new "relationship" pathways.

5. Know how to emotionally and physically deal with people in more skillful ways by volunteering to work with teens at a local Boys & Girls Club. Adolescents are attempting to learn the same relationship skills that you're trying to nail down—how not to act out their feelings with knee-jerk reactions, by sulking, or by otherwise behaving in an emotionally unhealthy manner. Also use the three-step process described earlier to catch up on learning the fourth-chakra relationship and emotional skills you somehow haven't picked up yet.

6. Change the negative thought pattern: *I can't tolerate the emotional pain and unpleasant feelings that relationships bring into my life . . .* to the healthier affirmation: *With the help of some good coaches and role models, I can set goals, strive for success, and create fulfilling emotional relationships that will lessen my pain and make me feel more in control.*

7. Follow the fourth rule for intuitive health—*Got to love her madly* —instead of alternating between making a scene and then withdrawing from society, learn how to attend to both relationships *and* your emotional sanity.

●—●—●

Creating health in the fourth chakra involves learning how to sing a different kind of love song. As a teen, you probably hummed along to angst-ridden bubblegum pop tunes about whether or not someone loved someone else. *If he doesn't call, I'll die,* you thought back then. In your early adulthood, you moved on to the more mature heartache, and often even rage, of the classic somebody-done-somebody-wrong song. Such tortured ballads about cheatin' hearts, roving eyes, and slashing tires are typically full of anger, vengeance, and grief.

But after all of these immature relationships, you're now generally ready for a mutually loving partnership characterized by emotional sanity. To resonate with this more evolved type of love song, you must follow the fourth rule for intuitive health—*Got to love her madly*—by balancing partnership and emotions. If your emotions are veering off-key, you can count on your fourth-chakra intuitive advisor to cue the refrain—illness in your heart, breasts, and lungs—to give you an opportunity to catch your breath and rediscover the harmony once more.

Chapter Seven

Fifth Chakra: "Baby Don't Go"

(The Health of Your Neck, Thyroid, and Mouth)

Your fifth chakra—which covers the region of your body around your shoulders, neck, thyroid, and mouth—is the intuitive advisor that lets you know how your communication skills are doing. The key to having health in this area is understanding that "communication skills" don't just mean talking. After all, two people talking *at* each other aren't really having a conversation. Communication is a two-way street that requires both speaking (getting information out) *and* listening and following along (allowing someone else's information to come into your psyche and change your actions).

One of the first times we learn how to have our say is during that dreaded developmental stage called "the terrible twos." Because at that age our communication skills are (pardon the pun) still in diapers, we tend to display more assertiveness than compliance. Ask any two-year-old to stop doing something ("Don't go over there, honey—it's dangerous. Will you please come over here?"), and how does she respond? With a loud, solid *"No!"* Even at that tender age, most of us discover that it's much easier for us to be assertive and communicate our point of view than it is to be compliant and bend to someone else's will, momentarily shutting our mouths and allowing other people to speak.

If you've ever suggested to a toddler, "Eat your cereal," "Let's get dressed," or even "Time for your nap," then you've probably experienced the quintessential example of the difference between talking and communicating. No matter what you say, even if an 18-wheeler is approaching and you're screaming out a warning for the child to stop running toward the road, she's likely to scream back at you, *"No! No! No!"* It's not an exchange of ideas; it's a struggle of *wills*. And it can drive you crazy.

With luck, we eventually learn the skill of communicating. This is easier for some of us than it is for others. For example, I have a public-speaking phobia, so I was very nervous about appearing at my first engagement lecturing on medical intuition. This was at a conference in Hilton Head, South Carolina, and I was told that it would be a small gathering of only about 40 people. When I got there, however, I saw almost 250 people seated in a room that seemed the size of a football field! Even though my friends Chris Northrup, Diane Grover, and Caroline Myss were in the front row for support, I was terrified.

Someone clipped a microphone to my silk blouse, and as the saying goes, I let it rip. The expressions on the faces in the audience were diverse. Some people laughed until they looked like they were going to pass out, while others looked at me as if I were something that landed from another planet. As I gave my talk—a mixture of slides and information outlining how intuition is a natural product of our brains and bodies—it wasn't *my* fault that my nervousness almost caused me to knock the podium off the stage twice. Or that the weight of the microphone kept dragging the opening of my blouse lower and lower, almost exposing me . . . much to the horror of the folks in the front row!

Regardless, I ended my first public talk on intuition more or less intact and no worse for wear. Or so I thought. Then I got my audience-feedback scores. My grades were, let us say, quite mixed. Some people said that I was a very nervous speaker and talked too fast, but they also thought that I was a diamond in the rough, and they enjoyed the class. It seemed that most people either absolutely loved me or hated me. Of course, it was the hate comments that sank into my fifth chakra. One person called me "an audiovisual nightmare with a speech impediment." Yes, a speech impediment! (Obviously, this person had never before heard a Rhode Island accent!) Needless to say, I was upset.

The next year, for some odd reason, I was asked back to speak at the same conference. Maybe they wanted me for comic relief—I have no idea—but the masochist in me accepted the invitation. The week before the conference, I came down with a fifth-chakra bronchial virus. Are we surprised? And of course, by the time I boarded the plane to fly down to South Carolina, I began to get a hacking cough and started to lose my voice. But if it was the last breath I took, by God, I was going to learn to talk to any kind of audience member, no matter how hostile. As if my fifth-chakra intuitive advisor was trying to signal that this might not be the wisest tactic, by the time I arrived at the venue, the only way I could speak without hacking was with a cough drop in my mouth.

Was my presentation any better? Well, I had the organizers take the podium away so it couldn't fall off the stage. The virus slowed down my hyperactive nervousness a bit. And I wore a higher-necked blouse so there would be no risk that the microphone would expose me. And guess what? The audience members still had the same mixture of odd expressions on their faces. Some people were laughing like they were going to lose it. And others looked offended no matter how hard I tried to win them over.

Months later, I got my audience feedback. And again, I got the same comments—I was a nervous speaker; I talked too fast; I was a diamond in the rough; I gave brilliant information, and people wanted to hear more from me. And then I came to this stinging comment: "It was rude that Dr. Schulz ate candy, gum, and mints throughout her entire formal presentation. If she had to eat during her talk, she should share her reasons for this with the audience." (Candy, gum, and mints? They were *cough drops,* for God's sake!)

Only then did I realize the wisdom behind my fifth-chakra intuitive advisor in the form of bronchitis. It had been trying to warn me not to try to communicate perfectly with everyone, not to attempt to get through to every type of audience member, no matter what. The simple truth is that regardless of how hard you try, you simply can't get *everyone* to understand your message.

●–●–●

As this story demonstrates, your fifth-chakra intuitive advisor will always try to get your attention one way or another, reporting on how well you're balancing having your say with allowing others to have theirs. It communicates with you through symptoms of illness such as bronchitis, strep throat, losing your voice or becoming hoarse, Graves' disease (hyperthyroidism), Hashimoto's thyroiditis (hypothyroidism), cervical disk disease, chronic arthritic neck pain, recurring tension headaches, temporomandibular joint (TMJ) pain, and various problems with your teeth or mouth. Improving your capacity for communication involves breaking down the walls that prevent people from understanding you, along with learning how to open up doorways of understanding when it comes to listening to others' points of view.

To attain optimal health in your fifth chakra, you must follow the fifth rule for intuitive health—*Sometimes you've got to be cruel to be kind* (balancing assertive and compliant communication styles). This involves developing an ability to know when it's appropriate to be bold and stick to your position and when it's better to be submissive and yield to another's will.

Most people who have fifth-chakra health problems tend to fall somewhere in between four extreme communication-style categories: the *Brick Wall*—those who firmly assert their points of view but don't very readily hear anyone else's; the *Screen Door*—those who are so good at listening that they tend to be overly compliant; the *Swinging Door*—those who know when to flexibly and expertly assert their points of view and when to diplomatically accede to others; and finally, the *Locked Door*—those who are either inappropriately silent and unreachable or who block out everyone else's ability to get in touch with them.

The Brick Wall

The first type of fifth-chakra extreme is the Brick Wall, those who talk more than they listen. I immediately realized that 17-year-old Quincy was a Brick Wall when his mother described him over the phone. Quincy had always been a very willful child. He had such a hard time settling down, following instructions, and getting his homework done that a doctor had diagnosed him with attention deficit disorder with hyperactive features (ADHD).

When Quincy's grades started going downhill in high school and his mother brought him into a psychologist's office, the therapist said that the boy was having a hard time acknowledging the teacher's authority and accepting the demands of his principal. Quincy was often late to class, refused to do his homework, and had been given several detentions for insubordinate behavior because he constantly talked back to his coaches and teachers. The therapist suggested that he learn anger-management techniques and take classes on how to improve his social skills. Around the same time, the teenager started to miss more and more school because of chronic neck pain that caused intense headaches.

Quincy, like a true Brick Wall, had definitely mastered *talking* (the first phase of communication), but he hadn't yet seen the benefits of *listening* (the second phase). Both phases are required for a true communion of heart and mind between two people. While Brick Walls are maximally assertive, they have a near-total inability to know how to comply with another's requests, so they often end up being isolated. Quincy's fifth-chakra intuitive advisor was letting him know through his neck-muscle tension and the resulting headaches that he needed to reevaluate his communication style.

If you, like Quincy, communicate like a Brick Wall, you're very good at standing up for your convictions. Initially, people think that you're a born leader with a very confident attitude, able to take charge when necessary. However, over time they realize that your one-way communication is truly dysfunctional, because such bulldozer approaches tend to backfire. You push your agenda with such force (especially when you're angry or frightened) that there's simply no room for others' responses or feedback, leaving everybody else tongue-tied. Even if your intention isn't to have such a one-sided conversation, your extremely brusque, overly confident tone makes you appear as if you don't care about how other people feel or what they think.

What I've learned from people like Quincy is that there are two types of Brick Walls, each with very different motivating forces:

— The first, whose imbalance stems from having ADHD, actually has a heartfelt desire to listen underneath that Madonna-esque confidence. When these men and women get called on the carpet for their interruptions, they feel awful and experience tremendous shame and remorse because they truly *want* to communicate and hear what others have to say. They desire relationships; it's just that they don't know how to withhold the impulse to say whatever pops into their heads, thus constantly interrupting and irritating the people in their lives.

— The other, more classic type of Brick Wall wants an audience, not a relationship. These folks are absolutely certain that their points of view are more valid than everyone else's. They don't have the patience, time, or interest to stop and think that it might be good to hear another opinion. And underneath all their posturing and bravado, they're actually terribly afraid—of change. They fear that if they really listened to others' opinions and then changed their minds, they'd lose their sense of control. This absolutely terrifies them.

Both types of Brick Walls, over time, end up feeling pretty lonely.

What signs indicate that you may be one of these individuals? In kindergarten, you were very energetic and a leader on the playground, but you rarely followed the teacher's instructions well in class. You always wanted to be the team captain, but you never enjoyed being a team *member*. You don't like anyone interrupting you, correcting you, or telling you what to do. You think that people talk and think too slowly. Others accuse you of talking *over* them all the time. In fact, you tend to finish their sentences so that you can go on with what you were about to say. You've had many failed relationships throughout your life because your partners never felt that they could get through to you or that what they had to say ever really registered with you.

You find cell-phone conversations difficult, because when the person on the other end is talking and the speaker on your end is temporarily disengaged, it's very irritating. If you looked at your phone records, you'd see far more outgoing calls than incoming ones. When you get excited about what you're saying, you may forget to ask what the other person thinks. You've become so wound up that you've interrupted teachers, bosses, or even police officers in midsentence and gotten yourself into trouble because you aggravated them. You're sure that if only you could say what you have to say in the right way, other people would agree with you.

If this describes you, you might as well go ahead and finish *my* sentence, because you probably can't help yourself anyway . . . you're a Brick Wall. Your fifth-chakra organs are eventually going to start talking to you so loudly that you won't be *able* to talk over them—at least not very effectively. The first such alarm you're likely to experience will be chronic neck pain and tension headaches. (And you have my sympathies, because I know from personal experience how disabling neck pain can be. I've blown so many disks in that region, had so many surgeries, and worn so many neck braces that I affectionately call my Maine home "Braceland.") These fifth-chakra signals are all indications that you need to develop a more balanced power structure within your communication style, or you'll be headed for an even *bigger* pain in the neck.

All of us have a Brick Wall hidden somewhere inside of us. Like Quincy, most of us have at times felt the urge to blurt out what's on our minds or to maximally stick to our guns during a heated discussion because we're so worked up for one reason or another. I was once 30 minutes late for a class and racing down a highway to reach the other side of Boston, only to get stopped by some poor, unfortunate police officer. When he took an inordinate amount of time to write up the speeding ticket, the time pressure, superimposed on enormous fatigue, frustration, and lifelong ADHD, became too much for me. "Can you *please* hurry up?" I snapped. "I'm in a terrific rush! After all, I wouldn't have been speeding if I wasn't pressed for time."

No rational person who was in the vulnerable position I was in, having just broken the law and all, would say something like that to a police officer. The cop looked at me with a mixture of shock, dismay, and sympathy and responded, "Lady, you've got to calm down!"

All of us need to have a voice, to learn to have our say at the right time and with the right intensity. However, when our communication skills become stronger in talking (or even screaming) than they are in listening, we aren't having relationships; we're having audiences—and we'll know that it's time to reexamine how well we're balancing the use of both these elements of communication.

Intuitive Advice for the Brick Wall

Do you suffer from chronic health problems in your neck, thyroid, and mouth; and do you tend to have Brick Wall communication-style issues? If so, you can learn to use mind-body medicine and medical intuition to break down those barriers to communication that you've erected and restore your fifth-chakra health. Your mind-body makeover begins by addressing your physical body. You could have any fifth-chakra health problem with Brick Wall tendencies. But if, like Quincy, yours happens to be tension headaches and musculoskeletal neck strain (and your doctor has ruled out the more serious problems of disk disease and arthritis), a physical therapist can teach you to relax the muscles in your upper body. If you play sports or lift weights, you might also see a sports-medicine specialist to see if any of your activities may be aggravating your neck.

If you're tempted to pop a pill for your discomfort, stay away from prescription pain relievers. Instead, stick with over-the-counter medications such as Advil, Motrin, or aspirin; and see an acupuncturist once a week for a while. (For other nonpharmacological pain-relief suggestions, see the advice for the Swinging Door, later in this chapter.)

Next, your mind-body makeover moves to your right-brain emotional state. As a Brick Wall, you have a tendency to interrupt in conversations, which may be aggravated by ADHD; if this is indeed the case, you need to learn how to manage your impulsive tendency to say everything that comes to mind. (See the chapter on the sixth chakra for more support.) If you have this problem, you can also try the mirror technique to help you recognize how your overly dominating communication style may be preventing you from having true relationships.

Here's how the technique works: Have a trusty friend, partner, or colleague sit in a chair opposite you while you have a trial conversation about a core issue that has been going on for a while. Set a timer for two minutes, and allow the other person to speak until it goes off. During this period, you're to say nothing—just listen and nod your head. If you're impulsive and have ADHD, you may actually have to clamp your hand to your mouth to prevent it from popping open with whatever ideas drop into your head. This hand-over-the-mouth technique works.

At the end of the two minutes, it's your turn. But before you can talk about what's on your mind, you must first mirror back to your partner what you heard the person say. Begin by stating, "What I'm hearing you say is . . ." and then paraphrase what you were told.

I know what you're thinking: that engaging in what seems like psychobabble may make you feel a little nauseated at first. And it might. But by reflecting back in words what's been said, you'll be correcting the salient feature that's missing in your communication style—that is, the listening component—which is preventing you from partaking in a true meeting of hearts and minds. By learning the rudiments of this simple exercise, you'll find that after a while you'll do it automatically. And the health of your fifth-chakra region will improve.

Here, then, is my seven-part program to rehabilitate the Brick Walls' tendency to dominate discussions and leave little room for others' input:

1. Identify that communication has two parts—both *talking* (your message going out to someone) and *listening* (the other person's message coming into your mind and heart). Although talking may seem like a priority, if there's no listening, then you're not truly communicating. Without the critical second step, you have an audience, not a relationship.

2. Recognize the emotional needs that partnerships fulfill, and see how listening truly helps give you an outside source of information in your life. After all, even if you're absolutely firm in your convictions, hearing other people's points of view is a reality check. There might be facets of the discussion that you weren't aware of or haven't considered.

3. Discern the difference between being confident and being close-minded. If you're confident, and comfortable with your opinions, you'll welcome hearing other people's input. But if you're close-minded, you're *not* confident; you're in fact frightened of what might happen if you heard something that threatened your argument and forced you to consider changing your mind. Understand that walls never last. Eventually, they fall down—unless they're continually reinforced (which in turn only builds up and reinforces your fifth-chakra illness).

4. Restrict your tendency to talk over people or to interrupt them in midsentence. After someone has completed a thought, repeat back to the person what you think he or she said. Although you may feel more in control when you try to dominate, lead, or bolster your opinion, understand that your impenetrable, brick-wall mentality will eventually make your relationships and career crumble to dust.

5. Know that the two-step communication style of both talking and listening, although frightening at first, will open you up to a network of partnerships with people who will support and nurture you.

6. Change the unhealthy thought pattern: *If I'm not right, I'll lose control* . . . to the healthier affirmation: *Inspired, I go after my bliss, but I am also open to the emotional reactions of others.*

7. Follow the fifth rule for intuitive health—*Sometimes you've got to be cruel to be kind*—and learn the benefits of being more compliant and yielding more often to other people's will instead of always being so forceful.

The Screen Door

The second type of fifth-chakra extreme is the Screen Door, those who are more open to other people's points of view than they are to expressing their own, and who listen more than they talk. Ralph, 38, is a good illustration of this. The perfect father and husband, living the good life in a three-bedroom house in the suburbs, Ralph had worked as a partner with his father-in-law, Sam, for more than a decade in a business that he was due to inherit any year now.

But since the economy had taken a downturn, Sam was dragging his feet about retiring.

Actually, Ralph wasn't in a true business partnership, because his father-in-law completely overpowered him. Sam had owned the company for years before the younger man was even in the picture. Because he had more seniority and clout, and because he was the father of Ralph's wife, there were no boundaries. Whatever Sam wanted got by his son-in-law like wind through a screen door, and Ralph completely yielded to his authority. He submitted, bowed his head, and acted like a lowly subordinate complying with the big boss. No matter how bad Ralph thought his father-in-law's idea would be for business, Sam prevailed. Although Sam *said* that the two of them were partners, the company could be more accurately described as a sole proprietorship owned by Sam, with Ralph as the lone employee.

When my client assumed his ever-complacent, lockjaw communication style, his feelings about the business had no voice—no skillful form of expression—so they had nowhere else to go but into his body, finally manifesting in the form of medical-intuitive warning signals. Ralph started getting tired and depressed, experiencing numbness in his hands, gaining weight, and becoming constipated. A routine physical exam revealed that he'd developed hypothyroidism due to Hashimoto's disease.

Although thyroid disorders are fifth-chakra illnesses, because they're also autoimmune conditions, they indicate first-chakra issues as well. As you may remember from the chapter on the first chakra, the health of this region of the body indicates whether you feel safe and secure in your family or some other organization. When Ralph developed a thyroid disorder, his immune system was going into overdrive attack mode to protect him in the area where he felt the most threatened: his fifth chakra (his voice box). His first- and fifth-chakra medical-intuitive advisors were working together to send him the signal that he didn't feel safe speaking his mind in his family or at work and that he needed to be more assertive in these partnerships.

If you, like Ralph, have the Screen Door communication style, you'll take in pretty much anything people throw your direction, the same way a summer rainstorm or even a strong breeze easily blows through a screen door. You'll follow orders rather than give them, listen as opposed to tell someone something, and be compliant more than assertive. To maintain harmony, you'll stand by what other people think and not stand up for your own convictions.

What I've learned from people like Ralph is that even though Screen Doors appear to be receptive during conversations, they hardly ever directly express what they want and how they feel. They use indirect styles of conveying their thoughts: talking with great hesitancy, hinting, or being very tentative; encoding their true feelings in a stammering, vague way of communicating that's designed primarily to avoid potential conflict. Their friends and colleagues use up enormous amounts of energy trying to pry things out of them, a rather maddening experience. Screen Doors tend to attract very dominating people as partners—ones who will talk and make decisions *for* them, generally take control, and possibly even abuse them.

What clues indicate that you may have this style of communicating? At some point in your childhood, you may have had a problem with stuttering, stammering, becoming tongue-tied, some other kind of speech impediment, or extreme shyness and social phobia. In high school, you never would have considered being on the debating team. If you're having a heated discussion—especially with a loved one— the other person does most of the talking, and you do most of the listening. Trying to get a word in edgewise is very hard for you. You've never argued with a cop when you've gotten a ticket. In fact, you've probably never even been pulled over. You've found yourself avoiding blowups and arguments in key relationships by saying a conflict-ending statement such as: "Whatever you say . . . never mind. You're right; I'm wrong."

You have trouble figuring out how to ask for a raise. At a flea market, you'd never try to bargain for a better deal; the very idea of it makes you feel very uncomfortable. When you're thrown together with a bunch of people, you like to sit at the periphery and listen to what everyone else is saying, and then when they're finished, you jump in and say a few choice words.

Sound familiar? Then you may have the Screen Door style of communication. The first sign from your fifth chakra that you're being overly compliant is that you'll start assuming a submissive posture during tense conversations—you'll bow your head, turn away, or slump. (The same body language happens in the animal kingdom when two creatures interact and one is clearly dominant and the other submissive.) Assuming this stance is a way of indirectly telling the other person, "I give in and give up. Whatever you say goes. Uncle!"

(By the way, in women who are Screen Doors, the fluctuating hormonal changes of menopause will often prevent them from censoring their emotions. As a result, long-buried desires, needs, opinions, and attitudes that they swallowed to keep the peace may, to their absolute horror, suddenly start spilling out of their mouths.)

If you've spent your whole life ducking and hiding from one conflict after another, listening to others more than speaking your mind, being ever receptive and never expressive, your fifth-chakra intuitive advisor is soon going to point this out through symptoms in your shoulders, neck, thyroid, and mouth.

If we examine Ralph's story, we'll realize that each of us has a Screen Door within us, a part of us that has at times felt that it was much easier to acquiesce to the desires of others and yield to *their* needs because it would keep things harmonious. We may think that diplomacy means listening and agreeing to another person's requests in order to maintain the peace. But nothing could be further from the truth. Although such no-questions-asked compliance initially avoids conflicts, if we repeat that pattern over time, we set the tone of the relationship. We'll also be allowing (or maybe even training) people to have power over us, possibly to an abusive degree.

On the one hand, we don't want to be demanding, oppositional, or provocative. But on the other, constantly yielding to the points of view of those around us sends the message that we're willing to pretty much go along with whatever they say. Is this really what we want to communicate? Sometimes we need to stand up, take a chance, risk disappointing someone, and say no. The relationship will survive; and if it doesn't, it's not a relationship—it's a fiefdom, and we need to move on.

Intuitive Advice for the Screen Door

Do you suffer from chronic health problems in your neck, thyroid, and mouth; and do you tend to have some aspects of the Screen Door communication style? If so, medical intuition and mind-body medicine can help you learn how to put up boundaries and get the words out of your mouth in order to be more assertive . . . and, well, mouthier in general so that people won't walk all over you. Your mind-body makeover begins by addressing your physical problems. You could have any fifth-chakra health issue with Screen Door tendencies. But if, like Ralph, you happen to suffer from a hypothyroid disorder, your doctor will prescribe a thyroid-replacement drug like Synthroid (which replaces T_4) and Cytomel (which has T_3). Some physicians go strictly by the laboratory definition of hypothyroidism, using the thyroid-stimulating hormone (TSH) level to make a diagnosis. Others prescribe medication if you fall within a range of what could be seen as a borderline case.

On the other hand, if you're *hyper*thyroid and so have too much thyroid hormone, your doctor may prescribe propylthiouracil (PTU) or knock out your thyroid gland entirely using radioactive ablation. After such treatment, you'll be hypothyroid, so you'd need replacement hormones for the rest of your life.

Although both of these Western-medicine treatments effectively address the most pressing physical problem—the fifth-chakra thyroid disorder—neither addresses the underlying issue associated with these conditions. Thyroid disease is a first-chakra autoimmune problem that occurs when your immune system attacks your thyroid gland, making it either under- or overactive. For that reason, I recommend also seeing an acupuncturist and Chinese herbalist who can treat you for immune-system disorders and any related chronic inflammation. If you don't address this autoimmune component, your tendency to make antibodies against organs in your body can progress to other, related illnesses, including rheumatoid arthritis, colitis, eczema, psoriasis, asthma, and so on. The list is endless.

Your mind-body makeover next addresses the emotional intuitive mind. If, as a Screen Door, you're so shy or anxious that you almost always say yes to a request (because you're so intuitively keyed in to the other person's imagined anger or disappointment that saying no would make you feel worse), you probably see yourself as perennially the low man or woman on the totem pole. Some of your friends might argue that you just need to "grow a set" (of balls) and fight back, being more forceful or demanding . . . or even delivering an ultimatum, if necessary. But solving a fifth-chakra conflict with aggression fueled by the second chakra (where sex hormones like testosterone originate) is the wrong emotional strategy here. Learning diplomatic communication skills (think Madeleine Albright, Henry Kissinger, or Jimmy Carter) is a better choice for a fifth-chakra problem than dropping an atomic bomb.

To maintain both your sanity *and* your relationship when you find yourself in a power struggle, you must balance compliance with assertiveness by using what I call the Four Rights of communication: saying the *right* words to the *right* person at the *right* time with the *right* amount of intensity. This form of diplomacy can help anyone (with any of the personality types) learn when to talk, when to shut up, when to push a personal agenda, and when to follow someone else's lead after considering a variety of critical factors.

Begin by choosing your level of assertiveness or compliance (your emotional tone) using the seven different chakras as a guide:

— **First chakra** (family or organization): Ask yourself, *Am I in the right place in this family or organization to be telling this person what to do or say?* In other words, does the other person have more authority? If so, then back down and be more compliant. Or you might ask, *Am I in a position to be taking orders from this person about what I should do or say?* If *your* place is the one of authority, then think about being more assertive.

— **Second chakra** (relationship): Ask yourself, *Is this relationship at the right stage for me to be asking this person for this?* If so, then be forward in making your request. Or you may ask yourself, *Is our relationship at the right stage for my partner to be asking me to do this?* If it isn't, then be more assertive and say no.

— **Third chakra** (self-esteem and responsibility): Ask yourself, *Am I going along with this person's request because I feel incompetent or helpless?* If you are, then increase your assertiveness and tell the other person what you want. On the other hand, you might wonder, *Am I asking this person to do this because I think that I always know the best way of doing things, and everyone should defer to me?* If that's how you feel, then you need to try to be more compliant and follow *other* people's leads at times.

— **Fourth chakra** (ability for emotional partnership): Ask yourself, *Is this partnership truly mutual and on the same level?* If not, then be more assertive. Or ask, *Has this partnership become estranged or somehow uncomfortable?* If the answer is yes, then be more compliant and listen to what's going on with the other person.

— **Fifth chakra** (communication): Ask yourself, *Am I interested in winning this conflict, no-holds-barred, and I don't care if I ever talk to this person again?* If so, then take your gloves off and increase your assertiveness. Or reflect on the question: *Am I willing to concede a disagreement to preserve a long-term relationship?* If that's indeed the truth of the situation, then become more flexible, lean back, take a few breaths, and prepare to give in on some points.

— **Sixth chakra** (information and intelligence): Ask yourself, *Do I have all the facts to deal with this matter?* If so, increase your assertiveness. Or inquire of yourself, *Do I have absolutely no idea what I'm talking about, but I just want to argue?* If so, then become more compliant.

— **Seventh chakra** (spirituality): Ask yourself, *How does it feel inside? What is the divine telling me to do? What is my gut telling me to do?* Then act accordingly.

After you've run through all seven of these factors in considering how assertive or compliant you're going to be, then you must choose which words you'll use. Once again, turn to the cue card of the seven chakras to guide you. Here's how Ralph might choose to approach his father-in-law using this model:

— **First chakra** (address the importance of the family or organization): "Sam, you're an important part of my life and family. You're my father-in-law and the grandfather to my children. You've built this wonderful business. I have so much love and respect for you."

— **Second chakra** (address your relationship and financial concerns): "But I'm worried about money, my job, and my future. I love my wife and family, and I want to do well for them. But I'm in my 40s now, and I'm not where I wanted to be at this point."

— **Third chakra** (demonstrate that you believe in yourself and are indeed a responsible person): "I've been working hard and feel confident about my contribution to this company. With my business degree, all the experience I've had so far, and everything that I've learned from *your* years of experience, I'm prepared to take over the way we've talked about. To that end, I want us to create a business plan for when you retire and I gain control, which we had originally discussed would happen two years ago."

— **Fourth chakra** (demonstrate your emotional affinity for the other person by validating his or her point of view): "I understand that it must be hard for you to hand over the reins of a business that you've so brilliantly crafted over the years."

— **Fifth chakra** (show that you're prepared to listen, the second step in communicating): "I know that you have some thoughts on this subject. I really want to hear them."

— **Sixth chakra** (address your desire for flexible negotiation): "Thanks for the opportunity to discuss this issue, because I've been wanting to share what I've been thinking about this lately. I'm sure we can come up with some compromise—you know I'm always willing to negotiate. I just want us to work together to start creating a business plan for when we'll be transferring your leadership to me."

— **Seventh chakra** (affirm your spirituality): *I am saying a silent prayer and maintaining an attitude of gratitude that I am now able to* *experience a true meeting of minds. I am ready to listen to Sam's response and, with an open heart and mind, try to comprehend what he says.*

Once you've used this guide to learn the Four Rights of communication—and you know how to maintain the delicate balance between assertiveness and compliance, between talking and listening—you'll be much less nervous about handling conflict and confrontation. And the health of your fifth chakra will show it.

The following is my seven-part program to rehabilitate your tendency as a Screen Door to be a pushover and not vocalize your own ideas:

1. Identify how you choose to avoid directly explaining what you want to someone because you fear a potential angry response.

2. Recognize that you prefer to hint at or indirectly express what you think because you believe that you don't command enough power, status, or respect to have a say and make it matter.

3. Discern that if you don't have relationships in which true communication occurs, you're not really *having* relationships. You're putting the people in your life on a stage, and *you're* merely their audience because you never get a chance to speak your mind. Avoid such polarizing relationships where you listen and others talk exclusively.

4. Restrict your tendency to agree and go along with people. Every single day, for the sake of developing your capacity to open your mouth and make a clear choice, resolve to say no in some situation. Don't worry—people won't think you're being mean (but they may be concerned because you won't be acting like your usual, overly meek self). You can start out small. For example, if the waiter at a restaurant asks, "Will French fries be okay?" choose this to be your assertiveness exercise and answer, "No, French fries are *not* okay. Can you please tell me what else you have?" Even if you feel like you're putting people out or wasting their time, you're exercising your brain/body fifth-chakra assertiveness pathways. Also, follow the two-part, seven-chakra diplomacy exercise given on the previous page.

5. Know that what you think of as being nice to others (being overly compliant) is actually being cruel to *yourself.* By disavowing your rightful voice and not communicating with the appropriate balance of assertiveness and compliance, you're disrespecting yourself and allowing other people to disrespect you along the way.

6. Change the negative thought pattern: *I can be happy if I let other people have their say; it's kind of me to allow their voices to be heard . . .* to the healthier affirmation: *I express my feelings with the proper amount of directness and assertiveness.*

7. Follow the fifth rule for intuitive health—*Sometimes you've got to be cruel to be kind*—and develop a sense of when to be more assertive. It may feel cruel, but it's not. It's being more assertive, sticking to your position, instead of always being compliant, yielding to someone else's will.

The Swinging Door

The next type of fifth-chakra extreme is the Swinging Door, those communication experts and diplomatic geniuses who know how to assert their own point of view and listen skillfully to others'. My client Raelynn, 52, was one of those extraordinary individuals. She was the go-to person for help solving a problem in the family. This woman would somehow be able to assemble everyone around a table—whether they liked it or not—and with a magician-like sleight of hand, get them talking, listening, and agreeing.

Raelynn raised her children as a single parent, and when they reached high school, she decided to go to law school. Afterward, she started working for a legal firm specializing in immigration. Raelynn had the most upbeat attitude, always letting her kids and clients know that if they wanted anything enough, and if they stayed positive and put in the work, their willpower could make it happen.

Unfortunately, willpower must have skipped a generation, because Raelynn's children developed numerous addiction problems. Her son was arrested for selling drugs and was given a two-year prison sentence, while her daughter was caught shoplifting four times and was finally placed in a juvenile detention center. Around this time, Raelynn started experiencing pain in her shoulders, neck, and head, which she ignored. Finally, she went to her primary-care doctor, who diagnosed her with degenerative disk disease in several neck vertebrae. Her physician then suggested she go on bed rest for at least a week and apply ice until the inflammation in her neck went down, but Raelynn responded, "Are you kidding? I'm not doing *that*. I have to take care of my clients and kids. This is nothing! I'll make this neck problem go away, but I'm not going to do it lying down!"

If you, like Raelynn, are a Swinging Door, you're an "I will make it happen" kind of person. Your flexible, successful communication style makes you a powerful diplomat and a force to be reckoned with. Like a swinging door, you deftly move in and out of negotiations— assertive when necessary and compliant when critical. You know exactly how to express yourself and push for what you want, but you also have an uncanny capacity to really listen and be receptive to the other person's message, factoring that information into the final analysis. But the way you assert yourself to get through life's problems is likely to take its toll on your body over time, through fifth-chakra illnesses.

What I've learned from people like Raelynn is that sooner or later, Swinging Doors forget who is really in charge. There comes a time when no matter how skilled they are, a higher design is put into motion that wreaks havoc with their diplomacy and genius communication style. Frustrated, they simply negotiate even harder, choose even better words, and listen even more . . . but still, the conflict isn't resolved. They simply can't understand why they're unable to make it go away, despite their Herculean will to do so.

These individuals are really good at saying to God or the heavens, "Hey, listen! I really need you to step in." And then they actually toss in the demand, such as, "Make these people sign my peace accord." They don't realize that their mantra has become "*My* will be done," not "*Thy* will be done." They're being overly assertive, even with the powers of the universe.

Swinging Doors may have mastered the two-way communication style on Earth, with balanced expression and receptivity, assertiveness and compliance; but when it comes to other realms, they're pushing it. Prayer is, after all, a form of communication. Therefore, it also involves both talking and listening, appealing to a higher power and contemplation.

If God or the universe (or whatever we believe in) is the higher power, and we are, let's say, not *nearly* as powerful, then all of us—Swinging Doors included—need to own up to the fact that the will of the heavens must come before our own. Ultimately, we must all surrender control to our higher power and realize that what happens next is in the universe's hands, not exclusively in ours.

What signs indicate that you might be a Swinging Door? Well, you could easily see yourself working at the United Nations, striking a peace accord or helping settle decades-old conflicts between many countries or clans who aren't getting along. You've always been the family mediator, and your friends usually turn to you to settle their arguments. Even in the most raucous, sticky, one-sided conflicts, you can make both parties feel heard and understood. You have a lifelong history of adversity, and against all odds, you've used your will to plunge yourself through the trauma. You've been able to manifest pretty much everything you ever wanted by setting your mind to it. You take on lost causes, such as people who have no voice or have been abused or disenfranchised. You advocate for these individuals, serving as their champions so that they, too, can manifest success. Your heartfelt belief is that if we could all just sit down together and talk and listen to one another, we'd end war and have world peace.

If this sounds like you, then you have the ever-flexible, genius-level communication style of the Swinging Door. However, such diplomatic skills can only bring you so far in life. Your negotiations won't always result in the harmony you envision. And if you continue to push to create an outcome, your fifth-chakra intuitive advisor will soon let you know—through symptoms of illness in your neck, thyroid, and mouth—that you're misusing your voice to impose your will on someone.

The first alarm that your fifth chakra will send is an awareness that your conversations are starting to sound like broken records. You'll keep going around and around, discussing the same points over and over again. However, no matter how many times you circle the issue, attempting different tactics and approaches, a consensus is never reached, and the negotiations lead to nothing except frustration . . . and fifth-chakra health problems.

All of us, however, have a degree of the Swinging Door in us. Like Raelynn, we've all sometimes employed every possible diplomatic or social-savvy device at our disposal to make something happen. Each of us has on occasion used our will to try to force an outcome, whether it's getting someone to fall in love with us, succeeding at a job, or having something turn out for our kids. But even after all the time, money, and sweat we've poured into a project; all the support we've garnered; and all the prayers we've said and intentions we've set, we may come to the realization that we simply aren't able to make that something happen. We can't force the universe. We truly don't create alone in the world. Rather, we do so in partnership with some higher power; and once in a while, for reasons we can't yet see, the idea of what we hoped to create is a "stillbirth" and our goal doesn't survive beyond the dream stage.

Intuitive Advice for the Swinging Door

Do you suffer from chronic health problems in your neck, thyroid, and mouth; and do you tend to have Swinging Door communication-style issues? If so, you can use mind-body medicine and medical intuition to learn to communicate your ideas without having to will them into place with your bobbing-and-weaving diplomatic style. Your mind-body makeover begins with attending to your physical health concerns. You could have any problem of the fifth chakra with Swinging Door tendencies. But if, like Raelynn, yours happens to be osteoarthritis in your neck and degenerative cervical-disk disease, a variety of approaches can address this. Surgery should be the last option.

First, go to a very conservative but reputable orthopedic surgeon or neurosurgeon to evaluate your serious nerve or disk compression. After giving you a neurological exam and possibly an MRI, most physicians will start by suggesting you apply ice and take anti-inflammatory aspirin, Advil, or Tylenol. For some cases, they'll recommend traction to help pull apart a compression on the disk, which can feel wonderful.

For other cases, they may advise removing whole disks or parts of them, fusing them, or possibly an artificial disk replacement when it becomes available in the U.S. Your surgeon could address your arthritis by cleaning out the bony fragments, called *osteophytes,* that may be causing you pain, although this might be a temporary solution because the osteophytes can return if you do nothing to prevent the local inflammation in your neck.

In the meantime, try acupuncture for pain relief. Sleeping with a Tempur-Pedic pillow or neck brace can help support your neck if it's hard for you to sleep flat. If at all possible, try not to use narcotic pain meds like oxycodone, Percocet, Flexeril, or any of their cousins. These are highly addictive; and they tend to cause problems with attention, memory, and constipation, making it almost impossible for you to work, let alone make the emotional changes necessary to help you heal your condition.

I also recommend that you ask your physician about taking what I call the *arthritis nutritional-supplement cocktail,* which is vitamin C (3,000 mg a day), grape-seed extract (360 mg a day), and glucosamine sulfate (200 mg a day). To that, add SAMe (800–1,200 mg a day, on an empty stomach) with a dusting of a prescription antidepressant, such as Wellbutrin (150 mg) or Prozac (10–20 mg). The serotonin from the SAMe and antidepressants tends to elevate your pain threshold, which can help immensely with neck- and headaches.

If the discomfort gets worse over time, visit your local teaching hospital's pain clinic, especially if it uses a variety of nonnarcotic modalities for pain control. Occasional steroid injections can ease the suffering caused by nerve inflammation. (The first time I had an injection in the patch of arthritis I have in my neck, I was amazed to be able to feel my hands again. I cried with joy and asked the doctor if he would marry me.)

Other ways to deal with chronic pain involve pumping up your opiates on a daily basis—without narcotics. Aerobic exercise for at least 20 to 30 minutes a day is critical for pain control, so try using an elliptical trainer or an exercise bike. Wearing Nike Shox or Asics GEL athletic shoes can also absorb the shock in a way that your own arthritic disks can't. Other methods to release natural opiates include working at least five days a week on something rewarding that you absolutely love, which uses all of your gifts, talents, and skills and also voices your identity. Finally, practicing the ancient disciplines of tai chi and Qigong will help you make this troubled part of your body more physically and energetically fluid.

Next, the mind-body makeover moves to the emotions. If the Swinging Door is your pattern, although your determination can be a plus when it comes to overcoming life's adversity, your willpower can turn into willfulness when you aren't seeing a perspective beyond your own. You need to learn to set aside your frustration and anger when you can't get your point across. Meditation, especially mindfulness exercises (such as the one described in the chapter on the second chakra), will go a long way toward helping you achieve that.

The following is my seven-part program to help rehabilitate the Swinging Doors' tendency to push their own will over that of heaven:

1. **Identify** the great joy you get when you can skillfully bring about consensus by communication. Admit that you feel powerful when you're able to introduce harmony and a true sense of compassion and communion into a situation that was previously fraught with antagonism.

2. **Recognize** those times when you've been unable to effect some deeply desired core change, no matter what stellar diplomatic tactics you employed. Realize that the situation left you feeling frustrated and powerless.

3. **Discern** that when your best efforts at diplomacy fail, it's possible that from a higher spiritual perspective, the currently unsolvable conflict may indeed exist for some reason that you might not humanly be able to consider.

4. **Restrict** your need to willfully push your earthbound point of view without first being receptive to a higher power's more spiritual perspective on the conflict.

5. **Know** that by balancing your capacity to excel at communicating on Earth with a newfound willingness to be open to the perspective

of a higher power, you'll truly be able to experience universal harmony and consensus.

6. Change the unhealthy thought pattern: *If I could only say it the right way, they would agree with me* . . . to the healthier affirmation: *There are multiple answers to every problem or block in communication. My role is only one part of the total solution to the conflict.*

7. Follow the fifth rule for intuitive health—*Sometimes you've got to be cruel to be kind*—and learn when it's appropriate to put aside boldly asserting your will and choose instead to serve that of the heavens or some higher power.

The Locked Door

The final type of fifth-chakra extreme is the Locked Door, those who have globally broken communication styles. My client Sierra fit the bill. A deeply spiritual person who had worked as an intuitive healer for years, this 61-year-old woman was easily the most interesting person in town. She lived alone, locked away with her menagerie of animals, including goats, cats, dogs, and llamas. The kids in the neighborhood were scared of her because they'd see her walking around talking to herself. Most people thought she was a little "touched."

When Sierra was 19, she'd been kicked out of a religious order for having a nervous condition, so she continued with her spiritual and monastic studies at home. She spent hours shut away in prayer every day and joined the local Catholic Charismatic Prayer Meeting.

Sierra made up for the time she didn't spend speaking to people on Earth by communicating with the other, more spiritual realms. Even if you were to manage to engage her in a conversation, probably about the healing properties of an herb or some metaphysical concept, you'd notice that she was much better at talking to God than humans. Sierra would ramble on and on—essentially preaching—not letting you get a word in edgewise. Most people at the prayer meeting began to say that this woman was arrogant and pompous: who did she think she was, anyway—the pope? Others thought that when her heart and mind became filled with the spirit, she just couldn't shut her mouth.

One day at the prayer meeting, people noticed that my client was sitting by the sidelines, uncharacteristically not saying much. Her jaw appeared swollen. Afterward, a friend went up to her to see what was wrong. Sierra told her that she'd been ignoring her sore jaw for many months. When the church members forced her to go to the dentist, my client found out that due to dental neglect, she'd developed eight cavities and four infected teeth. The infection had spread to the bone in her jaw, causing a condition called osteomyelitis.

If you, like Sierra, employ the Locked Door style of communication, chances are that you've spent much of your life separate from others because of a need for emotional solitude or spiritual communion. Due to years, perhaps decades, of minimizing input from people on Earth, you may have increased your capacity to get in touch with the spirit world or the divine; however, you don't have that same capacity to communicate skillfully with those around you. You're more focused on God and a higher power's plan ("Thy will be done") than on the concerns of mere mortals.

You're also more willing to sit, contemplate, and pray, waiting for the will of God to make everything happen, than to ask for what you want or need or to inquire about what others *around* you want or need. (In fact, you're mortified by the thought of discussing personal emotions openly because you don't want to invest energy wallowing in some "human" feeling.) For you, it's all about communication with the divine, not with earthly beings. In those rare circumstances when you do converse with people, you suffer from what I call "diarrhea of the mouth," talking nonstop, not allowing anyone else to express any other thoughts. These fifth-chakra challenges are likely to be reflected in a variety of physical problems that involve the mouth, including tooth, gum, jaw, and neck problems.

In addition, because you withdraw from others, you have a "people deficiency" in your life. While you might not think that this is such a bad thing at first, you need to know that when you're isolated from others and don't get their support (as you read in Chapter 3), your first-chakra immune system can end up having an increased risk of illness.

What I've learned from people like Sierra is that Locked Doors have some pride in their uniquely spiritual nature, but inside, part of them aches to be better understood by their friends and family. However, when they try to impart to others the same passion and knowledge that *they* find so fascinating, hoping those they know will be as inspired as they have been, all they get is a blank stare because people find their delivery so numbing. This inability to communicate their ideas in the helpful way they intend frustrates them and eventually leaves them in despair. They often feel lonely, lost between the two worlds of heaven and Earth.

What clues indicate that you may have a Locked Door style of communication? Well, people say that you're shy—and while that's true, when you open your mouth, you've been known to knock people over with the flood of information that ensues. In your house, there's a very high density of crosses and angel images, if you're Christian; or a plethora of pyramids and crystals, if you're a New Ager. Feel free to substitute the spiritual paraphernalia of your choice, but let's face it . . . there aren't a lot of empty beer cans in your kitchen, no one would find piles of romance novels in your bedroom, and there isn't a stack of *People* magazines (let alone issues of the *National Enquirer*) in your bathroom.

You can talk to God. In fact, you pray, chant, or meditate daily. You have two-way communication with all of your pets (including the goldfish) and your plants. Your response to the announcement of scientific studies showing that animals do indeed experience emotion was *Duh*—you knew that all along. You can't visit zoos because they make you depressed, even though you know that these preserves do a lot for worldwide conservation. You can sense the sacred in everything on Earth and can readily commune with nature in a very literal sense. But when you talk to people, you don't understand why they often give you odd looks.

If these scenarios match your experience, then you may be a Locked Door. The first alarm that sounds to warn you that your spiritual-centric, Earth-deficient communication style is becoming unhealthy is that you'll find yourself, when around people and in specific situations, more and more at a loss for words. During spiritual enlightenment and ecstatic states (and also during seizures, I might add—see the chapter on the sixth chakra), people lose the ability to speak. Neurologists might call this "speech arrest."

If this begins to happen to you, consider what you're doing with great caution. Do you really want to get so ungrounded that you become untethered, losing touch with planet Earth? Unless your heart is no longer beating and you've ceased breathing, you might want to keep your fifth-chakra communication pipeline to Earth open. It *is* possible to get too far out there spiritually, losing communication with the mother ship.

If we look closely at Sierra's story, we'll discover that we each have a bit of the Locked Door communication style within us. This is the part of us that just retreats and goes on emotional lockdown whenever we've exhausted every diplomatic tactic we know of and communication channels *still* break down. During these times, it *may* be necessary to temporarily remove ourselves from the situation and get a fresh perspective on what's needed. But then, after introspection and contemplation, we must revisit the conversation. However, we need to resist the tendency to retreat permanently. By patiently allowing time and distance to heal the situation, we'll be given the opportunity to hear guidance on how to approach the discussion from a different, more productive point of view.

Intuitive Advice for the Locked Door

Do you suffer from chronic health problems in your neck, thyroid, and mouth; and do you tend to have some aspects of the Locked Door communication style? If so, medical intuition and mind-body medicine can help you *un*lock the doors to communicating with fellow members of humankind on Earth, and your mind-body makeover begins with your physical problems. You could have any fifth-chakra health challenge with Locked Door tendencies. But if, like Sierra, you haven't been to the dentist in a while, this is an excellent time to pay one a visit. If you have phobia of dentists, chose from among the many who now cater to those like you who aren't fond of people poking around in their mouths.

If the dentist finds tooth decay, he or she might have to give you a filling, perform a root canal, or possibly pull some teeth (and then give you bridgework). If your gums are infected, you may need to see a periodontist, depending on the severity of the problem. Gingivitis, the early stage of gum disease, can be reversed with proper treatment and continued care. Its more advanced stage, periodontitis, may require surgery and low-dose or topical antibiotics. (By the way, adding a few drops of tea-tree oil to some mouthwash and gargling with it may also help ease pain and heal infection.)

Along with an extended course of dental procedures and surgeries, be sure to support your mood, immune system, and pain management at the same time. First, take SAMe or some other nutritional or pharmacological mood support that won't numb the part of your brain that's important for passion, spirituality, and mysticism. (See the chapter on the sixth chakra for details.) Second, consider going to a Chinese acupuncturist and herbalist; and ask about taking the herbs cat's claw, royal jelly, or *Acanthopanax senticosus* (eleuthero, previously called Siberian ginseng)—all of which help support the immune system. Acupuncture along with SAMe will help disrupt the pain pathways so that they won't become cemented into your system during prolonged dental work.

Next, your mind-body makeover addresses the emotional brain problems. If the Locked Door is your communication style, begin to work on feeling comfortable talking to other people—not just praying, meditating, or chanting—especially when you're experiencing any fear, anger, or sadness. You can still pray about it, but commune with someone who has a pulse as well. Every day, make sure you get out from behind your locked door and talk to some living, breathing people. Discuss politics, the weather, what's going on with your families, how you're feeling—just shoot the breeze. (For the purposes of this exercise, please avoid any profound, spiritual discussions; this is about practicing idle, lighthearted conversation, not imparting the mysteries of the universe.)

At first, this will feel awkward and uncomfortable, but understand that as you get additional practice with casual chatting, you'll strengthen more than just your fifth-chakra organs. Hanging out with more people and making friends will also pump up your first-chakra immune system—which, in turn, influences all the organs of your body, including your heart and brain.

Here, then, is my seven-step program to help rehabilitate the Locked Door's tendency to speak almost exclusively to (and often *for*) God or a higher power, instead of to other human beings:

1. Identify how you feel much more peace, harmony, and calmness when you're communicating spiritually, in prayer to the universe or in God-centered contemplation.

2. Recognize your fear that expressing many of your private feelings and thoughts to people around you would leave you overexposed. Further see how such sharing seems like an indulgence to you.

3. Discern that just as the health of your soul requires that you be able to communicate with a higher power, the health of your physical body requires that you be able to communicate with other humans.

4. Restrict your tendency to retreat into total monastic silence, becoming a communication anorexic with people on the earth. Make sure that every day, for at least one hour, you have a face-to-face conversation with another mammal who walks on two feet. (Internet chat rooms, e-mail, instant messaging, and other virtual forms of communication don't count.)

5. Know that spiritual and human communication are equally important. Be open to the fact that the more you come out from behind your locked door and relate to people on Earth, the healthier you'll be, and the more capacity you'll have to communicate with the heavens as well.

6. Change the unhealthy thought pattern: *What I say rarely matters . . .* to the healthier affirmation: *When my heart, mind, and soul are aligned, what I have to say reveals genuine insight and integrity, which makes people want to listen to me.*

7. Follow the fifth rule for intuitive health—*Sometimes you've got to be cruel to be kind*—and learn how to expand your comfort zone by developing your ability to successfully communicate with others around you.

• • •

To create health in your fifth chakra, you have to learn how to communicate with both give and take: getting your message across in an effective way while also being willing to bend to the other person's wishes. To accomplish that diplomatic feat, you need to follow the fifth rule for intuitive health—*Sometimes you've got to be cruel to be kind*—which involves developing a communication style that balances being appropriately assertive and compliant. As this chapter's title (and the song of the same name) urges, *baby don't go* . . . don't go too far in either direction, that is, because if you do, your fifth-chakra intuitive advisor will fire off a memo in the form of symptoms in your neck, thyroid, and mouth that will let you know that it's time to speak up or shut up.

• • • • •

Chapter Eight

Sixth Chakra: "If I Could Turn Back Time"

(The Health of Your Brain, Eyes, and Ears)

Your sixth chakra—the area of your body that includes your brain, eyes, nose, and ears—is your intuitive advisor that lets you know how well you see the world from all possible perspectives. The health of the organs in this area depends on how flexible and adaptive your mind-set is. Can you restrain yourself when necessary, and at other times allow yourself to be more indulgent? When it comes to having opinions, can you be flexible enough to have measured, traditional viewpoints on some issues, but a more innovative perspective on other situations? The health of this area of your body is affected by your ability to switch from one type of mind-set to the other, depending on the context and your ability to tolerate viewpoints other than your own.

Most people assume that as they age, their minds go downhill, but that's not true. Believe it or not, mental perspective *increases* with age. Children typically look at issues from only one (usually very concrete) vantage point. For example, most little kids would rather have 25 pennies than a single quarter because they believe that the phrase "More is better" is always true. But as they get older, they usually develop a capacity to look at the same phrase from a variety of points of view, extracting different meanings, depending on the context. If you're talking about pocket change, for example, less might indeed be better, because carrying 25 pennies around can be a pain.

Gaining increasing amounts of mental perspective also holds through adulthood. For example, the older you get, the better your remote memory (your recollection of events that happened a long time ago) becomes, giving you broader experience upon which to make decisions—something people may call "developing wisdom with age." True, your thought processing might be slower, so it could take you a little longer to come up with an answer. But the depth and breadth of your knowledge base is greater. And when you come to a decision, it's based on a wider, more flexible type of answer versus the knee-jerk childish response of vanilla/chocolate or no/yes. Faster but more impulsive isn't necessarily better than slower, wiser, and more astute.

The first time I saw sixth-chakra intuition in action was when I was nine years old and visiting my favorite godmother, whom I'll call Aunt Delancy. She lived with her husband, my uncle Joe; and her elderly mother, Mrs. Angelo. Although Mrs. Angelo had been in the United States for more than 40 years, you'd swear she'd just gotten off the boat from Italy, because her life had changed very little since she left Sicily. She spoke Italian, with some broken English. She would eat only food cooked from her own family recipes. It was clear that Mrs. Angelo had done very little to assimilate herself into the American culture. Whenever my family went to Aunt Delancy's house, we'd see Mrs. Angelo sitting in the same lawn chair she'd sat in for decades, in the same white frilly dress and wearing the same white frilly hat. Sometimes she'd sit inside, and sometimes she'd sit outside, watching the world go by. But otherwise, nothing much changed for her from one day to the next.

On this particular visit, we were to have dinner, and then the adults were going to play cards. Already hard at work earning perfect grades so that I could get into medical school, I was about to go do my homework in the den before we ate. But soon after we arrived, Aunt Delancy beckoned all of us into a side room to tell us a funny story about something that had happened with Mrs. Angelo—something that would embarrass the older woman if she heard it discussed.

Aunt Delancy told us that at 11 that morning, Mrs. Angelo had gotten dressed as usual in her white dress, hat, and gloves. She'd made her eggs and then went out to sit in her lawn chair in the front yard to watch the people go by, just like always. But within a few minutes, like a ballistic missile, Mrs. Angelo had come running back into the house, calling, *"Duhlanzeee!* Come-uh here! I got-uh talk-uh to you. Duhlanzeee! You have-uh no idea what-uh happened to me!" (If you could have seen my aunt Delancy performing this dramatic reenactment, you would have rolled on the floor laughing.) Her mother continued, "Duhlanzeee! Sit down! You don't know what I just-uh been through!"

So Aunt Delancy said, "Oh, Ma, what happened? I'm listening! Sit down. Don't be so dramatic!"

Her mother, who would not be calmed, responded, "Duhlanzeee, I get up-uh this morning. I brush-uh my teeth, and I wash-uh my face—"

Aunt Delancy broke in impatiently, saying, "Ma, hurry up! I've got a lot of things to do today."

Still, Mrs. Angelo wasn't going to be rushed. From her perspective, every detail was critical to this message. So she continued, "I put-uh on my nice-uh, clean-uh hat and a nice-uh, clean-uh dress-uh. I make-uh me a nice-uh breakfast, nice-uh eggs. I go out-uh-side and sit-uh on my chair and sit-uh back. And I say-uh to myself, 'Nice-uh sun'—"

Aunt Delancy cut in again: "Ma, you're driving me crazy with all these details! Get to the point, will you?!"

Again, Mrs. Angelo ignored her and continued: "I sit-uh back in my chair and relax and I say-uh, 'Nice-uh sun,' and then as I look up-uh at the sky, I see-uh a big-uh bird-uh. A big-uh God-uh-damn-uh bird-uh flying right over me. I say-uh to myself, 'What a beautiful bird-uh. This is such a nice-uh day!'"

One last time, my aunt Delancy tried to expedite Mrs. Angelo's rendition. "Ma!" she cried out, exasperated.

And then, finally, Mrs. Angelo wound up for her grand finale, hands wildly gesticulating. "The next thing-uh I know," she continued, "the God-uh-damn-uh bird-uh takes a big-uh sheet-uh right on-uh my nice-uh, clean-uh dress. A big-uh, huge-uh sheet-uh! God-uh damn-uh that bird-uh . . . !" At that point, Mrs. Angelo had trailed off into a litany of obscenities in Italian.

Aunt Delancy, realizing her mother was quite upset, had tried to put her arm around Mrs. Angelo to soothe her. But the woman was still very angry about her avian adversary, and she wouldn't be appeased. Triumphantly, she put up her fists and declared, "Duhlanzeee! Don't-uh worry. I fix-uh that-uh God-uh-damn-uh bird! He thinks-uh he's-uh so smart. I fix-uh *him*! Next time when he thinks-uh he's-uh gonna try to sheet-uh on-uh me, I'm-uh gonna fool him! I no gonna sit-uh in the front-uh yard no more! I gonna fool that-uh God-uh-damn-uh bird! I'm-uh gonna sit in the back-uh-yard!"

And at the ripe old age of nine, I knew that Mrs. Angelo didn't have all of her mental faculties intact. Just like the little kid who thought that 25 pennies was more than a quarter, Mrs. Angelo wasn't able to gain the perspective that to a bird in the sky, the front yard and the back one were the same. After decades of doing the same thing in the same way every single day, her mind was narrowing and becoming demented, concrete, and overly detailed. Ill informed and in the dark, she was missing the point.

•-•-•

The list of sixth-chakra illnesses that will let you know that your thinking is veering off in the wrong direction and you're too deeply entrenched in a specific mind-set includes migraine headache; eye problems (such as cataracts, glaucoma, and macular degeneration); ear disorders (such as tinnitus, vertigo and dizziness, Ménière's disease, sensory-neural hearing loss, and becoming hard of hearing); neurological and neuropsychiatric disorders (such as schizophrenia, Huntington's disease, Parkinson's disease, and multi-infarct dementia); and developmental learning disorders (such as dyslexia, obsessive-compulsive disorder, and attention deficit disorder).

To maintain health in this region of the body, you have to follow the sixth rule for intuitive health: *I know I'm different, but from now on I want to try to be the same (as other people)*—balancing conservative and liberal mind-sets. (Please keep in mind that this isn't about political parties; I'm referring to a style of thinking.) The health of your sixth-chakra organs involves having a flexible and adaptable mind-set: having the capacity to sometimes hold a more measured view and at others to be more tolerant and broad-minded. Successfully following the sixth rule for intuitive health entails striking a balance between being able to agree for the sake of agreeing and being able to allow yourself to be a mental free agent of change.

Most people with sixth-chakra health problems tend to fall somewhere in between four extreme categories: the *Bright Bulb*—those who worship facts and have a more structured, detail-oriented approach (along with a down-to-earth mind-set); the *Shooting Star*—those who employ a more unstructured, detail-avoiding, flexible approach (with a more extravagant, magnanimous worldview); the *Mind Like a Steel Trap* type—those who have a disciplined approach to the facts (as well as a freethinking mind-set); and finally, the *Blown a Fuse and in the Dark, but Spiritually Illuminated* type—those more mystical people who turn a blind eye to what's going on around them because they spend most of their time in spiritually illuminated prayer and contemplation.

The Bright Bulb

The first type of sixth-chakra extreme is the Bright Bulb, those more detail-oriented people who are all about structure and discipline and who have a more focused approach to the world. My client Eulie, 43, was a good example. This woman had always excelled in school, being both bright and a disciplined hard worker. Ever since her mother died of a burst aneurysm when my client was nine years old, Eulie had been a little on the nervous side, with several years when she was afflicted by panic attacks and depression. After she immersed herself in high school and later in college, Eulie was fine (other than a little bout with anorexia). However, after giving birth to four kids, she was suffering with a lot of physical symptoms and concerns, none of which her doctors seemed able to help her with.

In addition to a nervous habit of pulling at her hair, which was causing it to thin, Eulie experienced dizziness, vertigo, tinnitus, and numbness and tingling on the left side of her body. She also suffered from insomnia, nausea, and fatigue; and sometimes she had pressure in her chest, with heart palpitations. More than once, she ended up in the emergency room, afraid that she was having a heart attack, only to find out she was really having an *anxiety* attack instead.

When Eulie couldn't calm herself down or get to sleep, she'd compulsively organize the house. Then she'd go on the Internet and obsessively hunt for bargains. This woman spent hours searching for just the right backpacks, notebooks, and school supplies for her kids . . . beginning in May, four months before the start of the school year. Eulie would also spend hours compulsively stockpiling toiletries, stationery goods, and kitchen supplies that could last the family for decades.

Whenever her husband, Vernon, would protest that she was getting out of hand, Eulie would respond enthusiastically, "But I got a really good deal on it!" One day, when Vernon saw the UPS truck back into their driveway and the driver start to unload a huge pallet of toilet paper, he put his foot down. He insisted that his wife stop her obsessive-compulsive carryings-on and convinced her to call me for a reading.

If you, like Eulie, are a Bright Bulb, you like things focused, incisive, clean-cut, and tidy, filled with as many details and bits of information as possible. Like a spotlight, you want to put more and more light on a situation so that you can examine it more carefully. You can't stand not knowing and having any ambiguity or uncertainty. Obsessively and compulsively gathering and organizing information makes you feel as if you have some control over your life and your world. But collecting and controlling ultimately doesn't calm you down; rather, it just gets you more edgy, frantic, and anxious.

In fact, you're also likely to have compulsive routines or movements you do that seem to calm you down—nervous habits like biting your fingernails and picking at your skin. In cases where your emotions become extreme, you may start pulling your hair out (trichotillomania) or even cutting yourself (an act that releases opiates, which seem to have a calming effect). In Eulie's case, her anxiety became so overwhelming and her emotions so overloaded that the electrical signals in her body in essence flipped a switch that caused a temporary shutdown, a paralysis. This type of extreme stress response can occur in almost any tense, overwhelmed individual. The resulting paralysis is on the left side of the body, which is controlled by the right brain, the area for emotions. When you're overstressed, you may try to calm yourself down by ordering, scheduling, or double-checking. Likewise, when your body seizes you by leaving one side feeling numb and weak, this loss of control can feel akin to dying and sometimes leads to panic symptoms and heart palpitations that may make you think you're having a heart attack.

What I've learned from people like Eulie is that even though Bright Bulbs obsessively and compulsively gather as many facts as possible, they're actually blinded to the way all those details fit together to create a larger meaning—the bigger picture. As the saying goes, they can't see the forest for the trees, and this blindness to the bigger picture can make them anxious. Then, in an attempt to cope with the anxiety, they keep gathering more and more facts and details. Basically, they keep adding more and more trees to the forest . . . but without a greater perspective, all those trees just make the forest increasingly unmanageable.

I should point out here that many people believe being obsessive-compulsive means that you have to be like Jack Nicholson's character in the movie *As Good as It Gets*—the guy who couldn't walk on the cracks in the sidewalk and had to wash his hands 300 times a day. It's true that those with severe OCD spend so many hours cleaning their environment, reciting words silently, putting their belongings in order, and double-checking things repeatedly that they can't really hold a regular job or be in a normal relationship. But overly controlled, obsessive-compulsive behaviors can also occur in lesser degrees. When Bright Bulbs are nervous, they often engage in milder compulsive behavior, like frequently applying lip gloss, constantly tidying up their desks, checking their e-mail every five minutes, and similar acts that are attempts at ordering or otherwise controlling their environment.

What clues signal that you may be a Bright Bulb? As a child, you always colored within the lines. When you were a teenager, you cut out those coupons in magazines to send away for free samples of shampoo, makeup, and other personal-care products, even if you weren't sure you'd actually use them once you got them. In school, your term papers were always too long, and you did very well on multiple-choice tests. Your teachers liked you because they thought you were conscientious, diligent, and disciplined. When you took the SATs, your verbal score was higher than your math one. Even as an adult, your writing is wordy, your sentences compound and detailed. When composing a letter, you frequently add a PS or even a PPS. You have more books in your house than hairs on your head, and the mail carrier grumbles about how many magazines you subscribe to. Information is like Xanax to you—it seems to calm you down.

You try to be extremely tidy. You collect stationery products. You love eBay. You research things on the Internet for months before you buy them, never satisfied that you've found the lowest price. When you go shopping, you make a detailed list and tend to stick to it. You buy in bulk; and you never run out of toilet paper, paper towels, or Kleenex. You love warehouse clubs like Sam's and Costco. You've inquired about a lifetime subscription to *Consumer Reports*. When you buy a new car, you thoroughly research all the models first and then ask the salesperson to talk about every single detail.

You use a Day-Timer, PDA, or other daily organizer religiously; and you have at least three different calendars at any one time. When you notice products in the wrong place on a store shelf, you put them back the way they're supposed to be. Seeing misspellings or errors in punctuation or grammar on restaurant menus or on signs in stores grates on your nerves like nails on a chalkboard. You could be, or already are, an accountant, bookkeeper, lawyer, or copy editor.

Sound familiar? Congratulations—you're a Bright Bulb. But be careful! Your desire to know everything and never be in the dark when it comes to the day-to-day details of your life can get out of control. And when that happens, the organs of your sixth chakra will let you know by sounding the first alarm. In situations where you feel like you don't know every detail, as if you're in the dark, you'll start to panic, shake, pull your hair, or develop some other nervous twitch or habit.

If we look closely, we'll soon realize that all of us have a little Bright Bulb within us. Like Eulie, we all have a tendency to want to maintain mental control and clarify the details when we get anxious and tense about an uncertain situation. We try to find our way out of the confusion by nailing down the facts and reasoning our way out of the craziness. However, even though at first homing in on the details and locking down control may provide momentary relief, we eventually recognize that logic and rational explanation don't truly provide complete insight, nor do they give lasting comfort.

Intuitive Advice for the Bright Bulb

Do you suffer from chronic health problems in your brain, eyes, nose, and ears; and do you tend to have Bright Bulb issues? If so, mind-body medicine and medical intuition can help you learn to relax a little and not be so intensely focused on and compulsive about details. Your mind-body makeover begins by addressing your physical health problems. You could have any sixth-chakra issue with Bright Bulb tendencies. But if, like Eulie, your concern happens to be dizziness, vertigo, tinnitus, or numbness and tingling, your primary-care physician may refer you to a neurologist for some tests, including an EEG or an MRI. Often the diagnosis is a severe stress reaction or panic attack, but your doctor needs to rule out the possibility of other disorders. (See the information on panic attacks in the chapter on the fourth chakra.)

To reassure yourself that you are in fact monitoring and maintaining the health of your body, establish a supportive partnership with your primary internal-medicine doctor, whom you'll see every six months or so for a complete physical stress test, an EKG, blood work, a mammogram, a rectal exam, and other checks of your critical organ systems. Don't have these exams any more frequently (because doing so would be obsessive and compulsive) or any less frequently (or your anxiety and terror would escalate). Rest assured that when you see your doctor twice a year, you're doing everything that modern Western medicine can do to address your very sensitive, twitchy mind-body problem.

Next, your mind-body makeover moves to the emotional intuitive brain. To lessen your Bright Bulb feelings of anxiety and panic, try the nutritional, herbal, and medicinal solutions detailed in the chapter on the fourth chakra. High-dose prescription serotonin drugs such as Zoloft can be very helpful, but you may elect to try a supplement such as 5-HTP (100 mg, three times a day) instead. In addition, taking high-powered antianxiety medicines like Klonopin or nutritional supplements such as chamomile or passionflower may be a good first step in helping you reduce your anxious edginess.

However, you also need to run, not walk, to join a Cognitive Behavioral Therapy (CBT) or a Dialectical Behavioral Therapy (DBT) group to learn how to effectively funnel your right-brain anxiety into more productive activity than compulsive, controlling, or repetitive behavior. DBT is my favorite because it can teach you mindfulness techniques that help you identify whether your nervousness is truly an intuitive protective fear or a thought pattern that's more like a skip in a broken record that may scare you to death by repeating, "Watch out! Something bad is going to happen! Something bad is going to happen! Something bad is going to happen! . . ." DBT can help you identify such thought patterns that trigger anxiety and frantic obsessive-compulsive symptoms and teach you how to deal with them so that they aren't taking control of you and your life anymore. (For additional information about DBT, see the chapter on the first chakra.)

The following is my seven-part program to help rehabilitate the Bright Bulbs' obsessive-compulsive need for order and information:

1. Identify that the more facts you know about a situation, the safer you *think* you can feel. But note how collecting and concentrating on all those facts can get you so focused on the trees that you completely lose sight of the forest.

2. Recognize that no matter how much you learn about any situation, there will always be more information somewhere that you aren't going to be privy to. As a result, you'll always be somewhat in the dark, which terrifies you.

3. Discern that no amount of information is going to help you feel that you can have control over the world, because you *can't.* You need to be able to discern what is indeed an adequate amount and be satisfied when you've acquired that. Ultimately, you must have faith that you'll be able to handle whatever happens when you find yourself in the dark about something.

4. Restrict your tendency to schedule, control, and obsess about things. Pick at least one day every other week to be your "Spontaneity Day"—one when you know nothing about what will happen. A friend will pick you at 9 A.M. and will have planned the whole day for you already. You'll be given no facts, no schedule, and no information. You'll be left totally in the dark—you won't even be told how to dress. Your job is to sit back; indulge yourself; and learn how to tolerate a more liberalized, freewheeling, unrestricted way of living. You may think this is a lot to ask of a friend, but I guarantee you that if you're a Bright Bulb, someone in your life is *dying* to do this for you. Think of that person you know who always says that you should loosen up a little bit—that's the one.

5. Know that like a plant, you need a mixture of light as well as darkness to be healthy. Illuminating all the facts doesn't actually put you in a position of control; it could just make you feel controlling to others.

6. Change the unhealthy thought pattern: *I frequently find flaws, mistakes, and problems in myself and in others—I must try harder to fix them . . .* to the healthier affirmation: *I love myself and others unconditionally. Even though I love myself just the way I am, I accept the parts of me that need to change and grow. Even though I love others just the way they are, I accept the parts of them that need to change and grow, too.*

7. Follow the sixth rule for intuitive health—*I know I'm different, but from now on I want to try to be the same (as other people)*—by developing a flexible and adaptive mind-set, without fearing you're losing control of your world.

The Shooting Star

The next type of sixth-chakra extreme is the Shooting Star, those who avoid details and prefer a more unstructured, liberalized, and often more flexible mind-set. Shooting Stars like to approach a situation by looking at its overarching theme or gestalt, rather than scrutinizing the details. My client Tara was a good example: her Indian mother had chosen her name (which means "star" in Hindi) because she thought she saw a bright light in her daughter's eyes at birth. Tara, now 33, had always been a free thinker and favored a more unconventional way of approaching any situation. Her unstructured, unbridled learning style frequently clashed with those around her—including her father, a Marine, who ran their home like he did his unit. The children were kept focused and were trained to follow rules that would have been considered excessively restrictive by most people's standards.

From an early age, Tara was unable to thrive in the more conservative educational environment of the military base. She couldn't keep track of all the details required for the many tasks that involved rote learning. The classroom size of 36 kids made it difficult for the girl to focus on the teacher because her mind would wander to what was going on emotionally with all the other students in the room. Tara's parents sent her to a psychiatrist, who diagnosed her with ADHD. The psychiatrist prescribed Ritalin for distractibility, inability to pay attention, and hyperactivity. Her father argued that *he* had the same problems with hyperactivity as a child, but he'd never needed to take drugs. Joining the Marines, he insisted, was what straightened him out. Her mother was adamant, however, so their daughter started taking Ritalin.

Although the medication seemed to work for a time, after a while Tara felt that trying to learn in her school was like cramming a square peg in a round hole. So at age 18, leaving her Ritalin behind her, she ran away to California. She got a job as a waitress; took some art classes; and started to explore meditation, Eastern religions, and philosophy. A guru gave her the name Trayi (Indian for "intellect"), which she adopted. By the time she turned 33, Trayi found herself back in school, taking clothing-design classes in New York City. She hoped to take her unique and incredibly expansive artistic talents and channel them into a grounded career that could survive the constraints of the conservative, structured world of New York fashion.

But her freethinking, liberal, nonrestrictive mind-set was giving her trouble again fitting into the project limits and demands in her design-school courses. Her projects were given glowing praise for their overall creative genius, beauty, and innovativeness, but she was getting failing marks on attending to the details and precision of construction. Tara hit a crisis point when she was put on academic probation. Her advisor said that she clearly had the potential to be a rising star in the fashion industry, but her designs would easily get shot down because of the sloppiness, disorganization, and inattention to detail they exhibited. The aspiring designer then remembered her childhood diagnosis of ADHD and her problems with paying attention to fine points, organization, and conforming to the classroom structure on the Marine base—problems that were now being repeated at fashion-design school.

If you, like Tara/Trayi, are a Shooting Star, you have a mercurial, "Free Bird"–like mind-set, where your thoughts liberally fly from idea to idea. You tend to be unfocused, unstructured, and not easily controlled in the captivity of what passes for a normal classroom in our society. Yet your capacity to see the right-brain overarching themes in almost every situation gives you a unique viewpoint from those left-brain-dominant people who analyze the bit-by-bit details of any standard situation. If you're having a hard time fitting in to society, you may have a tendency to use stimulants such as cocaine, amphetamines, or anything else that involves adrenaline (which is pharmacologically related to Ritalin, the medication most commonly prescribed to treat ADHD). Over time, abusing such stimulants or living the life of an adrenaline junkie can increase your chance of having a heart condition called cardiomyopathy.

What I've learned from people like Tara is that while others may think Shooting Stars are ditzy space cadets, once they nail down a successful strategy for surviving in society, they can actually do quite well. While they're often most comfortable in creative environments (such as the world of art, music, drama, or design), that is hardly their only option. My client's father, for example, who was also labeled hyperactive as a child, joined the military. In doing so, he imported a structured, disciplined, and controlled way of eating, sleeping, dressing, speaking, and behaving. Consequently, he and others like him are able to hold a job without getting distracted and disorganized. Their rehabilitated mind-set enables them to function without jeopardizing or even annoying those around them.

What clues reveal that you may be a Shooting Star? Well, you were known in kindergarten for rarely coloring inside the lines. In fact, you only used a coloring book or sheet when a teacher made you, because you often got in trouble for scribbling on the wall with crayons. You may have even drawn extra pictures on the page or used other media to decorate the figures, including glitter, popcorn, cat hair, or table salt—anything you had access to. You had trouble finishing your schoolwork on time, and you had a hard time making your papers meet the length requirements. You never did well on multiple-choice tests. If you even took the SATs in high school, both your verbal and math scores were inappropriately low because you just couldn't focus on the test. Your teachers thought that you were bright but didn't try hard enough or work to your capacity. They wondered why you wouldn't just pay attention and follow directions.

You're fun to shop with or otherwise hang out with because you make every excursion an adventure—no one ever really knows where you're going to go, what you're going to do, or what you're going to buy next. You use many of the items in your house for functions that they weren't primarily intended for. A planter that looks cool in your bathroom, for example, might become a magazine rack, or you may drink out of Mason jars instead of tumblers because you love the vintage glass. You shun Pottery Barn and trendy one-size-fits-all attempts at design and pseudo-creativity.

You can hold only two or possibly three requests or directives in your mind at one time. Any item past the third on a list (or any point after number three in a presentation or a memo) goes right into your mental wastebasket. At least once every few days, someone will say something to you such as, "Like I already *told* you . . ." or a person will ask, "Didn't you get my e-mail?" but you'll have only a very dim memory (if even that much) of what the speaker is referring to.

If this sounds like you, then you may be a Shooting Star. Society has probably labeled you as ADD or ADHD. But as you can see from the preceding case history, this is only considered a disorder when you (or some authority figure or group) deem it necessary to fit your unbridled and unconventional, yet distractible and disorganized, learning style into a very detail-oriented, constrained, traditional, focused, and ordered environment.

If you've managed to balance your mercurial, creative mind-set by acquiring the more grounded, disciplined nature required to succeed in the world, then *your* shooting star is shining brightly indeed. If you haven't figured out how to fit into a more conservative, detail-oriented world, your star is on its way toward fizzling out. The first alarm that your sixth-chakra advisor will give you is that you'll zone out every time anyone tries to provide you with a lot of details all at once. Someone will be sending you information in an overly structured, controlled fashion and your mind will just go blank, you'll get lost in space, and the light in your eyes will dim and go out.

If we look closely at Tara's story, we'll realize that each of us can find within ourselves a Shooting Star, a part of us that feels like we can't focus, pay attention, or retain what we've learned during periods of crisis, illness, hormonal changes, or emotional overload. During these "spacey" moments, we feel our minds are truly in some other world. While we can indeed learn how to ground ourselves and focus on the details when we need to get something done in *this* world, sometimes we need to allow ourselves to have that creative free range as well. Not everyone can be corralled all the time.

Intuitive Advice for the Shooting Star

Do you suffer from chronic health problems in your brain, eyes, nose, and ears; and do you tend to have some aspects of the Shooting Star pattern? If so, you can learn to use mind-body medicine and medical intuition to make your freethinking, unbridled, unfocused mind work in a more detail-oriented, structured world; and your mind-body makeover begins with your physical health. You could have any sixth-chakra problem with Shooting Star tendencies. But if, like Tara/Trayi, you happen to be addicted to stimulants like cocaine or amphetamines—or even coffee, Red Bulls, or espresso shots—please seek treatment. (For more information on this, see the addiction section in the chapter on the third chakra.)

If you're very hyperactive, you need to learn that while this pumps adrenaline into your body to help you focus, the stress of being on overdrive all the time may tax your cardiovascular system. Consider taking heart-protective nutritional supplements, including a good multivitamin antioxidant that contains vitamin B_6, folic acid, and pycnogenol. (For additional suggestions, see the cardiovascular-health section in the chapter on the fourth chakra.) In addition, take alpha-tocotrienol and coenzyme Q_{10} (400–600 mg a day). I also recommend seeing an acupuncturist and Chinese herbalist who will help you learn to calm down as well as put out the inflammation in your body that tends to occur with such driven activity.

Next, your mind-body makeover moves to the emotional brain. The right brain, important for controlling emotions and intuition, also helps with divided attention between the inner and outer worlds. A variety of supplements can pump up its capacity for dividing attention so that you're better able to fit into and function in a more organized, detailed setting. You could start by taking DHA (300–1,000 mg a day) and SAMe (800–1,200 mg a day, on an empty stomach) to assist your body in making the neurotransmitters dopamine, norepinephrine, and serotonin—all of which can help you focus. Eleuthero, previously called Siberian ginseng (625 mg, two times a day); gotu kola (600 mg, three times a day); L-acetyl-carnitine (500 mg, up to three times a day); and ginkgo biloba (120–240 mg a day) can sharpen your mind a little, but work with a doctor if you decide to take them because they may elevate your blood pressure and act as blood thinners. Avoid aspartame, sugar, food dye, and MSG because these chemicals tend to have excitotoxins (substances that damage neurons), which may further distract you.

When it comes to being in a situation where your mind is reeling and you're overcome by all the possible choices when you have to make a decision, try the "two-step technique," which will ground you back to planet Earth and start the process of clarifying your mind. You needn't see *every* detail in the situation you're in to gain a clearer perspective; just jot down two simple facts that you know for sure, labeling them #1 and #2. Once you've nailed these two facts down, draw an arrow from each of them and write down the next piece of information that each one yields, labeling these new facts #3 and #4. As you keep repeating this two-step mind-grounding, focusing technique, you'll be creating a map that will guide you out of your confusion, step-by-step. Slowly, as you write down on paper what you know, the space-cadet feeling will dissipate and you'll have acquired a more focused map, a linear approach to your problem.

In addition, consult with an educational coach who can in essence donate to you a prosthetic left brain—in other words, someone who can help you acquire the left-brain skills of organization and focus that will help you learn in a more conservative, structured setting. Organizational tools like a Day-Timer scheduler, highlighters, and file cards can give a boost to the area of the brain that helps you process details and deal with them in a grounded format. Finally, choose either daily aerobic exercise or yoga to manage and transform all that extra energy you have.

Here, then, is my seven-step plan for rehabilitating the Shooting Stars' inability to stay focused and grounded:

1. Identify that you love to understand the big picture or the overarching theme of any situation, while the details drive you crazy. You like attending to the overall forest much more than dealing with all those pesky individual trees.

2. Recognize that even though your broad-stroke, freethinking mind might be truly innovative, your ideas may never get a chance to turn into reality if you can't also learn to attend to the details and meet the organizational requirements needed to make that happen.

3. Discern that no one person has all the answers to a problem, nor the capacity to see the complete picture of what's required to create anything. By acquiring some more conservative, focused organizational skills that you don't yet have, you'll be able to use your creativity more fully.

4. Restrict your tendency to balk at or shrink from details and order. Stop avoiding situations that require you to be more grounded, focused, and disciplined, even if they feel stifling and uncomfortable. Get an agent and a job coach to help you organize and market one of your creative or artistic projects for a more commercial audience.

5. Know that just as the world would be a sterile place indeed without your creative mind-set, it's also true that a freethinking mind at times needs structure to survive and thrive in our world.

6. Change the negative thought pattern: *Things have always come more easily to others than to me; my head has always been in the clouds . . .* to the healthier affirmation: *I am able to see things through a different perspective and can clearly communicate what I see to others.*

7. Follow the sixth rule for intuitive health—*I know I'm different, but from now on I want to try to be the same (as other people)*—by maintaining a flexible mind-set that can sometimes focus on the details and maintain structure and organization and at other times be more liberal, unstructured, freewheeling, and broad-minded.

The Mind Like a Steel Trap Type

The third type of sixth-chakra extreme is the Mind Like a Steel Trap type, those who have a disciplined approach to facts but who can also, when necessary, be more broad-minded freethinkers. Vance had just such a mind because he remembered everything he looked at. The 27-year-old could recall all the details of how a certain chemistry equation worked in the lab, as well as the specific dates of almost every significant war and treaty in American and European history. This young man was so smart that he had a double major in studio art and history. He was one of those fascinating people whom others loved to sit next to at a dinner party.

After college, Vance received a Fulbright scholarship to study abroad at the Sorbonne in Paris. Then he moved to New York City, where he started a very successful magazine with some friends. His world and future seemed bright indeed. But after being in New York for a few years, Vance started having vague symptoms—a lot of painful burning in his face, pounding headaches, and a pins-and-needles feeling in his legs and arms. He thought maybe he just needed a vacation, so he took some time off and went to the Caribbean with friends. He felt better right afterward, but six months later, after a particularly stressful magazine deadline, Vance woke up with blurry vision and had trouble walking. A neurologist told him that he had multiple sclerosis (MS), a neurological disorder where the immune system destroys the outer coating of nerve-fiber pathways in the brain and spinal cord.

If you, like Vance, are a Mind Like a Steel Trap type, you're truly blessed intellectually. On the one hand, you have a very disciplined mind that can absorb lots of details and process them in a rational, ordered, structured way. On the other hand, you also have an uncanny capacity to see overarching themes and patterns, so you can bring those details together in a brilliant, coherent manner in order to create innovative ideas. This combination is very rare indeed, and quite brilliant.

What I've learned from people like Vance is that Steel Trap types identify so strongly with their intellectual prowess that knowledge and brainpower become a trap, a prison of sorts. Sooner or later, they hit a wall when things happen in their lives that they simply can't think their way out of. After all, not every problem we encounter can be approached from a rational or even philosophical standpoint. Some dilemmas require a more "mindless," spiritual point of view. But to those of this type, emptying their minds and turning out their bright lights (all those IQ points!) for a little meditation or spiritual contemplation is frightening, because it would feel like it was flinging them into total intellectual darkness. For them, having their power plug pulled even for a moment is terrifying, because they would then be forced to look for other nontraditional, nonacademic sources of information beyond their very bright intellect.

What clues signal that you may be a Mind Like a Steel Trap type? You can do the *New York Times* crossword puzzle in ink. You read several (nontabloid) newspapers a day. You can speak at least three languages fluently; and you wouldn't bat an eyelash at learning one that involves a different alphabet, such as Chinese, Hindi, or Hebrew. You're never bored. Whenever you visit a city, you always scope out the museums, and as you drive around, you readily differentiate between the various architectural styles. You can identify the Chrysler Building in New York as Art Deco and the basilica in Vicenza as Italian Renaissance. You can recognize and intelligently discuss the subtle differences between all of Van Gogh's sunflower paintings.

You're so confident in your intellect that you never have to flaunt it. You understand the difference between the lack of education and the lack of intelligence. Your taste in music is truly eclectic: while you enjoy all manner of classical music, from German chants to English madrigals, Bach's fugues, Handel (of course, for Sunday-morning brunch), Schubert, Chopin, Debussy, and Pavarotti ("Nessun Dorma," naturally); Kylie Minogue, the Black Eyed Peas, Coldplay, Cher, Eric Clapton, Macy Gray, and Eminem are also all on your iPod.

If this description fits you, then you may be the Mind Like a Steel Trap type (but you're so smart that you probably already knew that, didn't you?). You've maxed out your IQ points in most subjects, but now you're meant to explore other frontiers of knowledge. Your sixth-chakra intuitive advisor sounds its first alarm through a feeling that your mind is fried, making it very hard to think and find rational solutions to a problem. Your eyes don't seem to focus the way they used to and can't seem to home in on what's going on around you. Your hearing feels like it might be off as well. For the first time in your life, you may find it difficult to pay attention.

This could be your mind's way of temporarily shutting down pathways of acquiring information in the rational world, forcing you to learn how to experience a catastrophic event in the darkness. Without your crucial pipeline to your intellect, you may panic at first, because you simply don't know how to feel safe and secure without intellectually seeing your way through something. But because you have no choice but to travel in the dark, your mind is being forced into a state of faith. You're learning to walk toward a different type of light—spiritual illumination.

All of us have a part of the Steel Trap type within us. Like Vance, most of us have had a time in our lives when we were focused on getting an education or some other form of training. It's during this time that we tend to believe that we've achieved our highest intellectual potential. But if that's what we *think*, then we need to think again. Just as we occasionally upgrade our computer, get a newer cell phone, rebuild the motor in our car, or remodel a room in our house, we're also able to physically upgrade our brains and our intellectual abilities throughout our lives. Through a process called *plasticity*—the ability of the brain to sprout new pathways when learning new material or rebounding from injury—we can remodel our minds for greater capabilities in every decade. So even if our brains shift and change and we fear that we're losing our intellectual abilities, we need to remember that in reality, new ways to learn and grow are always available to us.

Intuitive Advice for the Mind Like a Steel Trap Type

Do you suffer from chronic health problems in your brain, eyes, or nose; and do you tend to have Mind Like a Steel Trap–type issues? If so, don't panic—mind-body medicine and medical intuition can help you see your way to the other side of this turbulent river, as your mind begins to rewire new ways of acquiring rational and spiritual mind-sets. First, your mind-body makeover focuses on the physical body. You could have any sixth-chakra health problem with Mind Like a Steel Trap tendencies. But if, like Vance, *your* problem happens to be an immune-system disorder that affects your central nervous system, such as MS, a neurologist may try to stop the autoimmune attack by giving you steroids, either intravenously or orally. The doctor may also prescribe either interferon beta-1b (Betaseron) or interferon beta-1a (Avonex): both help fight viruses and infections and regulate the immune system.

If these don't help eliminate your flare-ups or if the side effects are too painful, you can take other medicines such as Copaxone that help block the immune-system attack. Muscle relaxers—for example, baclofen—can decrease muscle spasms in the legs, and Provigil and other stimulants can help with extreme fatigue.

A complementary medical neurologist might suggest a host of nutritional, herbal, and other solutions to help MS, as well as a low-fat diet, because dietary fat is thought to trigger inflammation in the brain. I also recommend a pharmacologic-grade vitamin source of thiamine (vitamin B_1), niacin (vitamin B_3), vitamin B_6, and vitamin B_{12}, because a deficiency in all these B vitamins is said to exacerbate MS. Omega-3 fatty acids, in the form of DHA (100–300 mg, three times a day), can potentially help repair the damaged neurons. (These solutions may well be helpful to those who want to protect the white-matter pathways in their brains from inflammation and injury, including but not limited to those who have MS.)

Your complementary-medicine doctor may also look at food sensitivities such as those to wheat and dairy, along with your exposure to toxins like mercury that could be triggering your condition or making it worse. As with every serious neurological disorder that involves weakness, pain, and debilitation, acupuncture and Chinese medicine can be very helpful in relaxing muscles in spasm as well as calming some of the fiery inflammation underlying your auto-immune problems.

In addition, by continually learning new things, growing, and changing multiple areas of your life, you can help your brain create new neural pathways, facilitating its normal upgrading and remodeling process. Whether you learn another language, read up on a different era in history, or study art or architecture, you'll also be learning to break down old mind-sets that you've been holding on to and to replace them with newer ways of thinking. This is critical not just for your memory and healthy aging but also for your total mind-body health.

Your mind-body makeover next moves to the emotional intuitive mind. When your life has been based on consuming facts the way kids consume Cracker Jack, either a gradual decline of your sight, hearing, or thinking or a catastrophic event that plunges you into darkness is especially hard to take. I'm familiar with this routine. I developed a sleep disorder and a seizure disorder starting at age 12 that caused me to fall asleep for longer and longer periods of time. Originally, I fell into short, unintentional naps. But by the time I turned 22, I was sleeping up to 17 hours a day. This means that at the height of the disorder, I was unconscious 70 percent of the time.

As you might recall from the Introduction, as a child I wanted nothing to do with developing my intuitive abilities. Since the age of seven, I'd been totally focused on cultivating my intellect for a career as a physician and a scientist. But after getting straight A's all the way through middle school and high school, I found myself sleeping through my freshman and sophomore years at Brown University. This yielded a 2.22 grade point average, which was obviously not going to help me get into medical school. I went to a neurologist, who told me at first that he could do nothing for me. My brain would keep flickering in and out, and I wasn't able to learn. After all, if I couldn't see the facts, my mind couldn't intellectually process them. The academic ideas wouldn't go into my brain. I was quite in the dark, in more ways than one.

What do you do when that happens? You turn to spirituality and faith. What else *is* there? Because my doctors didn't know how to wake me up, the only place I could turn to was a health-care facility that was definitely not covered by my Blue Cross and Blue Shield plan: faith and prayer. While I was falling in and out of sleep, in and out of the light and darkness, God was always there for me. I was never alone, and for some reason, I believed that I would eventually learn to wake up. And when that happened, I'd be able to learn again.

Over the course of five years, and after taking various medications, herbal remedies, nutritional supplements, and other treatments (some of which worked and some of which didn't), I eventually figured out how to stay awake. Throughout that whole process, my brain and intellect changed, and so did the way I learn. Because my sixth-chakra brain disorder prevented me from accessing my intellect, it also forced me to sprout new brain pathways of faith, spirituality, and intuition. From this experience, I was given a path to learn how to see in the dark—to make my way through a very difficult and daunting time, guided solely by faith.

Many people have talked about how faith forces you to see without facts, to learn to trust with a mind empty of assumptions and preconceptions. Sometimes the only way you can learn to believe in a power greater than your own intellectual problem-solving capabilities is through the catastrophic unplugging of your brain, eyes, or ears that comes with a sixth-chakra disorder such as MS, narcolepsy, epilepsy, migraine headache, stroke, brain tumors, or the like. When you can no longer shine the light of your intellect on a situation and you're plunged into your own personal darkness, you truly acquire your faith. And when you find yourself sitting in that darkness, you're also in a place that's ripe for spiritual illumination.

All of us go through this process at one time or another in our lives, a process that the Carmelite priest and mystic known as St. John of the Cross called the "dark night of the soul." And although I would never say I'm an expert on mysticism, I can very much relate to St. John's poem about fear of the darkness. (Have I mentioned that although I have narcolepsy, I'm also terrified of the dark?) This stanza of his is the only poetry I've ever been able to memorize. Hopefully, if you suffer the emotional pain of being thrust into the dark when you develop a serious illness, especially a sixth-chakra health problem, this will bring you as much comfort as it has brought me:

> Though I suffer darkness
> In this mortal life
> That is not so hard a thing;
> For though I have no light
> I have the life of heaven.
> For the blinder love is
> The more it gives such life,
> Holding the soul surrendered,
> Living without light, in darkness.

[From *Fear Not the Night: Based on the Classic Spirituality of John of the Cross* by John J. Kirvan (Ave Maria Press, 1998)]

Here, then, is my seven-step program to rehabilitate the Mind Like a Steel Trap types' need to learn how to rely on faith, a higher source than their intellect:

1. Identify the euphoria you feel when you think you have all the facts together in your mind, trying to formulate a total picture of the situation that presents a solution to a problem in a complete flash.

2. Recognize the panic and terror you feel when you can't think your way through a problem, when your mind goes blank (making reasoning impossible) and you're forced to move forward using only faith.

3. Discern that in the end, no matter how much intellect you have, many decisions that you'll make in life ultimately require a leap of blind faith—trusting the risks of not knowing everything. Ultimately, you have to balance knowledge with belief, facts with faith, in order to gain access to universal intelligence—a knowing that comes from a source beyond your brain.

4. Restrict your desire to understand why something is happening to you and to continually look for factual causes underlying your physical and emotional problems.

5. Know that some spiritual practices that involve mindfulness exercises can teach you to empty your head of images and ideas and to trust the stillness that results. Learn to travel into this inner darkness with contemplation or prayer.

6. Change the negative thought pattern: *If I don't have all my wits about me, if I'm not at my intellectual best, I can't succeed . . .* to the healthier affirmation: *When I balance my creativity, intellect, and spirituality with discipline and flexibility, I always succeed.*

7. Follow the sixth rule for intuitive health—*I know I'm different, but from now on I want to try to be the same (as other people)*—by developing a mind-set so flexible and adaptive that if your mind and your world shut down completely, you're able to survive with only faith and trust.

The Blown a Fuse and in the Dark, but Spiritually Illuminated Type

The last type of sixth-chakra extreme is the Blown a Fuse and in the Dark, but Spiritually Illuminated type. These folks spend so much time in the high altitude of spiritual contemplation, prayer, and mysticism that they don't see what's going on around them down here on Earth. Winifred, 33, who led a very solitary, monastic life filled with experiences of mystical states, was a perfect example.

But let me say this right up front: although you may feel at first that you have very little in common with Winifred, think again. As a brain scientist and neuroanatomist, I can assure you that we all have an area in our brains the natural function of which is experiencing emotion, passion, spirituality, and mysticism. During an extreme emotional crisis or tragedy, this area can get fired up, and as a result you may have a mini-mystical experience of intense spiritual feelings. If this has never happened to you, you might think it's simply not possible. And if it ever has, you may have thought you were losing your mind. But as I share Winifred's story about having a form of epilepsy, you'll see how each of us has within us a mini-mystic—that is, the neurological wiring for mysticism, a window of opportunity to have a spiritual experience.

Winifred was always unique. Starting in her teens, when every other girl in her class spent hours playing around with hair and makeup, as well as talking about school or the latest rock group, she was instead intensely interested in philosophy and spirituality. During this time, she became more moody, irritable, and fearful, but she only threw herself more deeply into her spiritual studies. Winifred spent hours in her room, poring over books on the angelic realm, Catholicism, Buddhism, Hinduism, and mystical Judaism. She didn't listen to popular music; she didn't read teen magazines; and other than watching the BBC, the Holy Rosary channel on cable, or the occasional show on Bible prophecy, Winifred didn't watch very much TV, either. The other kids started to call her Sister Winnie (Order of Perpetual Mercy), a nickname that stuck throughout her life.

One day in gym class when Winifred was 16, one of the other students noticed that Sister Winnie was having some kind of physical problem. When the gym teacher approached the girl, he found that she was pale; had a vacant look on her face; and was smacking her lips, repeating, "Uh-huh, uh-huh, uh-huh," over and over again. At the emergency room, a neurologist diagnosed Winifred with complex partial seizures. She eventually had to go to a behavioral neurologist at a nearby major teaching hospital to be evaluated for her seizure disorder because initial medications did nothing to control her "spells."

Over time, Winifred was stabilized on medication, but she continued to live a somewhat monastic life. Her seizures evolved to include visual experiences, such as seeing heavenly beings or a pillar of light, getting an overwhelming sense that God was with her, and then eventually falling and having a loss of consciousness. When Winifred had a seizure, she was rendered into a dark unconsciousness on Earth, but at the same time, she was experiencing a blindingly bright, illuminated spiritual reality.

If you, like Sister Winnie, are a Blown a Fuse and in the Dark, but Spiritually Illuminated type, you may have been born with this extreme pattern . . . or you might have acquired it through a brain injury, tumor, or lesion; a serious physical trauma; or emotional abuse in childhood. Either way, you're very comfortable having your mind go blank. In fact, you may spend hours in prayer and contemplation, emptying your mind of any ideas so that your brain can be a receiver of information from the heavens. You aren't driven to examine the facts of any situation; and you're not interested in broad-minded, liberal progress or thinking. These things just feel like cold intellectualism to you. You're more comfortable living in the dark, having blind faith, and relying on God or your form of spirituality to inform your existence and guide you through life.

What I've learned from people like Winifred is that the brains of Blown a Fuse and in the Dark types are likely to be shaped not only for deepening mystical experiences but also for intense emotional states. Emotions and spirituality go hand in hand because they're essentially in the same area of the brain—the temporal-lobe limbic system.

Many of the saints and mystics—including St. Paul, Mohammed, Margery Kempe, Joan of Arc, St. Catherine of Genoa, St. Teresa of Ávila, St. Catherine de' Ricci, Emanuel Swedenborg, and St. Thérèse of Lisieux—had epilepsy. They spent hours in deep prayer and contemplation, as well as in altered mystical states. But they were also known for their deep, dark moods, which included self-recrimination, irritability, intense tempers, and even attacks of rage. Although they experienced spiritual illumination, much of their lives were spent tortured in physical and emotional darkness and solitude. The reverse, by the way, is also true: those whose lives are filled with sustained states of despair, terror, frustration, love, and even euphoria may have been led to find clarity in the darkness of their minds via a spiritual practice. Either way, getting stuck for sustained periods of time in such extremely deep, dark states isn't healthy for the brain.

What signs indicate that you might be a Blown a Fuse and in the Dark, but Spiritually Illuminated type? You may have intense emotions . . . and when your feelings of irritability, despair, and anxiety escalate, you can get so overwhelmed that you feel like you're going to explode inside. Outside, however, you don't appear to be nearly as intense emotionally. After you experience extreme frustration, euphoria, passion, despair, or terror, you may feel numb. Your mind can go blank; and you may withdraw, fall asleep, or space out.

You spend a lot of time in self-scrutiny, feeling guilty, and examining how you can improve your flaws and receive redemption. You view most, if not all, of the events in your life as being related to destiny. You see symbolic spiritual significance and an element of divine guidance or Providence in almost everything that happens to you. You can feel God or a higher power as a spirit in your body when you pray or sit in contemplation, and you would never swear in church. Spirituality is more important to you than sex, TV, or rock and roll.

If this sounds like you, then you may be a Blown a Fuse and in the Dark type. Sooner or later, the organs of your sixth chakra will signal through symptoms of illness that you need to balance your search for spiritual knowledge with a stronger connection to earthbound ideas and attitudes. If you become so immersed in your faith that you're estranged from common-day knowledge of this world, the first alarm your intuitive advisor will sound is that you may have blackouts, pass out, fall asleep at an inappropriate time, or otherwise feel like your mind has gotten so overwhelmed with charged emotion that it's as if it has blown a fuse. With so much of your focus and attention withdrawn from Earth and concentrated instead toward the heavens, it may be that all that mystical information, faith, and spiritual illumination is too much for your brain to take. With too much demand on the circuit board of your mind, it shuts down physically and emotionally until its circuits can recalibrate.

If we look closely at Winifred's story, we'll realize that each of us can find within ourselves aspects of the Blown a Fuse and in the Dark type. This is the part of us that's become so intensely immersed in a difficult emotional or spiritual problem that we simply can't stand it anymore, and we wish we could somehow escape. We spiral downward, going deeper and deeper into more and more intense despair, asking one existential question after another in prolonged states of personal reflection and contemplation.

If we spend too much time in those dark emotional and spiritual states alone—untethered from the everyday hustle and bustle of life—

we're going to lose it. The chemicals in our brains and bodies will begin to become unbalanced; and we'll lose our health, our perspective, and our mental grip on what it's like to be a human being on Earth. When this happens, we don't need to pray or to contemplate—we just need to take a break, for a while at least, to enjoy life for life's sake and have fun.

Intuitive Advice for the Blown a Fuse and in the Dark, but Spiritually Illuminated Type

Do you suffer from chronic health problems in your brain, eyes, nose, and ears; and do you tend to have some aspects of the Blown a Fuse and in the Dark, but Spiritually Illuminated–type pattern? If so, take heart. You can use mind-body medicine and medical intuition to learn how to maintain your spiritual-centric life, but also have a healthier mind that's capable of attending to earthly details and relating to people around you. Your mind-body makeover first addresses your physical problems. You could have any sixth-chakra health challenge with Blown a Fuse and in the Dark tendencies. But if, like Winifred, yours happens to be epilepsy, your doctor may prescribe a cocktail of anticonvulsive medicines (including Lamictal, Topamax, and Keppra) that can treat staring spells and seizures—these medicines have the added benefit of decreasing moodiness and irritability and improving memory and the ability to pay attention. Acupuncture and Chinese herbs can also help calm seizures.

Even if you don't have epilepsy, if you allow intense emotions such as frustration, panic, and despair to fester long enough, the resulting firestorm-like activity in your brain called *kindling* is akin to a much milder form of the firing that occurs in seizures. After a while, the sustained firing of these brain areas puts you on overload, overwhelms you, and makes you escalate and in some cases pitch a fit (what we used to call having a "conniption"—and you know what I mean). After such episodes of blowing your emotional wad, you almost always need to retreat, lie down, and take a nap. The same thing happens with too much sustained spiritual illumination. It's as if excessive, prolonged, and intense firing of the brain's spiritual areas blows your fuses out; and as a mere mortal, you have to unplug and take a break from the intensity. If you don't consciously choose to take such a break at times when you've had too much spiritual intensity or when something bad has happened and you've hit the proverbial roof, your brain may pull the plug *for* you and you'll lose it—you'll space out, retreat, or fall asleep.

Stabilizing both seizures and moodiness is critical if you want to maintain a lifelong capacity for a healthy mind and memory. The long-term effects of inflammation and cortisol that result from either seizures or repetitive cycling of intense moods can ultimately fry the part of your brain responsible for memory, especially the hippocampus. To stabilize your mood and protect your brain, talk to your doctor about the possibility of trying the same anticonvulsant medicines used for epilepsy. In addition to these big-gun anticonvulsant mood stabilizers, you can also take nutritional supplements like DHA (100–300 mg, three times a day) and magnesium (200 mg, two to three times a day, on an empty stomach) on top of your regular calcium/magnesium supplement. Small amounts of serotonin-like drugs—especially if you don't have a history of mania—such as 5-HTP (100 mg, three times a day) or SAMe (400–1,200 mg a day, on an empty stomach) will take the edge off of your twitchy moodiness and fuse-blowing tendencies as well.

Doing 30 minutes of aerobic exercise a day can help regulate weight. You might also try avoiding meditation (which can sometimes make epileptic seizures worse) and even certain foods that might trigger seizures, including wheat, dairy, and refined sugars.

Your mind-body makeover next moves to the emotional intuitive brain. Take a break from doing too much intensely deep, emotional, spiritual work. Lighten up! Get out of your dark cave of emotional and spiritual solitude and do something lighter and more superficial. You'll initially feel ridiculous, frivolous, or at least like a fish out of water, but do it anyway. Find some family members, kids, or pets (or all three) and go to a park and get dirty in the grass. Have a few friends bring you a stupid movie, take you bowling, or play poker with you.

I've always maintained that in the spiritual and psychological community, there's an overemphasis on "deep healing," on going ever more profoundly into one's healing journey. Sometimes you'll notice that after all that spiritual activity, your brain feels fried or like it's about to blow. That's when your sixth-chakra intuitive advisor is letting you know that you need to lighten up and get a more grounded, rational, ordinary mind-set.

What follows is my seven-step program to rehabilitate the Blown a Fuse and in the Dark, but Spiritually Illuminated types' tendencies to shun the earthly in favor of high-voltage, high-altitude spiritual illumination:

1. Identify your discomfort with looking for rational understanding in any problem. See your resistance to viewing the world through objective knowledge—no matter how conservative, liberal, or progressive it may be—because you find that such information never completely answers humankind's fundamental problems; it still keeps everyone in the dark.

2. Recognize your tendency to choose faith over knowledge any day, believing that true guidance can only be obtained by emptying your mind of facts and images and going into the darkness of unknowing to become illuminated by a higher power.

3. Discern that ignoring the solid facts of any situation and going by pure faith alone may sometimes feel effective, but making it a common practice isn't healthy for your brain in the long run because it can increase your risk of mood and memory problems.

4. Restrict your need to lead a life totally in darkness and in *spiritual* illumination. If you're still on the earth, living and breathing, you physically need to see the light of day and to maintain a flexible and adaptive perspective in order to relate to other people.

5. Know that you can still be spiritually illuminated and also balance that solitude by having a part-time job alongside people in society. In other words, you can fire up your brain spirituality, but also cool it down to relate to a more grounded daily existence.

6. Change the unhealthy thought pattern: *The spiritual mind-set is always better; the rational explanation is always more superficial and shallow* . . . to the healthier affirmation: *True wisdom transcends the view that one mind-set is right and others are wrong.*

7. Follow the sixth rule for intuitive health—*I know I'm different, but from now on I want to try to be the same (as other people)*—by realizing that being able to commune with the heavens doesn't mean shutting down communication with others here on Earth.

●-●-●

To create health in your sixth chakra, you need to be able to bend and sway with the winds of change, moving from a dig-your-heels-in, stay-the-course stance in some situations to a more exploratory, free-form mind-set in others when appropriate. This balance allows you to grow and change with the times, focusing on what is unfolding in front of you, instead of clinging desperately to ways that have passed, wishing you could turn back time. This isn't the easiest of concepts to grasp in today's youth-obsessed culture, but it's absolutely vital to ensure the well-being of your brain, eyes, and ears.

Whenever you experience health challenges in these areas, know that it's just your sixth-chakra intuitive advisor prodding you to keep moving forward and stay flexible enough to change your way of seeing things and thinking about them. To accomplish this, you must follow the sixth rule for intuitive health—*I know I'm different, but from now on I want to try to be the same (as other people)*—appreciating that all viewpoints truly are valid and valuable and, just like you, can themselves age and mature.

●-●-●-●-●-●

Chapter Nine

Seventh Chakra: "The Beat Goes On"

(Life-Threatening Illness and Brushes with Death)

Your seventh chakra—your connection to the divine through any organ or part of the body—is your intuitive advisor that will let you know how in touch you are with your life's purpose, especially when your life is threatened in some way. After all, nothing makes you think about the meaning of life, and yours in particular, like almost losing it.

In the 21st century, we're obsessed with controlling our lives *and* our deaths in almost every way possible. We can increase the chance of a birth in the first place through procedures such as in vitro fertilization, donor eggs and sperm, and surrogate pregnancy. We even have the technology now to correct our genetic makeup in utero. Once our kids are born, we try to control the development of their IQs by getting them educational mobiles and stimulation toys, prepping them with Baby Einstein videos, and sticking them in intellectually enriching day-care centers.

Our thirst for control doesn't end there. Our society has invented the extreme makeover, where we revamp people's appearance and try to control their fate by making them attain a fairy-tale-like beauty and Hollywood physique. We even try to reverse aging by dialing up our hormones—including estrogen, progesterone, testosterone, and human growth hormone—to reach those of a 20-year-old female or male. We've even extended our life spans by decades through the development of antibiotics, immunizations, chemotherapy, and antiviral treatment for deadly viruses like HIV, hepatitis B, or hepatitis C.

But even though we buy into the idea that we're in control—that we can take our very definite opinions about what is desirable and acceptable, create a plan, and somehow make it work the way we envision—sooner or later, change occurs. Our plan hits a snag. I heard a Jewish scholar once say, "We plan and God laughs." So smart.

When a seventh-chakra crisis occurs, in the form of a life-threatening illness or a brush with death, life as we know it stops, and we're faced with our own mortality. We're forced to ask ourselves some sobering questions: Where do we go from here? Does the beat go on, with us continuing to exist on Earth? Do we still have a purpose? What path do we follow? When does our path on Earth end and another begin? Do we pass on to a different plane of existence, hopefully one of everlasting peace? And if we stay, what do we do with the time we have left? If we're given another chance, what do we make of it?

Balancing the energies of this chakra involves both living a purpose-filled life with every breath, as well as allowing ourselves to let go with dignity and grace when the time comes.

The first time I saw seventh-chakra intuition in action was with Mrs. Sousa, a little 76-year-old Portuguese woman with end-stage colon cancer. She'd suffered with this illness for three long years after having lived a very full life, which included three beautiful daughters, two handsome sons, twenty-one grandchildren, and four great-grandchildren. After her husband died, Mrs. Sousa's health started to fail; and the doctors found cancer that had spread to her liver, lungs, and brain.

Eventually, after having made peace with her illness and saying that she was ready to go home to heaven, Mrs. Sousa signed a DNR (do not resuscitate) order indicating that she didn't want any heroic measures taken to keep her alive. She said that if she started to die, she didn't want tubes shoved down her throat to make her breathe, a process called intubation, nor did she want to be put on any life-support system if her organs failed. Mrs. Sousa told her doctor that she thought what she was supposed to do on Earth was be a wife and a mother, and now that she was done with those jobs, she was ready to pass on.

To make Mrs. Sousa's life more comfortable, physicians started removing the cancerous fluid that had begun to accumulate in her abdomen. During one of these procedures, the elderly woman coded. If you watch TV medical dramas like *ER*, you know what that means. Her heart stopped, and she essentially started the process of dying. The only problem was that the other people in the room were Mrs. Sousa's youngest daughter, Ruth, and a very young medical resident. As the resident started to back away from Mrs. Sousa, thus allowing her to finish the process of dying and appropriately following the

DNR order, Ruth began to scream, "You've got to save my mother's life! You've got to save her life!"

Nurses came running with the emergency equipment on the code cart, but another one had the chart with the DNR order and was trying to stop resuscitation efforts, thus respecting the patient's request. But Ruth began to scream even louder, "You've got to save her! I'll sue you all! You just can't let her sit there and die when you can bring her back!" The medical resident was so terrified that he grabbed the code cart and intubated and resuscitated Mrs. Sousa.

Hours later, Mrs. Sousa woke up, speechless, connected by tubes to a respirator. A day later her heart was beating and she was breathing on her own again. The hospital lawyers were called, but there was nothing they could do, because Ruth wouldn't leave her mother's room. Her sole purpose now was to make sure that at all costs, her mother's heart kept beating. And Mrs. Sousa said nothing.

Days went by, and an x-ray was ordered to check the patient's lungs for possible pneumonia. Ruth stayed behind, as the resident insisted that she couldn't go down to the radiology department. As the resident and a medical student rolled Mrs. Sousa into the rickety elevator and started to descend, Mrs. Sousa coded again. They had no emergency equipment with them, and when they tried to get out of the elevator, the door jammed. Without any intubation or resuscitation equipment, they tried CPR, but they weren't successful and Mrs. Sousa died. She finally got what she wished for: she got to die because her purpose in life was complete. Ruth, however, didn't get what *she* wanted, and she was angry.

●–●–●

If you're diagnosed with a life-threatening illness, it can come from any chakra—malignant melanoma or HIV (first chakra), prostate or ovarian cancer (second chakra), colon cancer (third chakra), breast cancer or heart disease (fourth chakra), thyroid cancer (fifth chakra), or brain tumor (sixth chakra). Any and all of them tend to collapse the details of your life into a single critical item on your to-do list, one that trumps all other causes: *survive.* (Or sometimes—as in the case of Mrs. Sousa—*let go,* hopefully in a good way.)

On the other hand, if you develop a health problem such as chronic fatigue, fibromyalgia, environmental illness, Lyme disease, agoraphobia, post-traumatic stress disorder (PTSD), or severe depression, you can end up bedridden, crippled with debilitating pain, or on drugs that make you sleep all day. This is also a seventh-chakra crisis, because the disease or condition effectively stops you from living. The same is true of facing a diagnosis like HIV, sinking into the depths of an addiction such as alcoholism, becoming morbidly obese, or developing dementia. You're left tottering on the brink.

For a healthy life (not to mention a healthy exit plan), it's important to follow the seventh rule for intuitive health: *What doesn't kill you makes you stronger* (life-threatening illnesses and revising your life purpose). The health of your seventh chakra—your longevity and capacity to survive a life-threatening illness—involves learning two things: (1) how, at each stage of your life, to be able to pursue your life's purpose; and (2) how, when faced with potential death, to reconstitute your spirit and align yourself with a new life goal and focus.

Most people with seventh-chakra health problems tend to fall somewhere in between four extreme categories: the *Life Is a Highway* type—those who follow the straight and narrow, focused path through life, leaving little room for spontaneity; the *Accidental Tourist*—those who tend to saunter through life aimlessly, wandering from one adventure to another; the *"I Did It My Way"* type—those who have a focused purpose that guides them through life, balanced with intervening spontaneity; and finally, the *Undercover Angel*—those who believe that every single event in their lives is in the hands of fate and they're powerless to change any of it.

The Life Is a Highway Type

The first type of seventh-chakra extreme is the Life Is a Highway type, those who pin their hopes on a carefully crafted plan reflecting their life's purpose, pretty much ignoring the potential for spontaneous, unplanned adventures. Take Xola, 38, one of those people who live life on a mission. As if driven by an inner autopilot, Xola had mapped out her future by the time she was 12 years old: By 22, she would be married. By 24, she would begin to have the first of three kids. By 30, she would have bought a house, and by 35, she would have paid off the mortgage in full. By 36, she would have returned to school (for a law degree, or maybe an MBA). By 50, although she was uncharacteristically vague on the details, she wanted to be well on her way to stockpiling her retirement so that after having funded her children's college educations, she could quit working. A serious, studious child, Xola in fact followed her plan to a T. As if on cruise control, she proceeded to check off the items on her list.

When other people were taking the summer off after college to travel, Xola had no time—and didn't want to divert money from her plan—for such foolishness. She married her boyfriend, Ben, and proceeded to have the first of her three children, right on schedule. But then her husband's company was dismantled in an organizational buyout. Ben spent more than two years looking for a similar middle-management job elsewhere, living on their savings in the meantime. Xola could see her dreams going up in smoke, so she started an Internet business selling gourmet chocolate-chip cookies with a friend. It took off immediately and became a smashing success.

Xola went into hyperdrive, proceeding to have two more children, in keeping with her original plan. But her business was demanding, consuming her every waking thought. Soon Ben started to help her with it. Sales continued to climb, and by the time she turned 34, Xola had paid for her house. She was right on schedule, but at what cost?

Xola was working 14- to 16-hour days, and her house, which was supposed to be a home for her family, had been taken over by the business. Although she was on target with her life's plan, that plan hadn't factored in a specific critical element—*living*. Xola and her husband, and soon their kids, were living to serve a business that, like a parasite, had taken over their physical, emotional, and energetic lives. When Ben and the kids began to complain, Xola would hear none of it. She'd simply reply, "I'm doing this all for you."

At 36, Xola started gaining weight and having vague digestive complaints. She thought her stomach was distended from eating all those carbohydrates while sampling cookie dough in the kitchen. Then, after a routine visit, her ob-gyn sent her to the hospital for an ultrasound, which showed a huge tumor on her right ovary. Eventually, it was diagnosed as ovarian cancer. From the age of 12, Xola had a linear, rational, no-nonsense plan for her life that was like a freeway with no exits. She'd never allowed herself to deviate in any way from her plan. There had been no stopping to smell the flowers; no taking a break to laugh; no margin of error for accidents, mistakes, interventions, or even a revision of her plan. She just kept barreling straight ahead, full speed. But Xola's seventh-chakra intuitive advisor applied the brakes for her. Through a life-threatening illness, ovarian cancer, her intuitive advisor was signaling that she needed to reevaluate her life's purpose.

If you, like Xola, tend to live with such single-minded focus that you don't leave any room for random diversions, you may be a Life Is a Highway type. Going where the road takes you isn't an acceptable option. You move from one goal to another to make your life happen, but you never allow it to happen *to* you. You don't account for those random, spontaneous events that can interrupt your plans, even though that's just the way life is.

What I've learned from people like Xola is that these types are so busy being upset when things don't go exactly according to plan that, ironically, they can't see that things really always do go exactly according to *The Plan* (a greater, divinely guided one, that is). Let me give you an example of this from my own life. As you know from my previous stories, from the time I was seven years old, I wanted to go to medical school. My plan was to become a physician and scientist, so from the moment I entered middle school, I mapped out every course and credit to reach those goals. You could never have met a more purposeful person. And when all those years of schooling and planning were supposed to culminate in my placement in a program my mind was absolutely set on doing, my spine fell apart. Not just one or two, but *four* disks blew on two separate occasions, temporarily paralyzing a hand and a leg and essentially preventing the plan from happening.

I was devastated. So because my spine fell apart and I couldn't stand up to do the work required for the neurology program, I sat down in the psychiatry program. Instead of becoming a behavioral neurologist, I became a neuropsychiatrist. I just turned it around. And the medical leave of absence I was allowed to take while I was recuperating with my spine allowed me to work in the field of medical intuition. So even though I was thinking at the time that my plan didn't work out, it was only because I didn't see The Plan. Had my life gone according to *my* plan, there's no way I would have been able to see the value of intuition, to have the opportunity to study neuropsychiatry, or to envision the possibility of having two separate careers instead of just one.

At the age of seven, all I saw was one thing. I didn't have an understanding then of what was possible. And when I look back on it after the fact, like a Monday-morning quarterback, I realize that my plan did play out, but with a twist. It was a greater Plan—or as they say in marketing, a new-and-improved one—that worked out.

What clues signal that you may be a Life Is a Highway type? People have told you that you're one of the most focused, determined, driven, and indomitable spirits they've ever met. That song with the catchy chorus about getting knocked down and then getting up again could have been written for you. Nothing can prevent you from accomplishing your goals. No amount of adversity, no amount of discouragement, prevents you from continuing on your path. You have a hard time relaxing. People accuse you of being a work addict, a perfectionist. You never take a mental-health day or call in sick, unless you want to stay home and catch up on work or get ahead. You carry over vacation days from one year to the next, but then you never even use them. If you do take a vacation, it's always scheduled about a year in advance. You would never throw a bag in the back of the car on the spur of the moment and take off for the weekend.

You've broken engagements and ended relationships with potential partners whom you were truly in love with because they weren't practical choices and didn't fit into your life's plan. If you're in a committed relationship, you'd leave in a heartbeat if it meant choosing between your partner and your purpose. No one has ever accused you of being an incurable romantic.

If this description fits, then you may be a Life Is a Highway type. You're a sheer force to be reckoned with. Good luck to anyone who tries to get in your way! When those inevitable random events in life threaten to delay your plan, you simply contrive a detour. But in time, your seventh-chakra intuitive advisor will let you know that you need to loosen up and allow for some unforeseen adventures. The first alarm that you'll receive is that your life will come to a screeching halt. The day you get the diagnosis will become permanently engraved in your mind. From that point onward, you'll start to look for a new purpose. You'll describe your life as *BC* or *AC* ("before cancer" or "after cancer"— or insert the initial of your particular life-threatening diagnosis here).

The moment you hear those simple words *You have cancer* (or some other life-threatening illness), nothing feels the same. Life obtains a new urgency. As you look at the list of items you so seriously and deliberately put on your to-do list for the next several days, you begin to realize how ridiculous and trivial they really are. Instead, you're forced to strike out on a brand-new journey over which you have no control.

Yet all of us have a part of the Life Is a Highway type in us. Like Xola, each of us has a tendency to pin our hopes on certain life plans and allow little or no room for deviation. It's been said that those people whose lives are going exactly according to their plan meet each year at a convention in Chicago held in a telephone booth. (Yes, I'm kidding. Do you know *anyone* whose life has gone exactly according to plan?)

I remember when we had to take home-economics class in middle school, and the first project was sewing a jumper. All of the girls were instructed to go to Woolworth's and buy the same McCall's pattern. That's 36 girls with 36 identical McCall's patterns. You might think that the jumpers would have turned out pretty much the same because they were all made from the same plan. Not on your life! Some hems were crooked. Some were made from plaid material and had ridiculously mismatched seams. And some dresses actually came out looking pretty good. So it is with life: we can all start out with a general plan, headed toward a particular goal, but eventually we'll have to come to grips with the fact that our final product may turn out to look quite different from the "pattern" we began with.

Intuitive Advice for the Life Is a Highway Type

Do you suffer from any type of life-threatening health problem, and do you tend to have the Life Is a Highway approach to life? If so, don't panic—mind-body medicine and medical intuition can help you maintain your drive and aspirations while also allowing some spontaneity and flexibility in your life's plan, and your mind-body makeover first addresses your physical health. You could have any seventh-chakra problem with Life Is a Highway tendencies. But if, like Xola, you're diagnosed with ovarian cancer, your doctor will most likely schedule surgery right away, probably followed by both chemotherapy and radiation. If you're determined to do everything you can to rid yourself of the cancer, you'll seek both traditional Western medicine (checking the Internet for information on the latest experimental drug trials) and complementary medicine.

For example, an acupuncturist and a Chinese doctor with a complementary-medicine background may suggest that you try a macrobiotic healing diet combining fish, soy, and dark green leafy vegetables with miso soup and seaweed. This way of eating essentially removes all the toxins from your diet so that your immune system can focus on fighting the cancer without having to additionally deal with preservatives and allergens in the food you eat. This also makes it easier for your body to recover from the toxic effects of the chemotherapy and radiation.

Next, the mind-body makeover moves to your emotional health. But this is where the makeover gets a little tricky, because instead of *doing,* or following a plan overtly, the emphasis here needs to be on *allowing,* or learning how to mindfully be in the moment without intentionally trying to plan or control the event. This may be something you've never really done before . . . ever.

For example, let's look at how Xola eventually accomplished this. Through all the treatments, she refused to believe that her ovarian cancer was going to have any impact on her capacity to be a wife, a mother, and the head of her very successful cookie business. Xola told her friends that to let the cancer have any power to put a dent in her plans was to allow it to win, and with brute determination and sheer force, she proclaimed to everyone that not one part of her life plan would be compromised.

Then, Xola got pneumonia after one of her chemotherapy treatments, and as they say, the stuffing was knocked out of her. Xola spent a couple of weeks in bed and could not muster any energy to do anything but talk with a few friends and family members. Alone, without the distraction of schedules, her infamous to-do list, and e-mail for the first time in her life, Xola felt what it was like to have wide-open times of unplanned moments. Once, when one of her children came in with a new dog named Chase from the pound to cheer her mother up, the animal got a little rambunctious and knocked over some flowers. Water, stems, petals, and floral containers went flying, scaring the dog so badly that it dove under the bed for cover. Instead of being upset, Xola laughed and laughed, then cried, and then laughed again at the messiness amid the previously perfect order of her life. It was the first time she'd felt what it was like to experience spontaneous, unbridled life. Yes, it was a little chaotic, but it was hilarious, and it made her feel vibrant and very much alive—even if it had to happen in the setting of cancer.

People said Xola was never the same after adopting that dog from the pound while she was recuperating from her pneumonia and ovarian cancer. When she returned to work, her schedule was very much pared down (much to everyone's shock). At first, friends assumed that Xola needed extra time to rest after all the surgery and chemotherapy. What she'd gone through must have been simply exhausting, they thought. But when they visited Xola, even though she looked a little tired, she had this new, bright, shining light in her eyes. Every day, she closed the cookie-kitchen door at exactly 5 P.M. Even though Xola knew that this would decrease her production and the business's income for a while, she'd cleared her slate in the afternoons, in the evenings, and on weekends so that she could have fun just hanging out and spending time with the people (and dog) she loved.

Xola's life-threatening illness, although physically and emotionally devastating, struck a chord of euphoria in her, almost like getting a round of electroshock treatments. In psychiatry, there is a very controversial method for medicating nonresponsive depression that involves passing an electrical current into a patient's brain. This causes the person to have a seizure, which allegedly causes the patient's brain to dump a lot of antidepressant neurotransmitters, in turn helping them snap out of the depression.

A similar thing happens with individuals who have epilepsy. Essentially, although they may take anticonvulsant drugs that help eliminate their seizures, the electrical activity called *kindling* can still build up in their brains over time. When this happens, they start to get irritable, cranky, and more depressed (a syndrome called, believe it or not, *forced normalization*). And so the theory goes that when these people finally do have a breakthrough seizure, it may be akin to electro-shock therapy, because both processes dump an explosive blast of neurotransmitters into their system and relieve depression, and their mood greatly improves.

Similarly, when you have an emotional shock in your life, such as being told that you have a life-threatening illness, or experiencing some other serious catastrophic event, everything comes to a screech-ing halt. The trauma of this terrifying event literally rearranges your mind and your brain chemistry. The experience of being diagnosed with cancer or another life-threatening illness strangely feels like be-ing reborn, because from the moment you get that death sentence, you simultaneously get the opportunity to plan your life all over again—with a new direction, new rules, and the addition of some space for spontaneity and serendipity. Who knows? You might even begin to look for a higher plan, a greater divine purpose that had a hand in creating the whole life diversion in the first place.

Here, then, is my seven-part program that will help rehabilitate the Life Is a Highway types' rigid pursuit of their chiseled-in-stone goals or plans without allowing for any of life's inevitable deviations:

1. Identify the controlled, streamlined, powerful feeling you get when you remain on the course of the life plan you've pinned your hopes on.

2. Recognize that you have little room for any deviation from this plan. When some random life event happens to interrupt your momentum, you don't allow yourself to be diverted. You'll push hard and contrive a course to success at any cost and despite any road-blocks along the way.

3. Discern that there are a lot of other people out there (a universe of beings, in fact), all with their own plans. And every one of these people and purposes have to fit into a higher plan, a master plan, which you may or may not be privy to—depending on whether you stop every once in a while to listen. Reassess your life when you reach any critical juncture and listen for appropriate instructions. Putting on blinders to prevent interruptions, detours, and other aggravating disturbances may prevent you from seeing a greater purpose—one that you would never, ever consider for yourself given your limited perspective.

4. Restrict your tendency to have five- and ten-year plans without leaving open space in your schedule for spontaneous, unstructured fun or for other important activities that come up suddenly.

5. Know that you don't want to live to facilitate working; you want to work to facilitate living—however, you needn't wait until your 70s to enjoy your life.

6. Change the unhealthy thought pattern: *I'm afraid of change; I'm afraid of reevaluating my life's purpose* . . . to the healthier affirmation: *If necessary, I am willing to let go of an old identity and an old lifestyle, relationship, and career so that I can grow and develop my potential. I acknowledge that every ending is an opportunity for something new to begin.*

7. Follow the seventh rule for intuitive health—*What doesn't kill you makes you stronger*—by pursuing your life's purpose and also being open to the sweet serendipity of a new plan if it presents itself.

The Accidental Tourist

The second type of seventh-chakra extreme is the Accidental Tourist, those who tend to saunter through life, aimlessly wandering from one adventure to another, wherever life takes them, without a focused plan or life's purpose. My client Zachary was certainly like this. Ever since his father dropped dead at age 40 of a massive heart attack right in the family's kitchen, Zachary's mother had held on to her son for dear life. Everyone loved the boy because he had such a warm, carefree, fun way of approaching life. In high school and college, he was always the life of the party and could frequently be counted on to bring the beer. Zachary took six years to graduate from college, having lost a lot of credits from too much partying and also from transferring from school to school a lot.

After college, this overgrown child hung around the house for a while, and then his mother sent him on an extended trip to Europe with some friends. He stayed overseas for several years, teaching English as a second language, bartending, and even working as a "manny" (a male nanny) at one point. Then, when he turned 29, his mother told him it was time for him to come home and begin life as an adult. But when she picked him up at the airport, she was stunned to see that her son had easily gained 80 pounds. At 5'10" and almost 280 pounds, Zachary lumbered slowly off the plane and into the car. Then he took his place back in his old bedroom as if nothing had changed since before he went off to college.

For the next seven years, Zachary vegetated at home, sleeping until 1 P.M. on most days. He occasionally had a part-time job and intermittently mowed the lawn on his mother's riding mower. As the years passed, his weight climbed higher and higher. At 36, after a serious automobile accident where Zachary fell asleep at the wheel, he went to see a doctor at his mother's insistence. The doctor found that my client's weight had climbed to 475 pounds, his cholesterol was 300, and he had sleep apnea. Because of his weight, the fat on his chest had been compressing his lungs and heart, preventing him from breathing properly at night and interrupting his sleep. The resulting sleep deprivation was what had caused him to fall asleep while driving.

If you, like Zachary, are an Accidental Tourist, you occasionally have goals, but then you run out of steam. Without a grand purpose to your life, what plans you manage to make tend to fall through. Your life is a series of spontaneous adventures, but it's only a matter of time before your endless and aimless wandering catches up to you. Your seventh-chakra intuitive advisor will soon stop you in the middle of yet another detour and force you to face the fact that your life lacks direction of any kind.

What I've learned from people like Zachary is that Accidental Tourists are almost always surrounded by well-meaning, overly generous and responsive individuals (like Rocks of Dependability, described in the chapter on the third chakra) or people who act like parents (such as Perpetual Partners, described in the chapter on the fourth chakra). Accidental Tourists may have trouble leaving home, not wanting to physically, emotionally, or financially separate from their mothers. For their part, these moms are equally unable to give up nurturing their little girl or boy, who never grow up. Mother and (adult) baby continue to live in a symbiotic hell. (Incidentally, in some cases, a father can be stuck in this perpetual nurturing role with an Accidental Tourist as well. It's not as common in our culture for a father to want to infantilize a son or daughter, but it happens.)

What clues signal that you may be an Accidental Tourist? Well, you worked odd jobs as you traveled across the United States, Europe, Asia, or South America for more than three years before even considering college. And then if you did decide to go, you switched your major more than twice. In fact, you might have changed colleges two or more times, and you may have taken a year off to find yourself in between schools. Your job now is way below your intellectual ability, but you still don't know what you want to do when you grow up, although you're at least in your late 20s already and may even be in your 30s or 40s. About two or three times a year, you get wind of a new cool idea for a career, and you set up a whole business plan. Maybe you even get business cards and look into building a Website, but before long, you get distracted and move on to something else.

Someone may have told you that you have attention deficit disorder (ADD). You don't really work or learn well in a structured setting with someone looking over your shoulder and telling you what to do. (You weren't much into competitive team sports, either.) You march to the beat of a different drummer. Multiple wonderful family members have helped support you through college and then through your 20s and maybe even your 30s. Although it bothers you that you have to lean on people until you get on your feet, you try to be kind and personable, and you do odd chores around the house to defray your expenses. You like to sleep in, usually past 11 A.M., and go to bed later, after 1 A.M. You've had problems with using substances, such as alcohol, marijuana, or stimulants.

If this sounds familiar, then you may be an Accidental Tourist. You can't escape life by always being on vacation. Sooner or later, you must come home, unpack your bags, and start doing some hard work finding your real purpose. Otherwise, the first alarm your seventh-chakra intuitive guidance system will sound will be your body slowly and insidiously spiraling out of control. If you don't heed the wake-up call, eventually a serious crisis is likely to bring you bolt upright, shaking you awake from your lifelong slumber.

If we look closely at Zachary's story, we'll realize that each of us can find within ourselves an Accidental Tourist, a part of us that from time to time has absolutely no idea what our purpose is or what our goals or aspirations should be. Sometimes if a perfectly outlined, detailed life plan isn't apparent to us, we may feel lost. But not many of us are given such a clear and specific picture of what our life's purpose is. And even if we were to receive an itemized list in Technicolor, eventually the plan always gets revised anyway. The key isn't necessarily to *have* the correct purpose, but to try to *live* with purpose. Even if we have only our next two steps in mind, we at least have the general direction, if not an active destination. And eventually, as we add one or two more steps along the way, we'll create a path.

Intuitive Advice for the Accidental Tourist

Do you suffer from any type of life-threatening health problem, and do you tend to have the Accidental Tourist approach to life? If so, then you can use mind-body medicine and medical intuition to figure out a plan for your life, find a purpose that has meaning, and get on with it once and for all; and your mind-body makeover begins with the physical body. You could have any seventh-chakra health crisis with Accidental Tourist tendencies, but if, like Zachary, you're obese and have had a few incidents of falling asleep at the wheel, see a pulmonologist, a doctor who specializes in lung problems.

The pulmonologist may schedule you for a sleep study to see if you have sleep apnea, a potentially fatal condition where you actually stop breathing repeatedly during deep sleep, up to hundreds of times a night, for as long as a full minute per episode. The fragmented sleep that results is of such poor quality that it's almost like not sleeping at all. If you indeed have apnea, you may be given a continuous positive airway pressure (CPAP) machine that sends a stream of compressed air into your lungs via a face mask, keeping your airway open and ensuring that you continue to breathe.

You must also address your obesity at the same time, however, because your added weight could be further compressing your airways as you recline. You might be referred to a bariatric physician, a doctor specializing in obesity. In the most extreme cases, the physician may suggest inpatient treatment that would put you on a daily rehabilitative program for weight loss.

Next, your mind-body makeover addresses the emotional right brain. And not a moment too soon. With any life-threatening illness that involves an addiction that's left you anesthetized—whether you numbed yourself with food, drugs, marijuana, or alcohol; or you distracted yourself with the constant buzz of gambling, sex, or work—you wouldn't be able to recognize your life's purpose if you tripped over it.

Chances are that if your life has gotten this out of control, you're going to need a very structured environment to rebuild yourself physically and emotionally from the ground up. Look for an addiction treatment center that has an extremely controlled schedule— where someone else tells you when to get up, what to eat, where to go, and when to sleep. Because you've had no order and no schedule for such a long time, you'll now need to give up control for a while and allow someone else to set up some extreme regimentation that will, in effect, reset your life.

Here's an outline of what that rebuilding process can look like, chakra by chakra (but also refer to the previous chapters for further details on each step):

— **First chakra:** Take a look at the families in your life, including not just your biological relatives but other groups of people who surround you and fulfill a similar purpose. Try to stay away from those who have addictions and invite new people who have healthier values into your family.

— **Second chakra:** Take a fearless look at your intimate relationships. See if they have fundamental healthy building blocks that can survive the new kind of life you're going to lead. Also, identify how your substance abuse was the way you previously chose to medicate your problems with money or love.

— **Third chakra:** Identify how you take (or don't take) responsibility for yourself in the world, either in a job or in a relationship. Once you leave residential treatment, immediately find a job that involves duties you must perform each day. In this position, you should have a boss or a supervisor to whom you're accountable and who will give you orders, feedback, and rewards. This job needn't be one that's going to make or break your career. This work is meant only to get you started, once again, as a member of the workforce.

— **Fourth chakra:** Go to a 12-step program daily where you can talk about your feelings. Learn to fully feel and release all of the five basic emotions—*fear, anger, sadness, love,* and *joy*—allowing them to flow through you like a wave, swelling and then receding, letting them go without getting stuck in any of them. Take nutritional supplements and medications to treat depression, anxiety, irritability, and moodiness.

— **Fifth chakra:** Taking assertiveness training if necessary, learn how to maintain a balanced and flexible voice. Become skilled at being insistent and forward about your own ideas or needs as well as receptive and open to other people's thoughts and desires when you communicate.

— **Sixth chakra:** Learn compensatory strategies for any unusual or atypical learning styles you may have, including attention deficit disorder (ADD) or obsessive-compulsive disorder (OCD). Also, plan to sign up for classes—whether you attend a local community college, take online courses, or work with a vocational advisor—to build a foundation of intellect that you'll need for your new life's purpose.

— **Seventh chakra:** Address the lack of faith or spiritual purpose you may have, and begin to develop the ability to connect with a source of divine guidance through a daily meditative or prayer practice. Use this guidance to help identify the new life plan that you're constructing.

Once you've begun this long rebuilding process, the haze in your mind will clear, and your purpose and calling will slowly become apparent. Actually, you'll be reborn: just like a cancer patient who is pulled from the jaws of death by a lifesaving treatment, a person with a terminal addiction who leaves a recovery center has been born again.

Here, then, is my seven-part program to rehabilitate the Accidental Tourists' habit of living on semipermanent vacation:

1. Identify how you've traveled through life going from one unplanned experience to another. See that in your worldview, life is something that happens *to* you; it's not something you're likely to shape or create, because such control lacks the spontaneity and free-floating existence that you crave.

2. Recognize that your extended casual approach to life has led you to your present situation—where, without any goals or definitive plan, you also don't have any accomplishments.

3. Discern that once you decide to become responsible for your life, consciously making plans and following a purpose, you'll increase your chance of having a future and surviving your life-threatening illness.

4. Restrict your tendency to collapse into regret, blaming yourself for doing things that increased your risk of the catastrophic situation you're now in.

5. Know that you can still enjoy spontaneous adventures in your life even if from now on you live it with purpose, following an overarching plan filled with hope and aspirations for the future.

6. Change the negative thought pattern: *I don't know what my dreams and life's purpose are; I tend to get my joy through family and friends* . . . and replace it with the healthier affirmation: *As I pursue happiness through my dreams and life's purpose, I give birth to the unrealized potential within them, the unlimited splendor of my soul.*

7. Follow the seventh rule for intuitive health—*What doesn't kill you makes you stronger*—by discovering and reveling in your life's purpose, using spontaneity not to escape that purpose but to add joy to it along the way.

The "I Did It My Way" Type

The next seventh-chakra extreme is the "I Did It My Way" type, those who seem like experts at drawing detailed blueprints for their lives, certain that they've covered every base by even allowing for a little spontaneity. My client Yamini was the perfect example. From early on, this woman kept a journal outlining all of her hopes, plans, and dreams for the future. With an American father who was an Episcopal priest and an Indian mother who was a Hindu, the 47-year-old led a life steeped in ritual and spirituality. She learned the power of positive thinking early on by reading Norman Vincent Peale, and she spent hours examining her mind for any negative chatter she could eliminate.

After years of spontaneous spiritual pilgrimages, Yamini became very active in the New Age movement. She began to do visualizations and affirmations daily so that she could manifest what she wanted in her world. Her plan included a house on the water, an attractive partner, great Tantric sex, a single-digit dress size, and a six-figure income. Yamini had it all mapped out and daily would visualize all of it into place, creating her future. She even factored in periods of spontaneous spiritual exploration and play by planning various adventures and retreats. Over time, my client indeed attracted a handsome mate (whom she met at a spiritual retreat in the Poconos), great sex, a plummeting dress size, and a high income working in a hedge-fund trading company. She was thrilled to have manifested so much.

It all started to unravel when Yamini received a phone call in the middle of the night from her partner's wife . . . apparently he wasn't divorced, as he'd proclaimed when they met several months earlier. Within months, the stock market crashed, and the CEO of her company was under investigation for hedge-fund fraud. Yamini knew that she had to start looking for another job quickly.

Then my client woke up in the middle of the night with a kind of trembling in the side of her body. Over the next several months, she saw a series of neurologists who administered a series of confusing tests with conflicting results. She was given a tentative diagnosis of amyotrophic lateral sclerosis (ALS), commonly known as Lou Gehrig's disease.

Yamini told me that she always knew her life had a purpose. She'd pinned her hopes on an itemized list and a detailed plan that, even in the midst of her difficulties, she was continuing to beam out into the universe through her very focused affirmations and visualizations. She couldn't understand what had gone wrong. What Yamini needed to learn was the wisdom hidden in her Hindi name, which meant "night." Her seventh-chakra intuitive advisor had preempted her regularly scheduled life design in order to send the emergency signal that she needed to go into the dark night of her faith and yield to the wisdom of a higher power's plan.

If you, like Yamini, are an "I Did It My Way" type, you've always had a plan, as well as the ability to acquire the necessary skills and techniques to make it happen. You use affirmations and create visualizations to will what you want into being, without leaving much wiggle room for any dissenting point of view. You have a bull's-eye focus on your plans and purpose as well as an ever-flexible capacity to explore, be spontaneous, and go with the flow of life. However, even when you're having free-range moments and random experiences, you believe that you're choosing it all, calling it in, making everything in your life happen unilaterally.

What I've learned from people like Yamini is that My Way types depend solely upon their own point of view, their limited perspective and understanding, to outline what they think they can create for themselves. And as long as they think that what *they* want for their future is best, they'll never live an existence that transcends that. They don't understand that their limited human perspective also puts a cap on what they can accomplish.

In Yamini's case, she wanted to manifest a good-looking man and a six-figure income, and that's what she got on the surface. She didn't incorporate the perspective of a divine higher power into her plans and affirmations. Instead of making demands of God and the

Universe as if she herself knew what was best, she could have followed her affirmations with some core phrase that included humility and a humble appreciation that her human point of view was indeed limited. For example, when doing affirmations, she could have said what she wanted and then added, "I humbly ask that this or something better now comes to me in a totally harmonious way for the good of all concerned. So be it. Amen." Without having a personal purpose balanced with divine purpose, Yamini was in danger of living in a way that remained forever superficial. Her seventh-chakra intuitive advisor threw her a life preserver disguised as a potentially deadly illness to shock her into seeing life from this higher perspective and learning how to live in the darkness with faith.

What clues indicate that you're the My Way type? You believe that by yourself you can manifest anything you put your mind to if you hold enough intention. You do "command" affirmations and conduct your life as if you're solely responsible for creating your own reality. You don't make mistakes—you have "learning experiences." You think that pessimism and negative thoughts alone cause people to fail to get what they want. You keep a journal filled with detailed manifestation plans outlining what you want, including particulars about the type of house, car, and income you envision.

If this sounds familiar, then you may be the "I Did It My Way" type. You have strong intention and an incredibly positive attitude. But sooner or later, you're going to realize that you alone aren't responsible for creating your reality, because you aren't alone on the earth or in the universe. Yes, we all play a critical role in a higher plan, a master design. But if our goals don't fit into the destiny that the divine has in mind for us, then the blueprints we planned will get reworked or rejected altogether.

Your seventh-chakra intuitive advisor will sound its first alarm via what I call a rude awakening. Having become so conditioned to getting what you want for so long, all of a sudden at a key time in your life, your plan will tank. And you'll get handed a life-threatening or life-altering illness.

Somewhere within us we all have a part of the My Way type. Like Yamini, each of us can remember times when it felt like we had done everything humanly and spiritually possible to have success, and still things didn't go according to our plans—no matter how well we prepared, how hard we worked, how much help we got, how many affirmations we did, or how often we prayed. It's a sobering thought to realize something we've suspected all along: that we are, in fact, not the center of the universe and not in control of everything that happens in our world. But when yet another plan has fallen through, despite our best efforts and because of things that are totally out of our control, we might consider the possibility that the hand of the heavens is behind the failure.

My very good friend Naomi Judd taught me a great phrase I use to comfort myself in times like these: "Man's rejection is God's protection." Even if we don't see the protection we're receiving at the time, we must learn to summon blind faith that whatever has unfolded is indeed for our highest good.

Intuitive Advice for the "I Did It My Way" Type

Do you suffer from any type of life-threatening health problem, and do you tend to have the "I Did It My Way" approach to life? If so, you can use mind-body medicine and medical intuition to find your way in life without insisting that everything always go according to your plan, and your mind-body makeover begins by addressing the physical body. You could have any seventh-chakra health crisis with "I Did It My Way" tendencies. But if you happen to have been given a tentative diagnosis of a potentially fatal disorder or, like Yamini, of the neurodegenerative disorder ALS, your first step is not to panic.

However, during the time when your physician is monitoring you, watching your disease declare itself, there's much you can do to affect your fate. For one, you could reevaluate every aspect of your nutritional, environmental, and occupational life that could be related to your illness. In the case of ALS, you might look into the possibility of exposure to heavy metals (including mercury, organic solvents, and pesticides), as well as environmental chemicals that may be related to your condition. Many complementary physicians have protocols for nutritional agents that may help remove some of these toxic components.

With degenerative disorders, I also recommend aggressively working to regenerate tissue and renew function. Studies show that whether you've lost physical strength with a neuromuscular disorder or memory with dementia, you can regain some function if you work hard. Even Alzheimer's patients with mild to moderate memory problems can improve if they follow a daily exercise program and do assigned chores, such as taking care of a pet or a plant, every day. Stroke victims can also recover function through aggressive physical therapy. In addition, an acupuncturist and traditional Chinese herbalist may be able to identify the energetic imbalance that's increasing your susceptibility this illness. So even if you haven't been formally diagnosed with a life-threatening problem, now is the time to "stockpile" functionality and try to buffer against possible degeneration.

Theoretically, by aggressively treating your disorder, you may be able to arrest further development of your illness so that your condition forever stays at the preclinical, nondangerous level. The experience will give you enough of a rude awakening that you'll be inspired to continue to reevaluate how you live your life, without its being so serious that you think you're going to leave the planet any day now.

Next, your mind-body makeover moves to the emotional intuitive brain. If "I Did It My Way" is your pattern, up to this point you've been very good at moving through your life with purpose and spontaneity, all the while feeling that you're creating your reality. But once you have a potential diagnosis of a life-threatening illness, you get an opportunity to co-create your life path with a higher power. You have the chance to develop the faith to *listen* to how your hopes and plans might fit into your divine purpose, not to mention what divine guidance has in store for you.

In the case of ALS, this important step can actually save your life. A scientific study published in the late '80s showed that people with this disease who had a strong life purpose lived longer, with less disability. In the spirit of longevity, you might try bargaining with God, using the "Life Grant technique." I suggest this for all of my medical-intuitive clients faced with a life-threatening illness. This is like the grant proposals that researchers or nonprofit organizations write to get funding. But this is one that you send to the universe, God, or whatever higher power you believe in, outlining how much longer you want to live and what you intend to do with whatever additional years you're allowed to have.

To do this, take a piece of paper and write your name and date on the top. Then, along the top of the page, write: LIFE GRANT PROPOSAL. Follow that by a time period in parentheses, such as "for the interval 2009–2048," using the current year and whatever year reflects how much longer you want to live. Underneath this heading, break up the Life Grant proposal into five-year phases. So in the above example, Phase 1 would be 2009–2013, Phase 2 would be 2014–2019, and so on.

Under each phase, write what you propose your express purpose would be during that period of time, should you be granted the longevity to live until then. Then itemize what supplies you'd need to accomplish the plans you're proposing for that time period. Don't write down goals that you're already involved in, like volunteering at the soup kitchen or enjoying nature. If you're already doing it, it's not as convincing an argument. That's for a grant-renewal form—not a grant *proposal*. With this exercise, you're preparing a whole new purpose, not renewing the old ones. Also, avoid vague purposes, such as "creating world peace" or "loving my grandchildren." Chances are you already love your grandchildren, and creating world peace is such a nebulous phrase that it doesn't really mean much, weakening your proposal and making it less likely to fly.

A better life purpose would sound something like this:

> *Unlike my previous tendency to work 12 hours a day, 7 days a week, I intend to decrease my workday to 8 hours, 6 days a week. I will spend the rest of my day engaging in loving and leisurely activities with my grandchildren, including but not limited to going camping at least once a year, coaching their soccer team, and teaching them fishing and needlepoint.*

Got it? Be detailed, but not so much so that you don't leave room for a higher plane to be superimposed on your very limited viewpoint. The process of writing a Life Grant proposal is truly a profound exercise in reevaluating your life design, enabling you to set your divine purpose into motion, with humility and intention.

What follows is my seven-part program to rehabilitate the "I Did It My Way" types' tendency to guide their lives' purpose more than they *allow* them to be guided by a higher power's purpose for them:

1. Identify how you've been able to achieve quite a lot in your life by combining purpose, aspiration, and spontaneous exploration. Through your efforts, you've created a reality that has allowed you to accomplish almost any goal you set in front of yourself.

2. Recognize that up to this point in your life, you've used your own earthly perspective to project your plans and to determine your life's purpose.

3. Discern that as long as you cling to what you want to create in your life, you'll depend only upon your own efforts. You'll never truly enter into a world that transcends all that you are and all that you can achieve, because you aren't allowing for the possibility of a divine purpose that your higher power may have in store for you.

4. Restrict your need to make your plans happen, pushing them through, believing that you can unilaterally create your reality.

5. Know that in partnership with the universe, a higher power, God, or some other entity that isn't *you*, you can marry your life's purpose with divine purpose. You can pin your hopes on *your* plan but also have blind faith in a higher one, trusting that divine guidance will orchestrate your best possible future.

6. Change the unhealthy thought pattern: *Things should have worked out differently in my life* . . . to the healthier affirmation: *Things that have been out of balance will soon be back* _in_ *balance. If I remove confusion and gain greater clarity in my life, a perfect order and a divine purpose will become apparent.*

7. Follow the seventh rule for intuitive health—*What doesn't kill you makes you stronger*—by knowing, at every stage of life, how to pursue your purpose as well as how to be open to a divine one *for* you.

The Undercover Angel

The final type of seventh-chakra extreme is the Undercover Angel, those who believe that every event in their lives has ended up in the hands of a higher power or destiny, and they really are powerless to create a personal plan for themselves. This is the way 50-year-old Angelina felt. Over the years, this woman weathered a series of emotional, physical, and financial disasters, but somehow she always survived.

As a teenager, my client had a burst appendix and was hospitalized with a blood infection. At 20, she injured her lower back in an automobile accident and developed whiplash in her neck. This left her with headaches that never really went away and a weak lower back that would go out every time she was under stress. Her thyroid bit the dust in her 30s, causing her to gain a lot of weight—no matter what she did, she wasn't able to lose that extra 40 pounds she was packing on her small frame. In her 40s, she developed a suspicious patch of calcification in her left breast, which doctors diagnosed as ductal carcinoma in situ (DCIS) breast cancer. She was cured with a lumpectomy and radiation.

At 50, Angelina had a nagging cough that wouldn't go away. Her doctor ordered an x-ray, found a spot on her left lung, and referred her to a pulmonologist. No one knew if it was a recurrence of her DCIS or if it was lung cancer from smoking in her early years. Angelina was once again terrified about her health. But when the doctors biopsied the lung lesion, it turned out to be just a cyst.

Let's add up all of Angelina's health problems that had yet to kill her: a burst appendix that caused septicemia, a blood infection (first chakra); a lower-back problem (second chakra); a 40-pound weight gain (third chakra); breast cancer (fourth chakra); neck pain and hypothyroidism (fifth chakra); chronic headaches (sixth chakra); and the recent spot on her lung, which was suspected to be a form of life-threatening cancer (seventh chakra). Although Angelina felt that she had dodged yet another bullet, she was tired of living her life ducking health crisis after health crisis. She felt that no matter what she did, regardless of how hopeful and positive she was, her life was going to continue to be one disaster after another. It seemed to be her fate.

If you, like Angelina, are an Undercover Angel, your life appears to be a series of physical or emotional problems or catastrophes. No matter what you do, you can't seem to take control or have a hand in creating your destiny, and you're so worn down that you often feel hopeless and helpless. You think, as that classic song from the TV show *Hee Haw* went, if it weren't for bad luck, you'd have no luck at all.

What I've learned from people like Angelina is that even though Undercover Angels have one life-threatening problem after another, somehow, like a cat, these people always land on their feet. They're so distracted by all the misery and gloom that they don't see the rest of the picture: the fact that they always seem to live despite all odds indicates that they have an angel hidden in their pocket, an undercover one who is there to pull them out of the jaws of death each time. So although their lives are indeed filled with much recurring pain, they also have an extremely strong spirit within them that somehow manages to survive, and maybe thrive, even if their bodies are a little worse for the wear. These people's medical histories truly support that old saying that what doesn't kill you makes you stronger.

What clues indicate that you're an Undercover Angel? Well, you know which veins on your body are the easiest to draw blood from. You've had more than four chest x-rays and have been in an operating room at least three times. When you go to the hospital on repeat visits, you recognize the nursing staff and greet them by name. You're aware of the difference between a medical student, an intern, a resident, and a fellow. You'd know whether to go to a psychologist or a psychiatrist if you needed a prescription for Prozac. You've been to at least two illness support groups. You have a special color-coded file system for your pending insurance reimbursement claims.

You know the difference between an osteopathic physician, a naturopathic doctor, and a chiropractor; whether phosphorus is a Chinese herb or a homeopathic remedy; the location of the nearest acupuncture school; and where to get the best pharmaceutical-grade vitamins. At times, you've spent more money on health care than on rent or your mortgage. You would never confuse shiatsu with Swedish massage.

If the above scenarios describe your life, then you may be an Undercover Angel. I'm sure you've had several serious health scares that have forced you to face your mortality on more than one occasion.

Each time that you wondered whether your next disease was going to be your swan song, your seventh-chakra intuitive advisor was signaling a need to reevaluate your true life's purpose. The first alarm that you'll receive will be a tap on the shoulder, which could be upgraded to a familiar nudge, a push, a shove, or the ever-famous kick in the pants. The life-threatening event—be it an abnormal Pap smear, an elevated PSA, a funny spot on a mammogram, or a cyst on your ovary—will come in whatever intensity is required to inspire you to reexamine your aspirations and dreams. Rather than meaning that the universe just has it in for you, the scare occurs to keep you on notice that you have to live every day with intention and purpose.

If we look closely at Angelina's story, we'll realize that each of us can find within ourselves an Undercover Angel, a part of us that in moments of desperation—hopeless and helpless—feels that our future is indeed ill-fated and the heavens have it in for us. During these very bleak and dark times, some small sign often appears, sending us a lifeboat to let us know that we'll be okay. It could be getting an unexpected check in the mail when we're down to our last few dollars or running into a new treatment on the Internet for the illness that has us at the end of our rope. Somehow, if we maintain some faith and a little patience, the answer to a desperate time always comes. The undercover angels are hidden somewhere, simply waiting to give us a sign we need. We just have to keep going through our pockets until we find our undercover angel.

Intuitive Advice for the Undercover Angel

Do you suffer from any type of life-threatening health problem, and do you tend to have the Undercover Angel approach to life? If so, you can use medical intuition and mind-body medicine to help you feel like you're finally living instead of always dying, and your mind-body makeover begins by addressing the physical body. You could have any life-threatening diagnosis or health scare with Undercover Angel tendencies. Like Angelina's string of challenges, they all point to the same thing: for the rest of your life, you must nourish, support, and reconstitute every system in your body. That may sound a bit overwhelming, but it doesn't have to be yet another hurdle to jump over. Just take it chakra by chakra. Here's how:

— **First chakra** (bone, joints, and immune system): The cumulative stress of all these illnesses can increase your chance of osteoporosis, so maintain daily aerobic exercise for 30 minutes a day, and take calcium and magnesium supplements daily as well. To strengthen your T cells (those white blood cells that are known as natural killer cells), helping keep cancer at bay, buy a good multivitamin and/or consider taking a nutritional supplement called colostrum.

— **Second chakra** (hormones): For the time being, avoid hormone replacement therapy of any kind (including bio-identical, natural, or synthetic), because so many life-threatening illnesses have hormonal effects and can be precipitated by them.

— **Third chakra** (food, nutrition, weight, and addiction): Decrease your body fat by sticking to a diet that's one-third protein, one-third vegetables, and one-third starchy carbohydrates.

— **Fourth chakra** (cardiovascular system, heart, breast, and lungs): The cumulative stresses in your life increase cortisol, heightening inflammation, which in turn causes cholesterol to clog your arteries. Take the most potent anti-inflammatory available, such as alpha-tocotrienol and coenzyme Q_{10} (400–600 mg a day).

— **Fifth chakra** (thyroid): A history of chronic traumatic experiences will increase your risk for thyroid disorders, so be sure to have your levels checked regularly. Don't lowball your thyroid replacement because decreased thyroid-hormone levels will increase your cholesterol; but don't overdo thyroid hormone either, because if its levels are too high, it could worsen osteoporosis.

— **Sixth chakra** (brain, eyes, and ears): If you have to be on steroids, take antioxidants such as grape-seed extract (300 mg a day) to protect your eyes. Chemotherapy may save your life, but it can also wreak havoc on your brain, so guard against memory and attention problems with DHA (300–1,000 mg a day). Consider taking L-acetyl-carnitine (500 mg, two to three times a day) and eleuthero, previously called Siberian ginseng (625 mg, twice a day), to help protect your brain from the long-term effects of inflammation. If your mind gets dull from all the ups and downs of your various health crises, SAMe (800–1,200 mg a day, on an empty stomach) or the bigger guns like Effexor or Wellbutrin can help you achieve a more elevated mood and a sharper mind and memory.

— **Seventh chakra** (connection to the divine): Maintain regular follow-up visits with both your traditional and complementary-medicine health-care team to check for the recurrence of every serious life-threatening problem you've had. Once you've received a clean bill of health from your practitioner, congratulations! But hey, you know the drill: you're on notice from your body that every moment of your life is indeed precious. Constantly nourish your body with love, because it's taken you through so much—and because it's responsible for a core part of your intuition that lets you know, moment by moment and day by day, when your life is going in the wrong direction.

The next part of your mind-body makeover addresses the emotional intuitive brain. To say that someone with such serious health problems needs emotional support is truly an understatement. However, normal supportive psychotherapy or even cognitive or dialectic behavior therapy isn't very helpful when it comes to addressing the core issues of mortality, one's human vulnerabilities.

So, how do you simultaneously take care of your physical vulnerability (the first-chakra, day-to-day survival needs that get threatened when you have a seventh-chakra crisis) and your life purpose, including both your personal and spiritual aspirations? Start by getting a wide network of first-chakra emotional support. Your best friends will become critical now. Their capacity to present you with chicken soup will somehow take some of the sting out of your latest catastrophe. The fact that you can drop in on them unannounced if you get unraveled and crash on their couches while you stare into space, no questions asked, will be an invaluable healing tool—*as* invaluable as chemotherapy and radiation.

Similarly, it's time to get a seventh-chakra spiritual guide, an advisor to help you find a higher meaning and purpose in your health and emotional crisis. Whether this advisor is a trusted member of the clergy or a layperson doesn't matter. What does matter is the person's ability to help you get a new perspective on your situation so that you can gain peace by looking at the problem from the viewpoint of a higher power.

Finally, here is my seven-part program to rehabilitate the Undercover Angels' tendency to bounce from one health crisis to the next:

1. Identify your pattern of encountering one life-threatening illness or near-death scare after another.

2. Recognize that even though you're absolutely terrified by your most recent brush with death, you have to admit to yourself that you've covered this territory all too often before and have actually become stronger each time your body has broken down.

3. Discern how each major health scare you've experienced has forced you to take a serious inventory of everything in your life that you thought may or may not be part of your life's purpose. As a result, you've eliminated some inconsequential plans and elements of your routine as you've begun to acquire faith in a larger design or life purpose. Understand that this divine destiny isn't meant to punish you or make you suffer. Instead, it requires you to have wisdom and compassion so that you can be of service.

4. Restrict your tendency to believe that your history of health problems and bad luck are due to poor behavior or even bad karma. Resist the impulse to ask, "Why me?"

5. Know that every serious health problem you experience can provide you with a source of intuitive advice that helps you know day by day, hour by hour, when you need to change your mind-set and gain a new perspective. Further understand that accessing intuitive advice from a higher source (as well as having faith in this guidance) doesn't prevent bad things from happening in your life, but it does give you strength when they do.

6. Change the unhealthy thought pattern: *God has it in for me—the universe doesn't hear my voice . . .* to the healthier affirmation: *In partnership with the universe, I move through emotional conflicts to find a peaceful resolution. Listening to my own intuitive advisor, I simultaneously try to tune in to the intuitive advice that I receive from a higher power.*

7. Follow the seventh rule for intuitive health—*What doesn't kill you makes you stronger*—by developing the faith that you need to recognize your life's purpose, reconstitute your spirit, and set new goals, even in the face of potential death.

●–●–●

To create health in your seventh chakra, your connection with the divine, you must keep sight of your purpose in life and recognize the theme underlying every crisis or situation. This chakra determines your capacity for longevity and for bouncing back from a life-threatening illness (or the scare of having one). Remember Wile E. Coyote from the *Road Runner* cartoons? Every one of his carefully crafted shenanigans invariably went wrong: A huge anvil would smash him flat. A Mack truck would run him over. Dynamite would blow him up. But he always peeled his flattened or charred body up off the ground and got right back on task. He might change his plan a little, tweak his approach a bit, but his intense desire to catch his elusive prey kept him going, through one brush with death after another.

Both science and the seventh rule for intuitive health—*What doesn't kill you makes you stronger*—bear this out. Following this rule requires that you balance facing premature death with infusing your spirit with a mission . . . realigning yourself with a new life goal and focus and then carrying that out. When needed, your seventh-chakra intuitive advisor will continue to nudge you to recognize that no matter what, the beat goes on. Despite proverbial anvils falling from the sky and dynamite blowing up in your face, each day always brings you a chance to review and renew your contract with life.

●–●–●–●–●

Afterword
Why Not Me?

Of course, one of the biggest impediments to following the seventh rule for intuitive health is to find the inspiration and emotional energy it takes to reconstitute your spirit and realign yourself with a new goal and focus. It's hard to accomplish that when you've been hit over and over with one emotional or physical crisis after another. The human tendency is to simply ask, "Why me?" I'd like to end this book with the story of the powerful lesson I learned in my own life about asking that very question.

Back in 2005, at the age of 45, I was diagnosed with invasive breast cancer—first in my left breast. I was, to say the least, a little upset. And I knew that I was so grief stricken at the time that the invasive cancer would occur very quickly in my right breast as well, even though a mammogram indicated that it was healthy. So I planned a double mastectomy with reconstruction. Even though I expected it, I wasn't the happiest camper when the pathology report I got after the surgery reported invasive cancer in my right breast, too, confirming that I indeed had double breast cancer—bilateral invasive breast cancer.

I went off the deep end. For the first time in my life, the question *Why me?* flashed through my mind. *Why me?* All these ridiculous medical problems: the 128-degree curve in my spine at age 12, the year spent flat on my back, the spinal fusion, the epilepsy, the seizures, getting run over by the truck and suffering the fractures in my pelvis, the broken ribs, the collapsed lung, the Graves' disease, blowing ten disks, breaking my back, having the rest of it broken surgically so the doctors could re-fuse my spine again, and now the double breast cancer. *Why me?* I felt horrendous asking this because I'd always had a lot of faith, and I'd prayed and talked to God from an early age. Throughout all of my health catastrophes, I always kind of held it together. But there was something about getting invasive cancer in both breasts that completely undid me. I asked myself,

Is this it? Was I going to have to pack up my house, find new homes for my four sweet kitties? Was I really going to die?

As I kept asking the *Why me?* question, as if reading cue cards from a heavenly source (a higher power, God, or an undercover angel . . . who knows where it came from), I heard myself ask out loud, "Why not me?" Somehow this new question shut me up. Because these words had just flown from my lips (believe me, they didn't come from my brain), I got to thinking: *Well, why* _not_ *me?*

"Why *not* me?" meant it wasn't personal. I wasn't being punished. God wasn't somewhere flipping a switch and saying, "This time I'm *really* gonna mess this woman up and torture her good!" I could still learn from this illness, but I wasn't getting sick because God had it in for me.

Those words, *Why not me?* also happen to have special meaning, because that's the title of a Judds song from the 1980s (one that won them a Grammy, I might add), and Naomi and Wynonna are very close family friends of mine. I immediately ran to look up the words to the song to see if any further angelic messages were encoded in the lyrics that might help me survive this ridiculous breast-cancer problem. I'd love to tell you that I found more profound information about surviving tragedy and finding renewal. But alas, that's not the case. The song is about some guy going out with all these women all over the world, while a girl from his hometown in Kentucky bemoans, "Why not me?" She's wondering, what's wrong with her? Why can't he fall in love with *her?*

But the story doesn't end there. Angelic messages can sometimes be delayed. They come in universal time, not on ours—and not on demand, as they say on cable and satellite TV. The following year, right around the first anniversary of my breast-cancer diagnosis, plus or minus a couple of weeks, I was watching Naomi on TV. She was hosting an inspirational show called *Naomi's New Morning* on Hallmark Channel, and on this day, she happened to be doing a program on how to survive serious life tragedies. So there I sat, poring over my Sunday paper, eating my usual breakfast of eggs and oatmeal and watching Naomi's show.

Some of the interviews were about individuals with character, but most were about people with ridiculous kinds of catastrophes. At the end of the program, Naomi asked her guests what kinds of phrases helped them get through the trauma in their lives. I almost spit out a mouthful of eggs all over the place as this man, who was struggling with some ridiculous, obscure syndrome, talked about finding peace by hearing the words in his head, *Why not me?* (Of course, as I had, Naomi picked up on the fact that those words were also the title of one of her songs.)

It was then that I knew that there were undercover angels among people who had life-threatening illnesses, and God, fate, and destiny aren't behind these personal tragedies that every one of us has to endure. Instead, God (or whatever you call your higher power) is there when it happens, supporting you all the way. Faith in a higher power doesn't prevent bad things from happening; rather, it's there holding your hand and your heart when they do.

Incidentally, it matters not what your personal laundry list of catastrophes, tragedies, and health scares are. Mine is a little on the dramatic side, perhaps because I watched too many soap operas growing up with my aunt Edie. There's no such thing as the trauma Olympics, although judging from some people's life stories, they could have been gold-medal contenders. These individuals are known for recreating themselves over and over again, like a phoenix rising up out of the ashes of one disaster after another.

Cher comes to mind as a perfect example. When you take a closer look at the many songs she's sung over the years, you'll see that they seem to illustrate all the major life events that can affect the seven chakras—thus, the titles of the chapters in the second part of this book. It has been said that if there were ever a nuclear war, only two things would survive: cockroaches and Cher. And when asked about that comment in an interview, Cher herself said, "I think that pretty much sums it up." We can thank this musical icon for enduring one tragedy after another, right in front of our eyes, and inspiring us by coming out of each of them having not just survived, but grown and thrived.

In the end, I think it's part of the mystery of life that we're each dealt a genetic "poker hand." Some of us get crappy cards, and others get really good ones. But poker isn't just about luck—it's about learning how to play with the cards we're dealt, no matter how good or crappy they are. Sometimes we have to go by our skills; sometimes we win by sheer luck; and at other times we have to have faith that even if we lose a hand or two, at least we'll still be in the game. We'll survive.

Like Angelina in the case study from the last chapter, we all need to follow the message underlying her name—derived from a Greek word meaning "message of God." When any of us has a long, hard life filled with health issues and personal problems, we need to know that the message from a higher source isn't: "You're screwed. Your destiny is to suffer." When we instead look at the divine purpose behind the event, with the help of friends, family, and a higher power, we inevitably learn that what doesn't kill us *will* always make us stronger.

•—•—•—•—•—•

Acknowledgments

An intuitive advisor needs many advisors. I'd first like to thank God, without Whose continual help I wouldn't have written this book and you, the reader, certainly would never be holding it in your hands.

To my vast intellectual and professional advisors, who have steered my brain and my feet in the right direction, and without whom I wouldn't think straight and my career would have gone gonzo—Edith Kaplan, Margaret Naeser, Deepak Pandya, Joan Borysenko, and Chris Northrup, I would be nothing and know nothing without you.

To the wonderful staff of **Myss.com** and CMED, especially David Smith and Amy Myss, you are the most efficient machine, with a heart, that I know.

To Hay House, especially Louise Hay and Reid Tracy, for taking a chance on a little bit of an academic pinhead who's trying to loosen up—thank you for publishing this book. Thanks, also, to Jill Kramer and Alex Freemon for being sensitive, level-headed, enthusiastic editors whom I really needed; and to the guys and gals at Hay House Radio, especially Summer McStravick, Diane Ray, Emily Manning (the Web woman), and all the people in the booth who skillfully handle the hysteria every Wednesday at 11 A.M. PST (2 P.M. EST) on my radio show, *Intuitive Health* with Dr. Mona Lisa.

To the people who help me communicate my message out there, thank you to Mel Berger and all the folks at the William Morris Agency. Marshall Bellovin and Ken Lehman are the best lawyers that anyone could ever want. They sigh at the right place, look around, and always say, "I wish you would have called me before you went and did that." Thank you. Thanks, also, to the Web people at Ident Group inc. in New York City. I love your hours; the Tech-Geek Nation 24/7 always works for me.

Special thanks to Gil Levin and the staff of the Cape Cod Institute for the annual summer intuition camp that we do each year; I look forward to having my week with students on the cape every summer. Special thanks to Leslie Evans for incredible Dr. Mona Lisa business logos.

An intuitive advisor would be limping along without constant physical, emotional, and nutritional support. First, the physicians and healers—and there are many—who have worked hard to reconstitute my health. For the back, Dr. Paul Glazer, the wonderful Dr. Dean Deng, and maybe Dr. Rudolf Bertagnoli in Germany, too. For the breathing, Dr. Steven Dobieski. For the boobs, Dr. Dixie Mills, Dr. Rosemary Duda, and Dr. Michael Tantillo (it takes a village). And last but not least, for the brain, Dr. Fern Tsao (America's greatest female acupuncturist) and Diane Boyce, MSW (the brilliant Dialectical Behavioral Therapy expert and coach).

To the makers of the TV programs *Judge Judy, Ellen, Project Runway, Clean House* (with Niecy Nash), *Reno 911!* and *Kimora: Life in the Fab Lane,* thanks for the entertainment, education, and mental-health-inducing television viewing.

To those who, to the best of their ability, ensure that nothing will go wrong, Bill Goddard, your insurance agent, Phil Harriman, and John Doloff Investments.

Then there's the money. Thank you to Paul Chabot for sighing, pointing, and telling me to lose the credit cards—such a great advisor. Thank you, also, to Sarah; Sarah's father, Jorge; and Peter Dunn.

And last but not least, thank you to Cecilia at the Chicago O'Hare Mont Blanc store at Terminal One, Gate B7, for allowing me to frequent your store and demonstrate my fountain-pen and ink addiction.

Then there are the homes and the home-team advisors, of whom there are many.

On location in Chicago: Thank you to Donna at Heritage Travel for horsing around with all those upgrades on United, Maria Ugarte, and Phil, my home crew. Thank you to Miss Colleen Daley for the incredible graphics for this book. You're an amazing woman. Thanks to Jayme Marzillo, who lets me leave the salon with a wet head when I'm in a hurry, for great hair. And, of course, thanks to the fabulous and famous Miss Jill Angelo, who is one of those assistants who does everything effortlessly. Could you provide 7,000 copies of something collated, find and buy a 6½ foot giraffe, get an electrician and fix a plug, and bench-press 200 pounds, all before noon, without breaking a sweat or complaining? And thank you to the brilliant Andrew Harvey for not thinking that I'm intellectually deficient. To Winberies, thanks for those wonderful chopped salads, hold the onions. Life would be bleak without them. And thank you to Ellen and John and all the other Oak Park people who have welcomed me.

On location in Maine: Thank you so much to Miss Sue Abel for taking care of my home and my four sweet babies when I am away. You're a taproot of stability in my life. The house and grounds wouldn't be the same without Mike Brewer of Brewer's Property Maintenance, especially how you help me put up my yearly Christmas lighting and inflatables display. If it weren't for Joseph Saucier at the designer Escada in Boston, I'd dress like a slob. Thank you. Jerry Phair is the sweetest shaman you'll ever find. To my Petticoat Junction, the Harraseeket Inn staff in Freeport, thank you to Nancy and Rodney (Chip) Gray, the owners; Rhonda, bartender extraordinaire; waitresses Peggy and Denise; Mary Ann, the brilliant chef; Marsha, the manager; Theda, the head chef; Sharon, the pastry chef; and Elizabeth at the buffet. If it weren't for you, I'd be eating tuna and mac & cheese all the time. Thanks to L.L.Bean's Brenda Markee and Beth LeBlanc for always doing things for me when disasters, environmental and otherwise, are happening. Thank you to Ken and Lynda for overwhelming intrigue and boisterous mayhem at many a Sunday brunch and for chronically illegally parking with me in the no-parking-zone traffic circle. To Igor, the limo driver; and Pete, the other limo driver, how would I get in and out without you? Thank you to Steve Leen, the computer man who fixes my IBM, even though he thinks my house has been hit by a meteor.

Thank you to Katy Koontz, a writer who always pops up when you need her. Whether it's your extreme left-brain genius for details or your right-brain nuance and intuition, you are the bomb! (Ask your daughter what this means.) You took the book that I wrote and you put it into correct English so that I don't come across as either an overly academic pinhead or an audiovisual nightmare with a speech impediment. I am forever grateful that you continue to pop up. Thank you, also, to Karen Kinne for transcription.

To my Fall River friends, thank you to Liz and Julie for all the love (and sweet bread and malasadas); to Kate Grana and Sue Cotta for being Rhode Island relatives; and to my Aunt Nancy, Aunt Evie, and cousin Joseph.

To my New York City family, I miss you and appreciate your support always. Thanks to Laura Day, Samson Day, and maybe even Adam.

To my Franklin, Tennessee; and Nashville family, Jennie Adams (who is the sweetest friend) and Naomi Judd and Larry Strickland, thank you for your constant love and support. What would life be without my Tennessee home? To Wynonna and Roach, I love both of you so much it hurts.

Thank you to Linda Ward in Florida, who needs to write her own book. (Linda, we've been waiting.) Thank you, Priscilla, for helping me get incredible places to live at suicide prices. Thank you to Georgia Bailey for fabulous friendship and furniture assembly.

To my many readers, Janie Lemole, Elaine Rosen, and everyone else who is deep undercover, thank you for your honesty.

And finally to my family, I wish there was no such thing as order because I'd put all of you first and last. You're all equally loved and important. To Caroline Myss, Delores, Eddie and the rest of his family, Abby, Angela, Joe, Marilyn, Pam and Andy, Chrissie, and the rest of the Chicago cousins and their families, we play cards, we laugh, we cry, I cry, we cook, we eat. Thank you for being so wonderful.

To my Main Street family, Lisa and Leon Gorman, Wally, and Biscuit, what would life be without dropping by your house to watch *Curb Your Enthusiasm* DVDs or having other kinds of mayhem and foolishness? Thank you, Mr. Leon, a business genius, for picking the green beans of my business structure.

To my sweet Molly, Dolly, Jethro Bodine, and the famous Dr. Sigmund Feline, my sweet feline friends, you are my babies.

But Lisa Gorman and Caroline Myss get the last mention in these acknowledgments, and it is to these two women that I dedicate this book.

No animals were harmed in the making of this book.

•─•─•─•─•

About the Author

Mona Lisa Schulz holds a B.A. from Brown University, an M.D. from the Boston University School of Medicine, and a Ph.D. from Boston University's department of behavioral neurosciences. She is a practicing neuropsychiatrist, specializing in head injury, dementia, stroke, Parkinson's disease, and the psychiatric aspects of medical conditions.

In addition to her extensive background in health and brain research, Dr. Schulz has been a practicing medical intuitive since 1987, doing readings on people all over the world. During a medical-intuitive consultation, knowing only clients' names and ages, she discerns both their physical condition and the emotional state of their lives, helping them understand the connections between their health problems and their emotions.

Dr. Schulz is also the author of the books *Awakening Intuition: Using Your Mind-Body Network for Insight and Healing* and *The New Feminine Brain: How Women Can Develop Their Inner Strengths, Genius, and Intuition*. She hosts a live call-in radio show called *Intuitive Health* every Wednesday at 2 P.M. EST on **HayHouseRadio.com**®. She has also appeared on *The Oprah Winfrey Show* and the Discovery Channel.

Dr. Schulz lives in Yarmouth, Maine, with her four cats: Miss Dolly, Miss Molly, Jethro Bodine, and the great Dr. Sigmund Feline. Visit her Website at: **www.drmonalisa.com**.

•─•─••─•─•

Hay House Titles of Related Interest

YOU CAN HEAL YOUR LIFE, the movie,
starring Louise L. Hay & Friends
(available as a 1-DVD program and an expanded 2-DVD set)
Watch the trailer at: **www.LouiseHayMovie.com**

THE SHIFT, the movie, starring Dr. Wayne W. Dyer
(available as a 1-DVD program and an expanded 2-DVD set)
Watch the trailer at: **www.DyerMovie.com**

●─●─●

THE AGE OF MIRACLES: Embracing the New Midlife,
by Marianne Williamson

DEFY GRAVITY: Healing Beyond the Bounds of Reason,
by Caroline Myss

HEALING YOUR FAMILY HISTORY:
5 Steps to Break Free of Destructive Patterns, by Rebecca Linder Hintze

HEAL YOUR BODY: The Mental Causes for Physical Illness
and the Metaphysical Way to Overcome Them, by Louise L. Hay

THE POWER OF INFINITE LOVE & GRATITUDE:
An Evolutionary Journey to Awakening Your Spirit, by Dr. Darren R. Weissman

THE SECRET PLEASURES OF MENOPAUSE, by Christiane Northrup, M.D.

THE VITAMIN D REVOLUTION:
How the Power of This Amazing Vitamin Can Change Your Life,
by Soram Khalsa, M.D.

WHAT IS YOUR SELF-WORTH?: A Woman's Guide to Validation,
by Cheryl Saban, Ph.D.

YOUR DESTINY SWITCH: Master Your Key Emotions,
and Attract the Life of Your Dreams! by Peggy McColl

YOUR SOUL'S COMPASS: What Is Spiritual Guidance?
by Joan Borysenko, Ph.D., and Gordon Dveirin, Ed.D.

●─●─●

All of the above are available at your local bookstore,
or may be ordered by contacting Hay House (see next page).

We hope you enjoyed this Hay House book.
If you'd like to receive our online catalog featuring additional
information on Hay House books and products, or if you'd like to
find out more about the Hay Foundation, please contact:

Hay House, Inc.
P.O. Box 5100
Carlsbad, CA 92018-5100

(760) 431-7695 or **(800) 654-5126**
(760) 431-6948 (fax) or **(800) 650-5115 (fax)**
www.hayhouse.com® • **www.hayfoundation.org**

•—•—•

Published and distributed in Australia by:
Hay House Australia Pty. Ltd., 18/36 Ralph St., Alexandria NSW 2015
Phone: 612-9669-4299 • *Fax:* 612-9669-4144
www.hayhouse.com.au

Published and distributed in the United Kingdom by:
Hay House UK, Ltd., 292B Kensal Rd., London W10 5BE
Phone: 44-20-8962-1230 • *Fax:* 44-20-8962-1239
www.hayhouse.co.uk

Published and distributed in the Republic of South Africa by:
Hay House SA (Pty), Ltd., P.O. Box 990, Witkoppen 2068
Phone/Fax: 27-11-467-8904 • info@hayhouse.co.za
www.hayhouse.co.za

Published in India by:
Hay House Publishers India, Muskaan Complex, Plot No. 3, B-2,
Vasant Kunj, New Delhi 110 070 • *Phone:* 91-11-4176-1620
Fax: 91-11-4176-1630 • www.hayhouse.co.in

Distributed in Canada by:
Raincoast, 9050 Shaughnessy St., Vancouver, B.C. V6P 6E5
Phone: (604) 323-7100 • *Fax:* (604) 323-2600 • www.raincoast.com

•—•—•

Take Your Soul on a Vacation

Visit **www.HealYourLife.com®** to regroup, recharge, and reconnect
with your own magnificence. Featuring blogs, mind-body-spirit news,
and life-changing wisdom from Louise Hay and friends.

Visit **www.HealYourLife.com** today!**www.hayhouse.com®**